THE INTERRUPTED SYSTEM

THE INTERRUPTED SYSTEM
Israeli Civilians in War and Routine Times

BARUCH KIMMERLING
in collaboration with
IRIT BACKER

Transaction Books
New Brunswick (U.S.A.) and Oxford (U.K.)

Copyright © 1985 by Transaction, Inc.
New Brunswick, New Jersey 08903

Library of Congress Catalog Number: 84-23985
ISBN 0-88738-020-4 (cloth)
Printed in the United States of America

Library of Congress Cataloging in Publication Data
Kimmerling, Baruch.
    The interrupted system.
Includes index.
    1. Israel—Social conditions. 2. Sociology,
Military—Israel. 3. War and society. I. Backer, Irit.
II. Title.
HN660.A8K56 1985   306′.27′095694   84-23985
ISBN 0-88738-020-4

To all my friends—
sociologists, nonsociologists,
and antisociologists

Contents

List of Tables

Acknowledgments

Research for this study commenced approximately 11 years ago—an unusually long gestation period for social science research. There were numerous reasons for the delay in publication, foremost among which were my own procrastination, doubts, and hesitation, as well as my compulsive, ruthless preoccupation with 1,001 other interesting items. The extended duration of this study has perhaps concomitantly lengthened the list of people to whom the authors owe their gratitude. Not all such persons will be mentioned herein, lest the publisher demand compensation for increased production costs.

First, I acknowledge the generous financial support frequently tendered by the Hebrew University of Jerusalem's Levi Eshkol Institute for Economic, Social, and Political Research, without which this study would have been impossible. In 1978-79 I was the guest of the Center for International Studies of the Massachusetts Institute of Technology, where I revised a draft of this book. Recalling how I pressured the administration to complete the typing rapidly, I apologize to all Center staff members for the riots I caused and to Gene Skolnikoff, the Center's director, for his infinite patience and tolerance. I also thank my colleague Rivka Bar-Yosef, the director of the Institute for Labor and Welfare Research, for the captivating material that she placed at the disposal of this rival scholar.

During the 1973 war, scores of volunteers—students and nonstudents alike—assisted me in distributing a questionnaire among a wide sample population. This survey, which constituted a pilot study for the subsequent main research project, was undertaken during a period of universal war-induced anxiety and depression. In this respect, I especially note the assistance of Zilly and Sara Meiron and Rachel Zudkevitz. Gila Noam, Shmuel Himmelstein, and Zvi Ofer worked with me on the various English-language versions of this study.

Most important of all, I must thank my colleagues—and teachers who later became colleagues—for arguing with me in varying degrees of delicacy, expressing their opinions of my views and the manner in which they were presented. I am lost without such debate, as creative research can only take place within an atmosphere of intellectual tension. The order in which they are mentioned is entirely coincidental; it does not reflect the extent of their agreement or dissent to the conceptions published herein, nor is it affected by my personal opinions of them: Shmuel N. Eisenstadt, Moshe Lissak, Dan Horowitz, Irving Louis Horowitz, Elihu Katz, Victor Azarya, Joel Midgal, Russell Stone, Samuel P. Huntington, Reinhard Bendix, Robert Brym, and Eric Cohen.

Finally, I wish to add a few words about my collaborator in this study, Irit Backer. Irit served as a reserve soldier during the 1973 war, having filled a vital role throughout the war and for a considerable amount of time thereafter. When she was discharged from service and returned to university studies, I was just beginning to run the research upon which this book is based. I recognized Irit as a brilliant student, who made life difficult for her instructors with her thought-provoking questions. I therefore requested that she join me as a research and teaching assistant in my 1974-75 seminar on the subject of that war. I permitted her to use the material accumulated for her M.A. thesis. Chapters 2, 3, and 4 of this book are partially based upon Irit's work.

Shorter versions of three chapters were previously published. The author gratefully acknowledges the following publications for permission to use these materials:

Chapter 2 originally appeared as "Interruption and Continuity," in *International Review of Modern Sociology,* Winter 1985.

Chapter 4 originally appeared as "Voluntary Action and Location in the System," in *The Journal of Applied Behavioral Science,* vol. 18, no. 1, 1982.

Chapter 5, "Making Conflict a Routine: Cumulative Effects of the Arab-Jewish Conflict upon Israeli Society," *Journal of Strategic Studies,* vol. 6, no. 3, September 1983.

Baruch Kimmerling

Preface

Pitirim A. Sorokin's well-known book *Contemporary Sociological Theories,* published in 1928, included a chapter entitled "A Sociological Interpretation of the 'Struggle for Existence' and the Sociology of War," which was to have opened a new field in sociological research. Nevertheless, Sorokin's work enjoyed virtually no follow-up whatsoever; the sociology of war did not develop as an independent field, although the subject was occasionally covered within the framework of social conflict and so-called peace research. However, when phenomena such as ethnic conflicts, strikes, cultural and religious struggles (within society), class struggles, etc. are considered under a single semantic roof without distinguishing the unique characteristics of each, it becomes very difficult to construct a theoretical and conceptual framework to further our comprehension of social phenomena.

Several attempts at developing the sociology of war were undertaken during and immediately following the Second World War. The three most prominent efforts are most likely those of Quincy Wright, Hans Speier, and of U.S. Strategic Air Command sociologists, who attempted to analyze German society's endurance to World War II bombings. The British, too, accorded ample consideration to their "finest hour"; in the 1970s, they even reinvestigated the subject, questioning whether it was indeed so "fine." However, these few attempts were sporadic in nature; there was virtually no attempt to construct the conceptual and theoretical tools required for analysis of social systems at war. The lack of a sociology of war is even more evident in the light of the flourishing of military sociology and the sociology of civil-military relations.

The problems faced by Israel may be categorized according to two of that country's most outstanding features: First, Israel is a country of immigration, having absorbed immigrants from many different cultural backgrounds. These differences are subsequently translated into ethnic, economic/political, and even religious conflicts. Second, since its establishment, Israel has been involved in constant war with its neighbors. Most social research in Israel has focused only upon the first category, although a few studies dealing with the latter have appeared recently. According to all accepted criteria, Israel maintains a highly developed and sophisticated system of social science research, yet the sociology of war is utterly lacking. We offer no explanation of this interesting socio-logical phenomenon, yet feel it should have been taken into account, together with the universal attitudes of social scientists toward war. Furthermore, some scholars are of the opinion that by dealing with a topic one accords it a measure of legitimacy and perhaps even increases the probability of its occurrence. This assessment is apparently invalid, however, in light of the present compulsive (albeit nonsociological) preoc-cupation with nuclear weaponry and nuclear doctrine.

This book, as noted above, indeed deals with the sociology of war, or, more precisely, with the reactions of individuals, groups, strata, and the overall establishment system to the war situation. In this respect, it effectively continues from the point at which Sorokin left off. It concentrates upon one particular case study, that of Israel, investigating and analyzing the situation from various angles and points of departure, employing a number of research methods. The book attempts to bridge the gap between micro-sociological research and analysis and presentation of a macro-sociological framework.

The study therefore entails several limitations: it may tend to "over-explain" a phenomenon, restricting itself to analysis of the "case" within the society, while failing to present the broader context of "external factors" that likewise affect the conflict and its course and patterns within the system. The key issue under investigation is the manner in which Israeli society, in light of its particular limitations and character, has dealt with this situation of constant conflict—at times expressed as active war—with the neighboring Arab states.

The first part of this book concentrates upon a situation in which most of the Israeli system's human and material resources are recruited to deal with the conflict—whether or not active war is in progress—while nearly all remaining social goals are suspended or subject to a moratorium. The second part deals with the cumulative results of the conflict situation in toto—considering both the existing or developing institutional arrangements for facing emergency and conflict situations and the cognitive level of individuals and groups within society. The discussion focuses upon the transition phases between the system's routine social functioning and the optimal recruitment of society's resources for a specific, limited time, and subsequent return to the routine situation. Thus, the time dimension is a vital element of this study.

The first chapter provides a conceptual framework, representing an initial step in constructing a middle-range social theory. It attempts to utilize several concepts and evaluations developed within the traditional framework of disaster studies, yet emphasizes the vast difference between the subject of this discipline and the situations described herein. Moreover, the adoption of several features of disaster studies, and their inclusion within the original framework developed in this work, paves the way for a comparative study of entire societies and communities under special conditions, including not only states of war but also other situations involving society-wide recruitment. This book will not engage in such comparative study, however. Its goal is more modest—analysis and explanation of the Israeli case alone.

Chapter 2 is concerned with institutional arrangements that ensure the functioning of the civilian system during periods of war and emergency, including: supply and stockpiling of food and fuel; ensuring the sustaining of soldiers' families (the Israeli armed forces generally draft most able-bodied men, and many women as well, during times of emergency); evacuating the injured; clearing rubble; civil defense (where required); transportation and public transport; banking services; education; and continued economic production. Also reviewed are the principles according to which the system is supposed to work, its overt and covert basic assumptions, and the nature of practical implementation—considered in the light of the theoretical framework presented in the preceding chapter.

Discussion then continues in terms of social role fulfillment by individuals and groups within the system. Two types of roles have been discerned, together with their attendant questions: First, routine, year-round individual tasks—Who will carry them out and how are they to be implemented under the given special circumstances? Second, "new" roles resulting from the special situation—Who is to fulfill them? Are they to be implemented by "replacements" for draftees or as part of an overall contribution to the war effort?

At this point, we also note the question raised regarding the differential commitment of various segments of the Israeli system to the "agreed, overall goals of society," in accordance with their varying positions within that system. Chapters 3 and 4 deal with the implementation of civilian goals within the system during times of emergency and total call-up—the former is concerned with the routine roles ("father," "mother," "employer," "student," "housewife," etc.) while the latter considers the voluntary fulfillment of nonroutine roles. These two chapters are likewise analyzed within the conceptual and theoretical framework presented in the first chapter.

Chapter 5, which constitutes a second, complementary part of our research, breaks through the boundaries of the framework mapped out in the first chapter. It deals with the reactions of the system to the conflict situation in toto, of which the total call-up represents only one element. The chapter reviews the effects of the Israeli-Arab conflict upon various aspects of Israeli society (stratification, economy, political behavior, culture, etc). Its main thrust is provided by examination of the assumption that extended conflict is not considered to be an exceptional case, but rather one of the many overall "phenomena" or "problems" for which Israeli society must apply its aforementioned ability to ensure rapid social and military recruitment. The last chapter sums up several of the conclusions and limitations of this study.

The term "system" is employed as the key concept throughout this work. The use of this and all other concepts and basic approaches anchored in structural-functional sociology is by no means coincidental. I identify myself in a moderate and critical manner with this (stigmatized?) sociological approach—not because I "believe" in this, nor out of rejection of accepted critiques, but rather because I consider it to be a convenient and efficient *working method.* Thus, for example, use of the concept "system" does not postulate the actual existence of any such thing; rather, it is considered as no more than a convenient theoretical construct. This also explains the doubly sinful use of terms such as "degree of flexibility" or "capacity for interruption." We appear to posite the existence of a "system" and to personify its characteristics; yet these transgressions are apparently common to all sociological studies, even if carried out elegantly and covertly. In the present work, however, I have acted overtly and rather brutally—although hopefully not excessively so.

Finally, I wish to introduce myself in terms of my professional identity. I was educated according to the Weberian approach, which claims that sociological analysis, questions, and conclusions must be value free. Obviously, this goal cannot be achieved in any absolute manner, yet this does not render the aim of neutrality superfluous. Insofar as I am concerned, this is the only way that sociology may be "performed" without reverting to theology of one form or another. Such an approach will necessarily render the researcher somewhat skeptical regarding himself. Hence he must avow his intention to remain neutral while submitting his personal, political, social, and economic identity card for the reader's scrutiny. It is up to the reader to determine the extent to which the study is indeed free of the researcher's personal values. (As an interesting intellectual exercise, the reader is also invited to consider his own expectations in light of these values.) Therefore the writer feels that it is important to inform the reader that he considers himself to be a Zionist with highly moderate ("dovish") views on the Israeli-Arab conflict, nonreligious, and liberal in economic and social outlook.

PART ONE

1

The State of War and the
Interrupted System

In this study we describe and analyze a social system in the rare situation of a sudden but temporary interruption of many social processes. The system changes from one faced with many goals that generally conflict with each other—as in every open and modern society— to a system having only two main goals. Most of the social resources (manpower and material resources) are mobilized for the major or predominant goal, and the system must cope with a problem perceived as being of paramount significance for the collectivity's very existence. The second and complementary goal is to "maintain" the system so that it will be able to return to its previous state as quickly and inexpensively as possible once the predominant goal is achieved. Thus, *social interruption* is a concept totally antithetical to that of social change, inasmuch as the interruption is defined as temporary, and is aimed from the outset at restoring the previous societal situation at the earliest opportunity.

The concrete situation we will be dealing with is the Israeli case, and we will analyze the processes that did and did not take place among Israeli civilians in the so-called Yom Kippur War of 1973; included, too, are some reflections on the 1982 Lebanon war. As is known, on 6 October 1973 Israel was the target of a surprise attack along the cease-fire lines established with Egypt and Syria in the wake of the 1967 Six-Day War. Active combat continued until October 24 of the same year. Within approximately 72 hours of the attack the Israeli reserves were mobilized— that is, about 250,000 persons,[1] constituting about 30 percent of the total civilian labor force, were called up. A small number of persons, who potentially could have joined the armed forces but who were recognized as being indispensable for the operation of about 3,500 enterprises considered essential to the war effort, were not recruited. Likewise some public transportation vehicles were placed at the army's disposal as was about 90 percent of the total capacity of freight vehicles. This large-scale mobilization of material and manpower resources continued even after the cease-fire, although the partial and selective release of these resources began immediately after the cessation of combat and continued until approximately May-June 1974 (when the separation-of-forces agreements were signed with Egypt and Syria). Until then, 2,637 Israelis fell in battle, 7,500 were wounded, and 300 were taken prisoners of war.[2] From the standpoint of the civilians, though, what characterized this war was the lack of physical injury, bombing, etc., of civilians.

The 1982 war was different in most ways from that of 1973. On June 6 large forces of the Israeli army crossed the Israeli-Lebanese border. In the official Israeli communiqué, it was stated that the aim of the campaign—which was named "Peace for Galilee"—would be the creation of a security strip of between 25 and 28 miles, and to put Israel's northern settlements out of range of the cannons and missiles of the Palestinian guerilla organizations. On June 4 and 5, the Israeli Galilee settlements were subjected to a fierce barrage of Palestinian artillery fire, after a period of more than a year without shellings, the lull following a cease-fire negotiated by means of the U.S. as mediator. The Israelis claimed that the cease-fire included all types of actions against Israel, both in Israel and outside it, while the Palestine Liberation Organization (PLO) claimed that the cease-fire was limited to the Galilee region. On 3 June 1982 Palestinians shot the Israeli ambassador to London, wounding him gravely. On June 4, as retribution, Israeli planes attacked Palestinian bases in Beirut. Thus, the shelling of the Galilee was retribution for retribution. At that time, there were Syrian forces in Lebanon, and Israel announced that if they would stay out of the fighting, Israel's forces would not attack them. By June 8 it was already apparent that the campaign was going beyond the 28 miles stated in the first communiqué, after the Israeli forces had gone beyond Tyre and Sidon, and were on their way to Damur (about 11 miles south of Beirut). At the same time, the Israeli forces were advancing along two other axes: an eastern one, throughout the Lebanese Bekaa valley, and a central one. Here there were battles with Syrian forces (who were in Lebanon as the result of a decision of the Arab League, as an intervention force, and to keep order after the Lebanese civil war.) The battles with the Syrians were conducted entirely on Lebanese soil, and did not spread to the Syrian-Israeli cease-fire lines on the Golan Heights. On June 11 the Israeli forces reached the outskirts of Beirut, and in a few days linked up with the Christian militias in northern Lebanon. The controlling of the Beirut-Damascus highway and the entrance to eastern Beirut brought about the cutting off of the western part of the city and of a siege to that section. Western Beirut was a major stronghold of the Palestinians, and was the place where the central military and political commands of the Palestine Liberation Organization were located. As a result, the goals were changed completely from those first declared, and were now defined by the Israeli government as smashing the political and military strength of the PLO and of destroying its presence in Lebanon, while at the same time forming a stable Lebanese government.

In order to engage in this campaign, a large number of reservists were mobilized. They were mobilized not only to serve in Lebanon, but also to ensure against the intervention of any other nations in the war—here referring primarily to Jordan and Syria. The Israeli army did not publish the number of soldiers involved but it is almost certain that at the height of the campaign about one half of all the reservists had been mobilized. The massive mobilization continued for about five weeks, while even prior thereto (from the time of the signing of the cease-fire on June 26) a partial rotation of the mobilized forces was begun. The military situation stabilized—in the form of a siege and a mutual war of attrition around Beirut—while there were political negotiations, whose aim according to Israel was the removal of the fighters and commands of the PLO from Lebanon, and the stabilization of the political and military situation. When it became reasonably sure that the war would not spread, most of the reservists were released. However, as long as there were Israeli forces in Lebanon, and there was the continued threat of a military conquest of western Beirut, the homefront remained in a state of un-certainty as to the mobilization of a large number of reservists.

The purposes of our study are, first, to delineate and analyze the main reasons for the reaction patterns of (a) the general institutional system, or, more precisely, of the civilians not recruited to the armed forces, and (b) the bearers of societal roles[3] within the system to the special situation that was generated by the war's outbreak and the social mo-bilization that resulted; and, second, to analyze these patterns of reaction in the context of the unique situation of Israeli society, which from its very beginnings has been in a state of perpetual conflict with the Arab environment.

A Social System under Pressure

The civilian system faced four potential types of pressures in this period. First, pressures resulting from the nature of the Israeli-Arab war: In Israel, this war was perceived as threatening both the physical and socio-political existence of the collectivity as a whole. According to this conception, defeat in war would not only mean a loss of prestige or territory or a blow to national interests, but the total annihilation of Israeli society.[4]

Second, the threat of potential loss of life to each member of the collectivity (independent of the danger to the very existence of the collectivity as a whole)—both of civilians and (primarily) of soldiers on the front. This was accompanied by anxiety over the expectation of the loss of private property (e.g., if there had been bombings) and damage to the collectivity's economic capacity.

Third, the tension stemming from the very fact of reorganization of the system in various spheres in order to cope with the state of war and the snags in this reorganization constituted both emotional and instrumental pressures on the bearers of roles and severe constraints in the institutional system. The absence of many of the bearers of complementary roles, especially in the framework of primary groups and the family ("husband," "father," "son," or "boyfriend"), but also in the framework of secondary groups ("boss-worker," "supplier-client," "driver-passenger," etc.), brought about a situation whereby those (both men and women) who were not recruited into the military found it difficult to fulfill their roles, were not sure of the system's (or individuals') expectations in the situation created, or were suddenly exposed to contradictory expectations, as we shall see below. In such a situation we can hypothesize that the world of various individuals was shaken to a differential degree.[5] With the predominant task being to ensure the continued existence of the collectivity, a task translated into victory (or at least not defeat) in war, all roles not directly related to this task may be perceived as having lost their validity and the social rewards accruing to them (prestige, money, and power).

Fourth, pressures stemming from actual or potential shortages due to the mobilization of the system's resources for the purpose of attaining the predominant goal. Shortages were created in the supply of various goods and services (food, transportation and shipping, some of the educational services, fuel, etc.), and it was not clear when these services would be renewed, or until when services that did operate would continue to do so. These constraints and the uncertainty they created introduced both emotional and instrumental pressures into the system. However, these pressures were not necessarily present in every case and for all strata; nor was their intensity equal throughout the population. Even the connotations of these pressures varied from individual to individual. In order to better understand this whole matter, it is important to first look at the context in which the 1973 (and early 1974) war situation took place, as opposed to the 1982 war.

A Disaster Situation?

Until now, very few attempts have been made to analyze and explain the behavior of the Israeli social system as a whole and/or of groups and actors within it in times of active warfare.[6] The two most noteworthy attempts referred to the 1967 war (Kamen, 1971), and the 1973 war (Bar-Yosef and Padan-Eisenstark, 1977).[7] Both these studies were rooted in a common theoretical starting point—that is, that of disaster studies. Another series of studies that dealt with a fairly broad spectrum of problems appearing on the homefront during the war was based on various psychological and psychotherapeutic approaches.[8] But it seems that these two basic approaches could not provide a comprehensive response to the basic question of the nature of the functioning of the system and of individuals within it during wartime. The former approach reached a dead end because it ignored the fact that the necessary condition for the use of the theoretical framework of disaster studies—that is, the occurrence of a disaster—did not exist. The analogy to a disaster seems to stem from three independent sources: (1) the appearance of shortages was reminiscent of similar phenomena in disaster situations that stemmed, of course, from other sources; (2) there was a deep fear of (and also institutional preparation for) severe physical injury (by means of airplane bombings and enemy missiles); and (3) on the level of values, war is perceived as a disaster. The latter approach, that of various psychological and psychotherapeutic studies, did not present generalizations, but since it focused on extreme and deviant phenomena of negligible statistical significance, not only did not contribute to the understanding of the functioning of the system, but also unintentionally created a cumulative impression biased in the direction of severe difficulties in adjustment and of extreme malfunctioning.

Nevertheless, from the standpoint of the effectiveness of our conceptual framework and the analysis of our findings, it is worthwhile to summarize the disaster studies, which constitute a body of accumulated knowledge that can be used, at least in part, for our purposes. An additional factor which leads us to deal with the concepts of disaster studies is the fact that such studies categorize and deal with cases pertaining to the civilian population in wartime. Thus, for example, Hultaker's study classifies Swedish disasters by constructing a model of behavior based on the bombing of London in World War II; the study by Lang and Lang deals, among other things, with the World War II bombings of Germany and Britain and the life of the Jews in the Nazi concentration camps.[9] Barton and Sjoberg and others also mention that war's air bombings and the flight of some of the inhabitants from Paris.[10]

Many of those studying this area explicitly state the need for classifying disasters by their source—as for example, natural versus "man-made" disasters, with the latter including revolutions, military defeats, etc.[11] It is worthwhile noting that since World War II the tendency has been growing of dealing with events of war in the context of disaster studies, inasmuch as one of the practical goals of such research is the delineation, prediction, and treatment of sociological and psychological processes destined to occur as a result of which nuclear bombing is more likely to occur, than another conventional war. This trend is evident in much of the literature published in this area.[12]

In the beginning of his study, Barton[13] presents an introduction entitled "What We Can Learn from Disasters." Here he explains the need for disaster studies in the context of a nuclear threat, primarily in order to allow for the more effective treatment of nuclear disaster by means of an analysis of existing disaster studies and the construction of theoretical models. War situations seem to be more akin to the subject of nuclear disaster than are hurricanes, tornadoes, or floods. In this context, it is worth noting the study by Ikle, which claims that the appropriate analogy to serious nuclear bombing is to be found in the great plagues of the Middle Ages, and not in the natural disasters that are generally studied in the disaster study framework.[14] This trend of thought clearly contributes to a greater focus of the attention of students of disasters on wars and related phenomena, and—particularly relevant to our subject—on the functioning of civilians in war situations.

To this point, we have tried to analyze the sources of the almost intuitive tendency to relate to the functioning of civilians in the wars by use of the conceptual framework of disaster studies. Now we must examine to what extent our case is indeed appropriate for analysis under the conceptual framework of disaster studies, and to what extent such a framework would be beneficial. This examination will be conducted on two levels. First, we will examine to what extent our case correlates with the research definitions and questions generally accepted in the literature, and, second, we will attempt to determine whether the theoretical models generally accepted in the study of disasters are effective instruments for examining the behavior of civilians in the 1973 war.

The Theoretical Assumptions in Disaster Studies

It is quite difficult to find a definition that is sufficiently broad to encompass all or most disasters and, at the same time, does not include events that we do not relate to as disasters.[15] One of the most detailed definitions, which is relatively easily operationalized, is that of Marx and Fritz.[16] This definition includes several components. We will examine each of them in turn according to the degree of their suitability to our case.[17]

One, the event affects a community of persons—with the community here being defined as a group of persons sharing a common territory and linked by relatively permanent social relations. Israeli society as a whole may be viewed as a "community."

Two, the event confronts a large segment of the community with actual danger, or threats of danger, and loss of cherished values and material objects. It is certain that the 1973 war, which was perceived as a threat to the country's existence and security, fulfills this condition of danger or threat.

Three, the event results in deaths, injuries, the destruction of property and other losses and deprivations to the population, e.g., the disruption of community utilities and other community sevices. From our standpoint, this is the most problematic component. It is true that the civilian population did not suffer any severe damage to property and certainly not any loss of lives (except for the destruction of the property of a small number of settlements in the Golan Heights, which are by no means unequivocally "civilian"), but some of the mobilized family members serving on the front were hurt or were perceived as being in extreme danger.

For the civilian population, though, the war was generally expressed at the very most in several stays in shelters, maintenance of blackout procedures, and short-range and partial shortages in several products and transportation services (see chapter 2).

Four, the direct or indirect consequences of the disaster affect large proportions of the population. Inasmuch, as we noted above, as it is difficult to speak of the occurrence of a disaster in terms of the civilian population itself, this component is not relevant. The definition of Marx and Fritz thus presents us with the main problem in the use of the instruments of disaster studies: In the 1973 war, while the prerequisites for the case to be included in the framework of disaster studies were fulfilled, the disaster itself did not take place.

We chose to begin with the components of the definition of disaster presented by Marx and Fritz, since this definition makes explicit mention of the actual occurrence of the disaster. Other definitions do not specify the actual occurrence of the event per se, although it is clear from their analyses and models that they make the implicit assumption that the event has indeed occurred. Barton defines a disaster as "a sudden, large unfavorable change in the inputs of a social system."[18] The "social system" may be of any size—from a small group to a national or international community. The "change" can be expected or unexpected, can encompass all or part of the system, and the "inputs" may be physical conditions, economic relationships, power relations, or the belief system of the population. Thus, a case of war can certainly be included in Barton's definition, although it is clear that his definition related only to "change" that indeed takes place, while in the 1973 war, as noted, such was hardly the case.

It is worthwhile mentioning that the temporary changes in Israeli society during the war, such as a scarcity of workers (because of mobilization) and various partial shortages and difficulties in supply of services, may be viewed as "changes in inputs," but it seems that since these changes were very partial and short-lived, while a minimal level of functioning of the system in spheres perceived as essential was maintained, it is difficult to speak of a change in input in the sense noted in Barton's definition. A similar picture also emerges from an examination of the definiton of Thompson and Hawkes. "A sudden and disruptive event that overtaxes the community's resources and abilities to respond, so that outside aid is required."[19] This definition presents problems more complex than those noted above in terms of its compatibility with the case of the 1973 war, among other things perhaps because these researchers, as many others, are interested primarily in a specific type of disaster—natural disasters—and their work relates to studies conducted on tornadoes, hurricanes, floods, etc. But here too the central problem from our point of view is that Thompson and Hawkes assume *a priori* that the disaster indeed occurred.

Erickson[20] presents a completely different approach to disaster studies, and defines a disaster according to its results: An event is defined as a disaster if it arouses a traumatic reaction, with trauma being defined according to the clinical psychological usage of the destruction of defense mechanisms and damage to the delicate tissues underlying them. This definition is a broad one, inasmuch as it does not solve the problem with which we are faced, since (as we shall see later) it is difficult to speak of masses suffering from a trauma in the wake of the war (and it must be remembered that we are dealing only with the civilian population) in the sense used by Erikson with reference to the Buffalo Creek flood.

At first glance, the situation in our case seems to resemble several cases described in the literature as false alarms—cases in which, for various reasons, it seemed to the public that a disaster was occurring, although this had no basis in fact. The most well-known of these cases is the "invasion from Mars" analyzed by Cantril et al., and another example where an alarm warning of an air attack was sounded in error in a Washington business district.[21] But, actually, this type of study is not relevant to our subject matter: From the moment that people became convinced that a bomb had been dropped or an invasion from Mars had indeed occurred, these events became real from the standpoint of their results and the reactions to them. We, on the other hand, are dealing with a case in which a disaster—as defined in the literature— did not occur at all, not even in the people's minds.

Thus, we see that the case of the 1973 war is only partially compatible with the commonly accepted definitions of disaster, and for the 1982 war not at all. We are dealing with a situation in which there existed conditions suitable for the occurrence of a disaster and there was also an expectation on the part of the social system that it would occur, but in actuality it did not.

Many take issue with the possibility of generalizing and even with the importance to be attributed to the definitions of disasters. Barton claims: "It is not much use arguing over what to call a disaster. The best way to develop understanding of this set of events is to find several basic dimensions on which these situations vary, which will help account for a wide range of differences."[22] In the spirit of this approach, it is worthwhile to first of all examine the questions dealt with in disaster research. As Barton notes, these can be classified into several groups according to the time phases of the disaster process and according to the social unit constituting the subject of the study. On the level of the individual, he notes the following questions: Will people react to warnings? Will they behave rationally or panic and flee? Will they tender aid to each other or be indifferent? Will they indulge in looting? Will they emphasize cooperation or seek scapegoats at various stages of the disaster process?

On the family level, questions are posed as to the effect of the individual's role in the family, on his functioning as a whole, the behavior of those having a family versus those not having a family in terms of help to others, panic, the relative importance of family ties as opposed to other social ties in times of disaster, etc.

On the organizational level, questions such as the following are posed: Will people maintain their organizational roles in times of disaster or will they leave them in order to care for their families? What is the significance of the institutional system's organization for coping with the disaster prior to its occurrence? To what extent will organizations relinquish considerations of power and prestige in order to effectively deal with the situation?[23]

On the level of the community, these questions relate to the degree of the community's preparedness to deal with the disaster, the ability of the traditional community leadership to cope with the disaster situation, the degree of commitment of people in disaster areas to the community, and the way in which communities near the place of disasters react.

Again, it seems that some of these questions may be relevant at least to the case of the 1973 war while others, particularly those dealing with functioning and reactions from the time of the outbreak of the disaster, are irrelevant to our subject.

Research Instruments and Models

Despite the fact that a considerable portion of the knowledge in the study of disasters is composed of specific case studies having the character of a reservoir of data not necessarily comparable to data from other sources, researchers of disasters also attempt to develop models on a more general level whose purpose it is to classify and offer a general explanation for a specific aspect or component of human behavior in times of disaster.

On the level of the explanation of individual behavior, we may note various models on a continuum of explanations in purely psychological terms as opposed to explanations in sociological terms. As an example of the former type we may note the model of Wolfenstein,[24] whose starting point is depth psychology. His main claim is that disaster conditions may be viewed as an imitation of infantile conditions that arouse unsolved conflicts in the individual. According to this approach, we can predict various aspects of the individual's behavior in a disaster by referring to the basic theory and by examining the individual's unsolved conflicts. Another model that attempts to predict individual behavior in times of disaster from a psychological starting point is that of Janis,[25] which is also phrased in terms of arousal of anxiety and the means of dealing with such anxiety; he speaks of a group of concentric defense mechanisms that are put into effect by the individual in disaster situations. When the action of these defense mechanisms proves to be ineffective, frustration is created in the individual, and, in its wake, regression expressed in hostility. This hostility may be displaced to the ego, and in extreme cases lead to self-destruction. One should nevertheless not exaggerate the importance of models dealing with ineffective or nonadaptive behavior in times of disaster such as those presented by Wallace's disaster syndrome,[26] because of the tremendous difficulties and the biases in the definition of effective or adaptive behavior. Thus, Lang and Lang, for example, claim that behavior that is adaptive for the individual may be nonadaptive for the collectivity, etc.

The second reason for our reservation is the finding frequently observed in the literature that panic behavior and mass hysteria are much more rare in cases of disaster than one would imagine.[27] The problem of the validity of the predictions in disaster studies is clearly built into this sphere of study because of the inability, in most cases, of predicting the occurrence of disasters in advance, and the lack of any possibility for serious research at the time of their occurrence and immediately afterwards.[28] But when the actual disaster never occurs, this difficulty is much greater and significantly limits comparability with existing models.

Another type of model or general explanation focuses on individuals as part of a collectivity—generally the family, community, or organization. These models are generally stated in socio-psychological or sociological terms. Many deal with the individual's priorities in giving aid or his general functioning in times of disaster. Most researchers agree that the highest priority is given to the family. Friedson notes that a familiar finding is that the extended family comes to life during a disaster and is the most dominant factor in giving aid to the injured.[29] Killian noted that when people are faced with the choice between the family and other groups in the community, in a disaster situation most choose the family, at least in the short-range, and this is also the general conclusion of the Swedish disaster studies.[30]

Controversy exists as to the family's effectiveness at the time of the disaster. Many researchers agree that the family has a highly positive role in the physical, emotional, and social rehabilitation of those injured in the disaster. Thus, for example, Hultaker and Frost, after summarising the literature, claim that the findings indicate that it is good policy to maintain a whole family in times of war and other disasters, primarily because people seek and receive aid in their kin groups.[31] The explanation for the family's effectiveness is generally focused on the key terms of "responsibility" and "role." Hill and Hauser claim: "The more clear-cut the responsibilities—the more effectively a person meets a disaster."[32] They quote Quarantelli, who concludes that taking responsibility for another person is an almost sure means of prevention of panic (and escape). They explain the significance of responsibility in saying that when a person bears responsibility, he tells himself that others need him and his acts can save their lives or cost them their lives. They further claim that this trend of thought creates an "emotional check" that prevents panic, hysteria, etc. Fritz and Marx also argue that the functioning of persons having a family in a disaster situation is more effective than that of those without a family. Barton, who also relates to the work of Fritz and Marx, explains that strong motivation to help one's family prevents behavioral aggression.[33]

There is much data that supports Barton's argument[34] that in a situation of role conflict in the context of disaster, the family is revealed as stronger than the community, and the latter as stronger than formal organizations. Hill and Hauser[35] define this ranking in a more detailed manner: the individual will be ready to help others only after the welfare of those with whom he maintains intimate ties (the members of the primary group) is secure. Only then will he help other friends and organizations (secondary groups) with whom he identifies. Only afterwards will he help strangers, and later deal with property—first, his own, and later that of family members and intimate friends, and only then of others less close to him. Notwithstanding the family's salience and its significance in the disaster situation, it is worthwhile noting that the frame of reference of the research itself is generally the community. An explanation for the salience of the community as a unit of research in disaster studies can possibly be found in Nelson.[36] He believes, as does Bar-Yosef, that the disaster is characterized by a reconstitution of the *Gemeinschaft*.

We are generally dealing here with an injured community that is part of a broader society that is uninjured and that renders both immediate aid and long-range rehabilitation. Sjoberg, in noting this fact, even warns that in a case in which the broader society is injured and outside aid cannot be expected, it is very likely that we will witness social processes different from those known from existing disaster studies. To a certain extent this point again limits the similarity between disaster studies and the case of the 1973 war in which the disaster—to the extent that it was to occur—was perceived as equally threatening to all parts of Israeli society. Nevertheless, the question of the relative importance of various social groups and the possible role conflict among them may be relevant to the case discussed here: Inasmuch as the disaster itself did not take place, we are not interested in actual decisions and choices of individuals in the disaster situation, but rather in the relative priority of various social roles as perceived by individuals in the emergency period in which there was a clear danger of the occurrence of a disaster. These priorities were expressed in (among other things) routine performance of roles in the framework of primary and secondary groups and the organizations to which the individual belonged, and in the performance of additional roles in the context of the community or collectivity (volunteer roles).

It is clear that we cannot accept a priori the model presented above as to the ranking of commitments to various social roles as described on the basis of disaster studies. The reasons for this are, first of all, that we are studying a situation of a disaster that did not occur, and this may be totally different from a disaster situation in terms of (a) the pressure of the situation, (b) the definition of alternatives, and (primarily)

(c) the *implications* of the choices that the individual must make; and because of a basic difference in the perception of various social roles, and possibly also in the degree of their legitimation. In cases of disaster the routine role is generally perceived as ineffective, and behavior expressed in the continuation of such functioning is perceived as nonadaptive and undesirable. On the other hand, in the Israeli case not only was the continuation of routine functioning not viewed as nonadaptive, but rather it was or might be perceived (as will be discussed later) as a normative imperative of the social system. In a situation of shock, uncertainty, and change or the danger of change characteristic of a disaster situation, it is clear that this difference in the perception of the routine role may completely change the individual's perception of reality, and, as a result, his functioning.

Thus, in our case it is difficult to accept a priori the model of ranking role priorities characteristic of disaster studies. Nevertheless, in the framework of this study we also include the problem of the perception of the role, possible conflicts between roles, the search for new roles as opposed to the carrying out of routine roles, and the criteria for classifying the routine roles themselves in terms of commitment to them in times of emergency as expressed in a situation of threat of disaster.

Another type of argument of general significance, although not characterized by well-formulated models, relates to the sphere of stratification. Some researchers in this area claim that the existence of a situation of stress tends to eliminate the differentiation inherent in social stratification and drastically reduces the number of significant reference groups. The society tends to become organized on two levels, as is characteristic of nonmodern societies.[37] This approach is also supported by Sorokin, who claims that war, and particularly revolutions in their earliest and most destructive stages, release powerful forces that tend to eliminate economic inequality.[38] But the relevance of this claim of Sorokin's to our case is relatively limited, inasmuch as he clearly relates to the possibility of social change in the system in the wake of disaster. Other researchers present a different argument. Some stress the expectation of a return to the status quo as the key point, and focus on the integration among social strata when this factor of expectation of a return to the status quo indeed exists. Sjoberg writes that in the wake of a disaster, cooperation among various social strata is created, and the differences among them are blurred, but only in those cases in which there is a conception of at least partial control. High morale and integration appear only when the population believes in the restoration of the status quo and one cannot expect the appearance of integration and unity when restoration is expected.[39]

As will be demonstrated later, one cannot speak of the collapse of the stratification system and the (temporary) integration created among the various social strata only on the basis of the explicit expectation that stratification will be restored after recovery from the disaster situation.

At the same time, the disaster does not necessarily have an identical meaning for various strata, although objectively it applies to all those belonging to the injured collectivity. Hill and Hauser note, in relation primarily to studies on the Depression in the United States, that theoretically the vulnerability of lower-class families is not greater than that of the middle class. Each stratum has its own Achilles' heel. While the lower-class families have fewer resources at their disposal, middle-class families tend to overestimate difficulties because these constitute threats to their status and aspirations.[40] This reasoning as to the magnitude of possible loss as a result of the breakdown of the existing social order receives certain support from the findings of Quarantelli and Dynes,[41] according to which in disaster conditions the middle class (whose possible loss is greater) tends to evacuate less than does the lower class.

It is perhaps necessary to clarify the source of the incompatibility among the approaches presented above—that of Bar-Yosef and Padan-Eisenstark arguing that the stratification system collapses in times of emergency, and that of Sjoberg, who argues that no such process is in evidence. Bar-Yosef and Padan-Eisenstark define the goal of the system subject to a disaster situation (in this case, the 1973 war) as follows: "Fighting for victory in war is the first and central task of a society in a situation of crisis or war."[42] This contrasts with most disaster studies, including that of Sjoberg, which view the system's goal in a disaster situation as the return to a situation of normalcy or to social equilibrium (whether this means a return to the previous equilibrium or to a different equilibrium because of the change in the balance of forces among various social groups).[43] According to this approach, the victory in war that Bar-Yosef and Padan-Eisenstark speak of will be an intermediate goal or possibly a means to attaining the ultimate end of a return to an equilibrium situation. Thus, even if Sjoberg would accept the argument of Bar-Yosef and Padan-Eisenstark according to which the emergency situation will lead to a change in criteria for the allocation of societal resources,[44] he will still view this new criterion for the allocation of resources only as an additon to the previous criteria that continue to exist. Furthermore, according to his approach, which stresses the perceived temporariness of the emergency situation, this additional criterion will be only temporary, inasmuch as even at the time of the emergency situation the injured population is aware of the temporariness of this criterion.

As we shall see below, the 1973 war should be viewed as an event with a dual meaning, perceived on the one hand as a one-time trauma, similar to a flood or hurricane in the classic disaster studies, and, on the other, as a temporary intensification in the constant process of confrontation.

This dual conception has a special significance in terms of the suitability of the Israeli case to the theoretical framework of disaster studies. Most of the cases dealt with in the framework of disaster studies are, as noted, one-time traumatic events. In this connection, Merton states that the concept of disaster as sudden and acute collective stress as opposed to chronic suffering focuses our attention on the high visibility of such events, and the social results of this visibility. He again asks Barton's question: Why is not climate, for example, defined as a disaster worthy of a mass reaction?[45] Erikson, who also discusses this point, reaches the general conclusion that we must differentiate between "acute" and "chronic" disasters which, although differing in terms of individuals' reactions to them, are both included in the category of disasters.[46] Classic disaster studies focus first and foremost on events of acute significance, while in our opinion the Israeli case, as we will see later, should be viewed as an acute outbreak of a chronic phenomenon existing at any given point in time. It is clear that this point also limits our ability to make use of models suggested by disaster studies.

Another subject dealt with in the framework of disaster studies is the organizational sphere and its functioning. There is no doubt that the efficient functioning of at least some organizations is an important component in the rescue and rehabilitation of the injured social system. Nevertheless, as noted above, most of the researchers conclude that the organizational role is low vs. the individual role in times of disaster. One of the central problems dealt with by those studying the organizational system in disaster conditions concerns the cost of institutional preparation. Sjoberg defines this in discussing a dilemma of industrial society: whether the society should invest to preserve what it has or live dangerously in order to arrive at a higher level of technological attainment.[47] It is clear that the specific response to this dilemma is related to variables concerned with the frequency of disasters in a given society—to economic variables of the price of the disaster and the cost of the investment in defense against it, and to cultural and social variables relevant to the perception of the disaster. Barton argues, in this connection, that the reason for the absence of investment in institutional defense against disasters stems from their great rarity: Serious preparation for a disaster requires long-range planning and a readiness to invest without any promise of receiving returns from the investment—matters far beyond the capacity of most local agents.[48]

On the macro-level, the possibility of war—as a specific type of disaster—is dealt with more efficiently: Most countries maintain a skeleton force of professionals to deal with the problem, and this force may be expanded in times of emergency by the recruitment of nonprofessional manpower. Barton notes several examples of civilian organizations of this nature—the Red Cross, public health services, the fire department, and the local police force.

Under what circumstances can we expect an organization to function effectively in disaster conditions? In the light of his examination of the effectiveness of the functioning of various organizations in times of disaster, Barton concludes that the following are necessary: First, leadership should be recruited to organizations on the basis of technical skills (rather than on the basis of ascriptive criteria). Second, the organization must have plans prepared in advance for functioning in times of disaster. Third, the organization needs to practice the implementation of these programs.[49] This point of the efficient functioning of the organizational system is very relevant to our case study, particularly in light of the chronic aspect of the Israeli-Arab conflict. Although the disaster itself did not occur, the threat and the situation of emergency were sufficient to activate those organizations that were prepared in advance to function in such situations. We can thus examine to what extent there indeed existed organizations aimed at dealing with the situation, how they functioned and at what level of efficiency, what spheres they defined as having high priority and what others were neglected, and to what extent their activity was based on the implementation of preconceived and pretested programs, as opposed to the ad hoc improvisation of solutions to problems. Such subjects will be dealt with in the framework of this study.

We have surveyed a variety of models, theoretical hypotheses, and generalizations as to various aspects of disaster studies. It should be noted that considerable doubt is expressed in the literature as to the possibility of arriving at general models that will be valid for all the events included in the category of "disasters," primarily because of the tremendous variety of phenomena characterized by this term.[50]

Before we leave this area, though, one should note the structural dimensions of Barton, which include: (1) the extent of the injury (geographically, the number of persons, etc.); (2) the rate of the outbreak (immediate, gradual, chronic); (3) the duration of the injury itself (short, long); and (4) social preparedness (low or high).[51]

As is the case with Lang and Lang's dimensions, here too we can demonstrate that the Israeli case of the 1973 war (but not of the 1982 war) was relevant to some of the dimensions—particularly that of preparedness. Barton writes that a society that has experienced external pressure in the past is likely to learn how to deal with it and to develop a high degree of social preparedness. A system is "highly prepared" for a given type of pressure if it has well-defined roles for individuals. These individuals receive appropriate training for these roles and the roles are organized in organizations and plans that can be put into effect. We can relate to the degree of preparedness of the Israeli social system as expressed in the war periods. Nevertheless, some of Barton's dimensions are not relevant to our discussion, primarily because the disaster did not occur at all.

But Merton's comment quoted above as to why climate is not defined as a disaster raises the possibility that the situation should be analyzed in a different or additional context—that is, that of the general Israeli (or Jewish)–Arab conflict. This is so as from the beginnings of its existence as a sovereign state, and even before that, in the long formation period that preceded sovereignty, Israel has been in a state of constant and chronic conflict with its Arab neighbors. This situation introduced a permanent element into the system known as "security tension."

The Interrupted System

When dealing with Israeli society, we are referring to a situation of prolonged tension of a cumulative nature which on a certain level has actually become an immanent part of the social structure. The new Jewish community in Palestine has existed under the threat of annihilation since its establishment in the 1880's. Despite this situation's permanence we can note peaks in the outbreak of tension: the riots of 1921, 1929, 1936, and 1939, and after the establishment of the State—the War of Independence (1948-9), the Sinai Campaign (1956) and the so-called Six-Day War (1967). The respite between these periods was perceived as a continuation of the crisis which preceded it and as bearing a higher potential of threat for the future within it.[52]

If indeed the wars in which Israel has been involved are perceived as being on a continuum of conflict or constant but differential amount of security tension,[53] then the context of our analysis changes. But in order to fully comprehend the difference between this context and that of the "disaster" paradigm, we must expand on this approach by what will be the central hypothesis of this study. The argument is that if indeed conflict has become an immanent part of the social structure, it is very likely that organizations, institutions, and institutional arrangements will be established whose function it is to deal with the continuous conflict. We may hypothesize that the very existence of a perpetual conflict—whether active or dormant[54]—demanding limited and controlled use of power, allowed for the construction of a flexible social system that could reduce the total cost of involvement in the conflict to the bare minimum while constructing effective and flexible institutional arrangements for dealing with the conflictual situation. An important example of such arrangements and organization is the Israeli reserves system,[55] which cuts down to a minimum the time needed for transition from a dormant to an active situation of war. This flexibility enables the system to act even in a large-scale mobilization of manpower and material resources for dealing with the conflict. Conflict management is only one of a conglomerate of social goals that have to compete for the allocation of various social resources. Eliezer Schweid posed this situation as a constant and basic dilemma with which the system must cope:

> In order to exist we must mobilize all the forces of existence. But if all forces are to be mobilized exclusively for the defense of mere existence, then we cannot exist. How can we deal with the struggle for life without the war destroying life and economically, socially, and spiritually enslaving all creative activity to it. . . . pioneering Zionism can be proud of the fact that it withstood this dilemma. It found ways of social and political organization which allowed for continued creativity and the continued existence of a meaningful and purposeful life in a situation demanding constant alertness.[56]

We hypothesize that this is a permanent dilemma that would exist even in the extreme situation of an acute increase in the conflict's intensity whereby coping with the conflict would become the system's predominant goal. This dilemma would be expressed in a cluster of conflicting expectations and cross-pressures of differential intensity on actors who were not mobilized for roles directly relevant to the war situation (armed forces, war industries, etc.) through the institutionalized channels. On the one hand, every individual is expected to contribute to the attainment of the common goal to the best of his ability. In addition, if the institutional system does not provide access to "contributing" positions, individuals are expected to initiate such roles and positions and, at the very least, to allocate time resources to them. On the other hand, those who "stay at home" are not only expected to continue with their routine lives as much as is possible but also to maintain their private and collective "world order." However, at the same time the system also offers an opportunity for a moratorium from the fulfillment of some or all the routine roles that are not relevant to the predominant goal at hand.

It is the conflictual frame of reference that enables us to relate to those activities and roles that are defined as irrelevant to the attainment of the predominant goal by the conceptual framework of disaster studies as legitimate outputs of the system and an integral part of general social processes, rather than as "nonadaptive" or "pathological" reactions. Even in a situation of very intense conflict and maximal mobilization of the system, "conflictual outputs" are not necessarily in a zero-sum relationship to "routine outputs."

The Israeli-Arab conflict is also a chronic situation that caused the system to develop mechanisms that were to deal with it quickly and effectively. But at the same time, the sudden changes in the conflict's intensity (i.e., the passing into a stage of warfare) and the threat inherent in it are components that liken it to the patterns of social inputs and outputs known to us from disaster studies. Therefore, in order to analyze this special situation we will have to synthesize the two approaches: One that analyzes the processes and phenomena that appeared among civilians in the 1973 war, and to a lesser extent in those of 1982, from the perspective of a prolonged conflict, along with the approach that views this period as a special ("disastrous") occurrence, although comparable to similar events at other times and in other contexts. It seems that this combination will help us construct a framework for analysis and comprehension of an interrupted social system.

A dialectic process is engendered in the Israeli society with the sudden (or gradual) increase in tension up to the development of a situation to be defined as warfare. On the one hand, there is a tendency to interrupt all social processes that do not directly serve[57] the predominant goal— which is "making war" most effectively (according to the military doctrine prevalent in a given society at a given time). On the other hand, the tremendous effort invested in the attainment of the central goal is legitimate only in terms of the original social purposes prior to the interruption of social processes. Thus, "interruption" is not social change, but rather its very antithesis.

Bar-Yosef and Padan-Eisenstark state that "the existence of the pressure tends to dramatically eliminate the differentiation in the stratification system and decrease the significant reference groups. The society tends to organize itself on two levels [as in non-modern societies]—the level of society as a whole, and that of primary groups."[58] Thus, Sorokin also states that "war, and especially revolution, in its initial and most destructive phase, releases powerful forces tending to rectify economic inequalities."[59]

But Bar-Yosef and Padan-Eisenstark certainly did not refer to this nor to the expected (short-range) pattern of war between Israel and the

Arabs, but to one of the derivatives of the intensification of social integration in wartime. Coser (in his Proposition 9) indeed states that an exogenous enemy intensifies social integration, but is careful not to claim far-reaching changes in the internal structure of the collectivity under exogenous pressure. Thus, for example, he states that "a common enemy promotes coalition, but more than a common enemy is required to transform coalitions into unified systems or groups."[60]

At least in the short range, the wars in Israel until today have not brought about a significant reallocation of social rewards *after* their conclusion. As long as the war situation prevails, it seems that we can note a certain change in the allocation of rewards, inasmuch as rewards are channeled toward roles dealing with the predominant goal, but these rewards are not necessarily in a zero-sum situation vis-à-vis those granted to the fulfillers of complementary roles, and it is very difficult to convert rewards and resources acquired by virtue of participation in the fulfillment of the predominant goal in warfare to resources of tradable value in a routine situation.[61] Social interruption includes three elements that are essentially antithetical to social change, whatever its definition: (1) it is temporary, (2) there is *a desire for restoration of the order* that existed before the appearance of that factor which led to social interruption, and (3) there is the promise that the mobilization is *conditional.* Mobilization focuses on the fulfillment of essential and specific needs of the interrupted system (not on other broader or unspecified—even desirable— purposes).

The component of temporariness stems from the fact that the very interruption of routine social processes and the reorganization of the system around the predominant goal can be carried out only when there is an explicit awareness of the temporary nature of the total social mobilization. The component of restoration is connected with that of temporariness but they are not one and the same. The purpose of social interruption or of the suspension of most societal activities is the restoration of the collectivity's relative security or its rehabilitation, after which the organization around a predominant goal (created only to fulfill needs arising in an emergency) will cease, and the collectivity will again return to its form of a multipurpose system. Moreover, part of the collectivity's members' motivation to fulfill the predominant goal is anchored in the very promise of the temporariness of the mobilization and the eventual restoration of the system's multipurpose order. This does not imply that changes will not occur in the system in the wake of social interruption, but rather that the interruption itself is not change (or is actually change for the purpose of preservation). It is likely that the system will not be able to return to the "order" that prevailed within it before the interruption, but it is not the goal of the interruption to bring about change; the opposite is the case.

Temporariness cannot be equated with "a short time," or any amount of time that can be determined a priori. Temporariness is a sense that the institutional order that directs society to realize one goal that predominates over all others is not a permanent order. Thus, we do not include in our definition of interrupted societies all those societies whose governmental systems organize them around one predominant goal (national, economic, ideological, etc.) for the purpose of permanent mobilization of the periphery, since such a social organization strives for permanence (even when in some Utopian future the goal is presented differently).

The factor of temporariness is thus in direct contradiction to the hypothesis of a tendency for the elimination of social differentiation. This contradiction results from the fact that temporariness by its nature implies a return to the previous condition rather than a significant and permanent reallocation of general social resources; the latter in turn being an essential condition for the abolition or limitation of social-class differentiation. It is true that prolonged wars, and especially those that were dealt with ineffectively or that ended in the defeat of the society being examined, often brought about a new allocation of resources and drastic changes in the stratificational map. These changes were generally a byproduct of the dissipation of social resources. However, even when such changes in the distribution of resources occurred during wars or in their wake, they were not necessarily in the direction of greater equalization.

The third element—that is, making the social mobilization for the performance of the specific task a conditional one—is aimed at preventing "taking advantage" of the mobilization for other purposes, and this too serves to maintain the situation extant prior to the interruption.

Sometimes there is only a partial rather than a full interruption. This was the case in June-July 1982, in the military campaign that Israel dubbed "Peace for Galilee." At that time only a part (evidently about half) of all the reservists were called up. Such a situation is different for the society than a full interruption. Experience has shown that in such circumstances it is almost possible to run the system without disruption, simply because those left behind cannot find any legitimation in taking a moratorium from fulfilling their duties. It is true that there were some problems, for example, in the schools, different companies, entertainment, public transportation, etc., which, while showing the strain here and there, nevertheless continued functioning. The moratorium was individual (for example, those civilians who were mobilized were exempted from fulfilling their civilian duties, such as making payments of various debts and of their mortgages), and not collective. A person who was not mobilized could not absent himself from his work or stop paying his bills, claiming that the country was at war.

The very act of a large military venture, the fact that many soldiers were killed and many civilians—but not all—were mobilized, made the system very ambivalent, if not lead to a situation of anomie. This ambivalency was seen clearly in the inability to define the situation— in the mass media, in official publications, and in private conversations there was an inconsistent use of the words "military operation" and "war" interchangeably. (We use the term "war" [e.g. the 1956 war], and not "operation," only for the sake of convenience—to be consistent with our convention of labeling Israeli military actions according to the years in which they occurred.) This situation led to a number of internal tensions within the system:

1. The partial mobilization evoked major problems of equity in dividing the burden and dangers fairly among the members of the collectivity— a problem that does not exist when there is a full mobilization, but it is of the nature of such a large organization that it cannot afford to pay the "high prices" that a full rotation would have demanded from it in terms of confusion among the forces.
2. The uncertainty about the developments during the war created a great deal of personal uncertainty for all those who were subject to mobilization but who had not been mobilized, or were mobilized and then eventually released (provided that the war would not spread any further).
3. Neither the institutional system nor the value system knew whether to treat this as a state of war (as is the case of total interruption in the homefront), or whether business should go on "almost" as usual. And then, if it was to be "almost," which areas should continue and which not? For example, the "emergency economy"(EE—see chapter 2) was not employed at all, while, on the other hand, the mass media (radio and television) went onto a war footing, at least for the first month of the campaign. Some of the economic processes were stopped (for example the market for housing), but the places of entertainment and vacation areas lost almost no clientele (a fact that increased the feeling of an unfair sharing of the national burden).
4. The 1982 war was the longest active war (not the longest interruption), except for the 1947-48 war. Except for the latter, Israel has never been involved in any war that lasted a month or more. But this condition was somewhat blurred by the nondefinition of the situation (war vs. operation) and the sporadic nature of the fighting.

Here we must add that this war, more than any other of Israel's wars, showed almost no break in communication between the front and the homefront. A few days after the fierce battles had broken out, most of the soldiers were able to call home, and within two to three weeks were able to come home for short vacations. Many people, as a result of their vocations (journalists, government workers, etc.), or even without any specific reason for doing so, were able to move freely from the front to the homefront and back, without being stopped. This made things much easier for both the soldiers and those at home, but did not make the situation any more clear. There are signs that the phenomenon that followed, which had no precedent in Israel—i.e., the casting of doubts as to the justice and necessity of the war (primarily after the change in its declared aims) and the formation of protest groups against it while the battle was still raging—began at the front and spilled over speedily into the homefront. From that point of view, the 1982 war has been the only in Israel to this time that affected adversely the social cohesion in Israel and did not strengthen it (see chapter 5). All these factors together— the partial interruption, the problem of defining the situation, the lengthy duration, the inequity of the mobilization burden, the raising of doubts as to the logic and justice of the war—evidently worked together to increase the uncertainty and anomie in the system during the 1982 war.

Relevance to the War Situation Versus
Fostering Continuity of the Existing Order

Bar-Yosef's and Padan-Eisenstark's claim[62] concerning the reevaluation of situations, activities, roles, and even individuals within the system according to the degree of relevance or proximity of their roles to the predominant goal, stems from the very fact of the conversion of the previous state of the system to one oriented to a single dominant goal. Stinchombe also poses the same question: What happens to various roles in a situation of war?[63] He hypothesizes that the roles relevant to the attainment of "victory" will be rewarded more than those that have no connection to this goal. But as already indicated from the Israeli case in the general context of the Jewish-Arab conflict, the trend to the creation of a basis of social differentiation and stratification parallel to the existence of a predominant social goal will still be in a state of tension with all the other bases of differentiation and criteria of resource allocation anchored in norms and values that determine the general social goals in the routine situation of "no active warfare."

This is so for two principal reasons. First, as stated above, the other social goals do not lose their validity, but rather their attainment is deferred to various degrees. Second, civilians continue to exist as a complete society, some of whose needs and goals may indeed be subject to a moratorium, but the other instrumental and expressive needs (sometimes defined as "minimal") not only continue to exist, but the demand for them becomes even more salient. In general, the interruption of social processes does not stem from the fact that these processes serve purposes no longer deemed valid, but rather from selective mobilization for the fulfillment of the predominant goal, which creates a great shortage of an entire series of role bearers. In a complex *Gesellschaft* society, this even paralyzes many areas in which there is not a manpower shortage even after mobilization.

Furthermore, in such a situation the performance of some of the routine roles that are not connected with the predominant goal may be temporarily rewarded even to a greater degree than in "normal" times, because of the manpower shortage.

This is so because the system, even when not "fully active," must be "maintained" in order to ensure its existence as a complete society and in order to allow for the possibility of a quick return to the routine situation after the attainment of the predominant goal.

This argument constitutes an expansion of the hypothesis as to the nature of social interruption, and is anchored in the conception that along with the existence of a predominant goal within the system, there also exists a complementary goal of preservation of the order that preceded the interruption. Thus, the interrupted system is conceived of as having a dual purpose.[64] However, we hypothesize that while for a limited period (until the predominant goal, i.e., victory or the prevention of defeat in war, is attained) the dilemma discussed by Schweid is decisively resolved in favor of "existence," the tension between the two types of purposes ("to exist" versus "how to exist") will continue, particularly in the area defined geographically, societally, and psychologically as "civilian." On the level of social organization this will be expressed in tension, or even in struggles in certain areas, as to which of the two goals will be allocated the resources not yet allocated to the predominant goal. Such struggles sometimes take place even before the event triggering social interruption (since the interruption is not unexpected, and a system existing in a context of constant conflict of varying intensity is by definition always in a state of alert for social interruption, just as it is on alert for a situation of active warfare).[65]

In a situation of social interruption, the institutional level is divided (both in the areas of the predominant and the complementary goals) into spheres in which (1) there exist structured and regular institutional arrangements and spheres in which (2) the institutional system does not supply a priori organizational responses to situations which are likely to

TABLE 1.1
Structured and Unstructured Spheres in the Achievement of the Predominant and Complementary Goals

Nature of Organization	Predominant Goal	Complementary Goal
Structured	Mobilization of manpower and means of transport (the Reserves)	Supplies and transport (Emergency Economy), Civil Defense, and evacuation of injured populations and casualties
Unstructured	Achievement of goal ("flexible response")	All other societal goals and needs (e.g., volunteering)

arise, but rather leaves these to entrepreneurs, improvisations, and "the free play of the market."

In Table 1.1, the row of structured institutional arrangements indicates institutional arrangements and mechanisms that are built into the Israeli system. The most conspicuous among them is the reserve system (which we will not deal with directly in this study). It is perhaps surprising that even with reference to the predominant goal, very extensive spheres of activity remain unordered (unless we call the doctrine of disorder "order"). Thus, as shown by Dan Horowitz,[66] the entire Israeli system of warfare is based on a "flexible response" of local officers to various situations at the front that generally cannot be predicted in advance. This flexibility and the ability to improvise are what grant the Israelis the advantage in complex situations of modern warfare. But the entire sphere of the predominant goal—to the extent that reference is made geographically to civilians—is not in the sphere of our discussion, and the classification is presented only to round out the picture and to understand the activities of the system as a whole.

With reference to the complementary goal, we find several institutional arrangements. These are limited primarily to a part of the achievement of this goal—that part aimed at the system's "upkeep" and minimization of the damage likely to be incurred, both as a result of the interruption itself and as a result of the threat of physical injury to civilians. Almost all other spheres of the complementary goal are not ordered by the institutional system and are left to initiative and improvisation when the interruption comes. But as such periods become more frequent, the institutional system will tend to construct new organizations and institutions—or adapt existing institutions—in order to organize ever larger options of the complementary goal and include them in the structured frameworks (see chapter 2).

On the level of the fulfillment of social roles, we may delineate four patterns (or strategies) of behavior since each actor can act—or not act—simultaneously in two different spheres: (1) in the sphere of fulfillment of routine roles filled by every actor in the context of the social system in times in which there is no interruption;[67] (2) in the sphere of attainment of the predominant (or at least complementary) goals, for although the actor is "stationed" among civilians by virtue of institutional arrangements, he can try to fulfill roles associated with the predominant goal, or can assume new or additional roles in order to aid the system to continue to function (driving a bus or truck, distributing bread, volunteering to teach schools, etc.).

We can justify the elimination of the differentiation between activities relevant to the predominant goal and those relevant to the complementary goal in the light of several interconnected factors: From the institutional standpoint, the behaviors analyzed in this study are located in the area of complementary activities (the civilians). At the same time we can assume that the system is constructed in such a way that in a situation of social interruption most rewards (in the form of prestige stemming from participation in collective tasks) are allocated to tasks performed in the area of the predominant goal or connected with it. From the analytical standpoint (and even empirically—see chapters 2 and 4) the shortage of roles linked with the predominant goal (e.g., ammunition production) among civilians is most salient and these roles are very much in demand.

However, in order to ensure that roles in the zone of the complementary goal will be attractive as well, there will be a tendency to eliminate the differentiation between the two zones of activity and to redefine the meaning of the activities from the zone of the complementary goal, so that they will be linked to the predominant goal. Thus, a reservist general who volunteers to drive a garbage truck[68] will gain publicity, because if a general collects garbage then this and similar activities are perceived as relevant to the war effort. This tendency to eliminate the differentiation between the two zones constitutes an integral part of the functioning of an interrupted system. However, we cannot *analyze* such a system without emphasizing the separate existence of each one of the two task zones.

The actor in the complementary zone acts in the framework of different kinds of constraints, the three main ones being:

Role constraints: Inasmuch as routine roles are characterized by differential degrees of rigidity, and since, from an objective standpoint, time is a zero-sum resource in its allocation among various roles, the individual is not completely free to abandon certain roles, nor is he completely free—in terms of the time at his disposal—to adopt new roles. Thus, for example, the rigidity of such roles as "housewife"or "mother of small children" is much greater than that of the roles of "student" or "single student" at a time when there are no classes in the universities. Situational and normative constraints make it almost impossible for the former to take on a legitimate moratorium from the fulfillment of her roles (although the level of performance of the roles may decline considerably), while the situational constraints stemming from the situation of full social interruption almost compel the latter to do so.

Institutional constraints: These stem not only from a shortage of goods and services, but also from a scarcity of certain types of roles, primarily those connected with the predominant goal, and also those belonging to the zone of fulfillment of the complementary goal. Even when such a shortage does not exist, there are barriers and a lack of information as to the demand for certain roles. In the framework of our research we often came across situations in which on the one hand there was a demand for certain types of manpower, and on the other there was a supply of such manpower. However, a "perfect market" also requires an effective stream of information. In short, there was differential scarcity in the demand for various roles just as there was a limited supply for others. The supply available did not always meet the existing demand because appropriate institutional arrangements did not always exist, and there was a lack of channels of information (see chapters 2 and 4).

Personal constraints: Included here is a varied spectrum of constraints involving a lack of professional and social skills, lack of personal contacts (in order to acquire information as to the existence of or means to approach scarce roles), or lack of mobility (not having a car in a situation in which there is no regular or reliable public transportaion)—all of which reduce the individual's chances of acting in accordance with his predispositions. Subsequently, however, we shall find that at least some of these constraints are significant in a broader context.

Location in the System and Strategies of Role Fulfillment

If indeed various individuals employ different strategies of role fulfillment in times of social interruption, what will be the main predictors of the behavior to be chosen by given social categories? We hypothesize that, beyond the constraints, the choice will be primarily a function of the original routine time location of the actor on the center-periphery continuum, in the sense used by Shils.[69] The degree of the actor's centrality in routine periods is determined by the degree of his proximity to that zone in the system in which, first, one can participate in the creation of central values that determine the goals to be defined as significant or in the right to interpret these values, which are: "The order of symbols, of values, and beliefs which govern society . . . is felt to be such by many who cannot give explicit articulation to its irreducibility. The central zone partakes of the nature of the sacred. In this sense every society has an 'official' religion."[70] Second, one can participate in making decisions which, to a differential degree, bear on the collectivity's fate, inasmuch as the center is not only a "value zone" but also a "power zone," since it is "a structure of activities, or roles and persons, within the network of institutions."

Two of the three generally accepted components of the stratification system—prestige and power—will, by definition, also be determinants of the location of individuals and groups on the continuum of center-periphery, while the degree of importance of the third component—wealth—as a determinant of centrality is an empirical question that varies from society to society and from time to time.[71] Thus, some of the indicators that predict socioeconomic status will also predict "centrality." Here we refer of course to indicators that predict prestige and power (for example, education, occupational status, and ethnic origin), but not income or wealth.

In a situation of rapid and extreme fluctuation in the conflict's intensity, with national security being not only a central value but also predominant over all others, the degree of an actor's centrality is no longer determined by many parameters (for example, the extent of the contribution to the attainment of the predominant goal, and the extent of the contribution to the attainment of the complementary goal, although particularly among the civilians there is constant pressure to eliminate the differentiation between the two and to include the latter in the former). Thus, in such a situation the stratificational position of an individual does not change, since there is no reallocation of most social resources (except for the specific resource of the prestige of participation in the collectivity). *What tends to change or what may change temporarily is the actor's location on the center-periphery continuum.*

In fact, as an integral part of the phenomenon of social interruption, the system separates into two subsystems according to the functional (and geographic) division of the front and the civilian "homefront." In each of these two subsystems a separate scale of proximity to (and distance from) the center is created. Centrality in the zone of the predominant goal is determined relatively simply by the accepted scales of military status (rank, job, unit, etc.).[72] On the other hand, measures of centrality in the social area of the complementary goal are a combination of the actor's location in the initial uninterrupted system and his ability to perform roles that are relevant to the interruption (or to interpret his original roles as relevant to the new societal demands). The two are not totally unrelated to each other.

In contrast, as part of the phenomenon of social interruption, the system exerts pressure to maintain the routine way of life including the location of actors on the center-periphery continuum. This location will also be one of the predictors of the strategy to be employed by actors in a situation of social interruption.

The orientation towards fulfillment of roles can be of two basic types: totalistic or selective. An actor with a totalistic orientation will perceive the normative imperative as requiring him to fulfill *all* types of roles; he will be committed both to his routine roles and to those stemming from the situation of social interruption. He will be characterized by a perception of "all or nothing." If for any reason (see below) he does not succeed in fulfilling roles in each of the two goal zones, he will appeal for a moratorium from the obligations stemming from his other roles as well. This will occur primarily if the actor is oriented toward the predominant goal, while the institutional arrangements place him among the civilians.

Those with a selective orientation will perceive the situation as obligating them to choose between the fulfillment of routine roles and an attempt to fulfill or to initiate new roles necessitated by social interruption. The two types of roles will be perceived as related to each other in a zero-sum relationship (in terms of time, physical and/or emotional effort invested, etc.).

However, we hypothesize that the key variable for predicting the strategy of behavior in a situation of social interruption is the location of the actor on the center-periphery continuum.

We may divide actors into those possessing skills relevant to the situation of interruption and for which there is a demand, and those who do not possess relevant skills. In the context of the performance of disaster roles, Barton indicates that the motivation to fulfill such roles indeed constitutes an essential but not sufficient condition for their performance. In order to fulfill such roles, two social skills are necessary: the knowledge of *whom to contact* or where to turn, and the knowledge of *what to do*. The first type of skill is intimately bound up with the actor's location in the system (the more central the location, the greater the probability of having more social ties), but the second type of skill is not necessarily connected with centrality but rather with the temporary shortage created as a result of the situation of interruption.

In such a situation an actor suddenly finds himself in possession of a scarce resource and is faced with the dilemma of what to exchange this resource for. If the actor acts according to the normative system's prescriptions, he will engage in activity in the framework of one of the institutions coping with the situation of interruption, and in exchange will feel that he is participating in the fulfillment of the complementary goal (and may even enjoy a certain amount of economic reward). In the framework of our analysis, we will not deal with situations in which an individual acts in conflict with the prescriptions of the normative system. Such behavior may be rooted in a broad range of reasons, the main ones being: (1) interruption is a temporary state, and so (2) the rewards offered by the system for fulfillment of the new roles are not perceived as satisfactory or relevant; (3) some of the formal members of the collectivity ("citizens of the state") may feel like deprived non-members, or even opponents of the collectivity's existence in its given form and with its existing contents. In such a case they, at least theoretically, may not only refuse to fulfill a role in the zone of the central or complementary goal, but may also view the situation of war as an opportunity for the fulfillment of their aspiration to fundamentally change, or even destroy, the collectivity.[73]

Thus, those members of the collectivity who do not wish or are not able to fulfill roles in the zones of the predominant and complementary goals, but on the other hand cannot or do not wish to request a moratorium from the fulfillment of their routine roles, will coninue to fulfill these roles—and only these roles—while taking the constraints of the institutional system into consideration. We expect that the strategy of routine activity will be most prevalent in the interrupted system among all those actors who have been placed in the "rear" civilian zone, since this strategy constitutes a "solution" of many and varied dilemmas. It constitutes an alternative for relatively central actors who did not succeed in the "race" for new roles or in initiating them, for relatively peripheral actors who do not bear a totalistic orientation, and, finally, for some of the actors who are not committed to the system.

We must also stress that the choice of one behavior is not necessarily an indicator of the degree of commitment and ideological identification with the collectivity—although we may hypothesize that the more central the actor's location, the more likely he is to identify with the collectivity and its goals. Shils has already noted that "there are persons, not many in any society but often of great importance, who have a very intense and active connection with the centre, with the symbols of the central value system, but whose connection is passionately negative."[74] In this context Shils notes the well-known distinction made by T.S. Eliot between the atheist who feels strong "religious" feelings against religion, and the person who is indifferent to it. In our study we do not deal with those marginal groups (who, according to Shils, are not peripheral) who feel a strong negative tie to the collectivity, its goals, and the definition of its boundaries, but we definitely do include in our discussion all those—especially in the periphery—whose identification with the collectivity is indifferent or whose active identification is at a very low level. In this sense we hypothesize that a strong identification with the collectivity and with the order which originally prevailed within it may serve as a motivation for more active behavior: An actor located in the periphery, who strongly identifies with the collectivity, may attempt to take a moratorium, since this is the strategy that is perceived (particularly in the more peripheral area) as contributing more to the collectivity. But it is probable that the opposite combination—that is, location in a relatively central zone and indifference toward the collectivity, will not necessarily mean a moratorium or any other pattern of behavior. On first glance indifference toward the system should eliminate the orientation toward both the central and complementary goals. But we hypothesize that indifference will generally arise only in a routine social situation when the system can function even when some of the members of the collectivity do not identify with or do not have a strong interest in the maintenance of its internal order. However, in a situation perceived as severely threatening the collectivity there may be a high price for indifference. Indifference as to the existence of an order is not necessarily identical to indifference as to its destruction.

Role Fulfillment in the Zone of the Complementary Goal

In this section we shall reexamine the strategies of fulfillment and focus primarily on the fulfillment of roles in the zone of the complementary goals. In analyzing the institutional system we may note that these roles may be fulfilled in two ways. First, roles may be fulfilled according to the prescriptions of the normative system and the demands of its institutions whose function it is to deal with the situation of social interruption or with the system's "upkeep." For example, if an actor is licensed to drive a heavy vehicle, he may (for a salary, as a volunteer, or by injunction) undertake various transport operations for the "emergency economy" (EE; see chapter 2) or for any other body dealing with the situation of social interruption. Second, the actor can act outside the prescriptions of the normative system (for example, earning a great deal of money by undertaking private transport jobs) or even in violation of these prescriptions (for example, while being mobilized by EE an actor may undertake private jobs at EE's expense and/or with the illegal use of its vehicles). In the two modes of action, on a macro-societal level the actor is serving the complementary goal; that is, contributing to the existence of a transport system. However, in the latter case this is not being done in accordance with the priorities set by the official organization whose function it is to deal with the phenomenon of interruption. When the demand is so much greater than the supply, and the rewards for performing tasks beyond the realm of the prescription of the normative system are so high, it is difficult to assume that a supply of the nature described above will not appear. But such behavior can also appear in the opposite situation—when a great demand exists for roles (in the zone of the complementary goals) and there is a limited general supply (in contrast with the demand for the fulfillment of specific roles). In such cases there are likely to be actors acting outside (and even in violation) of the normative arrangements and prescriptions of the system, in order to fulfill certain roles even when these require skills that the actor does not possess (for example, utilizing pressure and social connections in order to teach in school without having been trained in dealing with social deviance). However, we will not deal with activities not in accordance with the prescription. This is the situation of an actor who decides to convert the resource in his possession to maximum material benefits. In addition, there is an entire series of roles with reference to which the normative system does not dictate any prescriptions (plumbers, garage mechanics, etc.). Nevertheless even with reference to them the dilemma still exists of whether to supply their services according to those criteria which were acceptable before the interruption (prices, selection of customers, etc.) or to take advantage of the new situation in the market for the maximization of material profits. As with reference to all other spheres of social activity, the solution of this dilemma depends on many and diverse variables. However, we will continue to claim that the location in the system—on the center-periphery continuum—will be a key variable and may predict a greater portion of the variance than any other variable.

We will hypothesize that an actor who possesses a resource that is both relevant to the situation of interruption and scarce, and whose location in the center is more central, will tend to exchange this resource according to the prescriptions of the normative system. On the other hand, the more peripheral his location, the more he will tend to exchange the resource for money not in accordance (and sometimes even in conflict) with the prescriptions. The rationale behind this hypothesis is as follows: an actor located in a relatively central position has two incentives (not independent of one another) to act according to the prescriptions of the normative system. First, there is an intrinsic incentive of "centrality oblige," and, second, that this will offer him an opportunity to preserve his centrality in the system to a certain extent, inasmuch as this centrality has been reduced to a certain degree by the very fact of the actor's placement in the zone of the complementary task. For an actor located in the peripheral zone, the exchange of the resource for participation yields a very marginal profit, since a significant degree of centrality is not attained merely by temporary participation in a specific collective task. Such a profit will generally not be equivalent to the material, immediate, and effective profit inherent in attaining considerable material benefits.

And what happens to those actors located in central zones of the system but who do not possess skills that are in demand in the market? They too are subject to the rule of "centrality oblige" and they too will try to improve their status (which as suffered a relative decline) in the framework of the total civil-military system. While it is true that they do not possess scarce and desired skills, they have other resources stemming from their centrality that they may attempt to exchange for positions connnected with both the predominant and the complementary goals. The following can be done by utilizing one's position of centrality: New roles connected with one of the goals can be initiated by using skills possessed by the entrepreneurs (for example, the creation of bodies for locating trouble spots and granting aid and services connected with the situation of interruption; see chapter 2). What this amounts to is the linkage of skills to the complementary collective goals—skills that were not connected with them at the outset. This actually constitutes an initiation of needs so that there will be someone to fulfill them. Second, social ties may be utilized in order to obtain a role connected with one of the goals, either predominant or complementary, whether a special skill is needed for the fulfillment of the role or not. Finally, one can continue to fulfill routine roles and attempt to connect them with the predominant and complementary goals in a more salient fashion than by the general legitimation that is granted to the continuation for fulfillment of routine roles (for example, a professor of sociology who claims that the research he conducts is clearly connected with the understanding of the public's wartime morale). By the very nature of the situation, the vast majority of the actors located in peripheral zones who do not possess skills that are scarce and in demand also do not have other social skills that can be exchanged for roles that would emphasize their participation in the collective goals. Nevertheless, as we saw, not all the roles in the zone of the complementary goal require a specific skill. Thus, for example, almost every woman can serve as a teacher's aide and any physically able male who for some reason was not recruited can play a significant part in the system's upkeep. Generally, extensive material rewards are not attached to such roles, and thus those fulfilling them must be satisfied with the relatively modest reward of participation at the margins of the collective effort.

Links among Activities on Different Levels

Another type of question arising in this context is that of the relationships among types of activity on the individual level; for example, the connections between the degree of performance of routine activities in the interrupted system and the initiation of, or at least participation in, activities new to the actor or the system as a whole. An additional question is that of the connection between the structuring, range, and the effectiveness of institutional organization and the nature of activity of individuals within the system. In other words, does an institutional system that operates efficiently in the period of interruption and satisifes various needs of the members of the collectivity encourage them to continue in their routine activity—independently of their location in the system—or does it discourage them from doing so and thus create conditions more suitable for taking a moratorium?

The same question can be posed as to the nonroutine activities related to the new roles created in the system: Will an efficient and organized system that satisfies various needs encourage or discourage the entrance of individuals into new roles (i.e. volunteering) or taking initiatives for the creation of new roles?

A much broader and more far-reaching question is that of the possible effects of institutional organization in the period of interruption on the social system as a whole, even in its routine (i.e., uninterrupted) phase. Conversely, do certain characteristics of the system in the routine period affect the form of the interruption, or *the very capacity to be interrupted?* In this section we shall deal with these questions only on a theoretical level. In subsequent chapters we will go into greater empirical detail.

At this stage we may propose three general hypotheses. First, no necessary connection exists between the extent of performance of routine roles stemming from an individual's role and the performance of "new" roles in the period of interruption. Furthermore, it is not necessary that there be a connection between one type of routine activity and another. Thus, in the period of interruption an individual may take a moratorium from care for himself (e.g., personal hygiene) while at the same time going to work with the same frequency and working with the same (or perhaps even greater) intensity than in the routine period. If, indeed, a (direct) connection is found between two activities, this may stem from our previous hypothesis as to the individual's location in the system. This hypothesis is based on the following assumptions: (a) by definition, the interrupted system issues contradictory messages that allow for differentiation among demands for the performance of various activities; (b) various activities are subject to the constraints in the interrupted system to a differential degree; and (c) there may arise a zero-sum situation (or what is perceived as such) in the dimension of the time at the actor's disposal when he has to choose between the performance of routine roles and that of "new" roles.

Second, an institutional structure that is efficient in a period of social interruption may be of considerable help in facilitating the performance of both routine and "new" roles. The more such a structure overcomes institutional bottlenecks, the more some of the constraints will be reduced and individuals will be able to perform their routine roles. This is the case in the creation of an institutional infrastructure for the regulation of "new" activities, and the institutionalization and planning of the transition to new roles. Thus, an institutional structure that is efficient and prepared for the possibility of interruption will constitute a necessary condition for individual capacity to perform routine and nonroutine roles. At the same time, a political center that is too efficient, intervening in too broad a range of spheres, and that creates a paternalistic atmosphere will no doubt be harmful to the individual's motivation to fulfill nonroutine roles.[75]

Third, without discussing it until now, we have assumed that the Israeli social system has a certain capacity for interruption. This is actually a special case of the general degree of *flexibility* of the social system that is generally associated with its degree of modernity. If this is indeed so, only a relatively modern social system can interrupt itself efficiently. But the more interesting question is in the opposite direction: What does the capacity for interruption do for the general social system in the context of its constantly being in latent (and sometimes manifest) conflict with its environment?

Part of the answer was hinted at earlier when we discussed Israel's dilemma as presented by Eliezer Schweid. The interruption is meant to respond to a very defined need—not to be totally mobilized at all times, despite the constant threat to survival. The success of the system in "learning" to be interrupted at (1) the "right" time for (2) a minimal period, and (3) later to return to the point at which the interruption occurred, seems to have far-reaching social implications. We hypothesize that the more the capacity for interruption developed, the more Israeli society *avoided* many of the characteristics expected to be found in a society subject to a continuous and total conflict (characteristics of a "besieged society").[76] Thus, the contribution of the capacity for interruption lies in several features that *are not* characteristic of Israeli society, rather than in those features that are. But it is obvious that the capacity for interruption is not necessarily a constant, just as the general societal flexibility does not exist at a fixed level, but may increase or decline, [77] and any deviation from the delicate societal arrangements and principles or their abuse (like in the 1982 war) may transform an interrupted system into a disrupted one.

Notes

1. The datum is taken from Z. Schiff and E. Haber (eds.), *Israel: Army and Defence: A Dictionary* (Tel Aviv: Zmora, Bitan, Modan, 1976), p. 255 (Hebrew).
2. For a description of the 1973 War from the military perspective, see E. O'Ballance, *No Victor, No Vanquished: The Yom Kippur War* (San Rafael, Calif.: Presidio Press, 1978).
3. "Social Role" is a key concept in sociology that links the abstract entity of the "system" to the individuals interacting within it. The role is a cluster of recurring institutionalized activities that regulate contacts between individuals. The individual may fulfill many roles ("father," "soldier," "employer," etc.) but cannot be defined by only one role. For a discussion of this point, see the well-known eighth chapter of Ralph Linton's *The Study of Man* (New York: Appleton-Century, 1936). In the framework of our essay we will often use an alternative concept to that of "role-bearer," that is, "actor." The latter is less comprehensive and refers to isolated activities of role bearers.
4. Until Sadat's visit to Jerusalem there was complete agreement among most Israelis that the final goal of Israel's Arab neighbors was the destruction of Israel as an independent political entity. It seems that this conception was not far from the truth. See Y. Harkabi, *Arab Attitudes Toward Israel* (Jerusalem: Keter Publishing House, 1972).
5. E. Shils, "Charisma, Order, and Status," in *Center and Periphery: Essays in Macrosociology* (Chicago and London: The University of Chicago Press, 1975), pp. 256-75.
6. Active warfare is contrasted with a situation of *dormant* warfare threatening to "awake"—a situation that characterizes the Israeli social system from its beginnings. The situation of war can also be viewed otherwise, not dichotomously in terms of active warfare, but as a continuum of differential exogenous pressures exerted on the system.
7. S.C. Kamen, "Crisis and Social Integration: The Case of Israel in the Six-Day War" (Ph.D. diss., The University of Chicago, 1971). R. Bar-Yosef and D. Padan-Eisenstark, "Role System Under Stress: Sex Roles in War," *Social Problems* 25 (1977): 135-45. I refer mainly to the Hebrew enlarged version, *Megamot*, 22 (1975): 36-50.
8. See papers by Anson, Bernstein, and Antonovsky; T. Breznitz; Benyamini; Goldberg; and Yinon presented to the International Conference of Psychological Stress and Adjustment in Time of War and Peace, *Abstracts* Tel Aviv, 6-10 January 1975. This is particularly evident in Amia Lieblich's book, *Tin Soldiers on Jerusalem Beach* (New York: Pantheon, 1979). Although the study is not limited to the period under discussion, it creates the impression (as a result of its focus on psychotherapeutic topics) that the members of the

collectivity are constantly in a state of emotional distress that sometimes also interferes with their effective functioning, as a result of the external pressure and the problems aroused.

9. See O.E. Hultaker, "Evakuera," *Disaster Studies*, no. 2 (Upsala: Upsala University, 1975); K. Lang and G.E. Lang, "Collective Responses to the Threat of Disaster," in G.W. Grosser, H. Wechsler, and M. Greenblat (eds.), *The Threat of Impending Disaster* (Cambridge: M.I.T. Press, 1964), pp.58-75.

10. A.H. Barton, "The Emergency Social System," in G.W. Baker and D.W. Chapman (eds.), *Man and Society in Disaster* (New York: Basic Books, 1962), pp. 222-67. G. Sjoberg, "Disaster and Social Change," in *Man and Society*, pp. 356-84.

11. H. Cisin with W.B. Clark, "The Methodological Challenge of Disaster Research," in Baker and Chapman, *Man and Society*, pp. 23-53; Sjoberg, "Disaster and Social Change."

12. See, for example, Grosser, Wechsler, and Greenblat, *Threat*, Introduction, pp. 3-8; and Upsala University, *Disaster Studies*, 7 vols. (Upsala), no. 7.

13. A.H. Barton, *Communities in Disaster: A Sociological Analysis of Collective Stress Situations* (New York: Anchor Books, 1969).

14. Sjoberg, "Disaster and Social Change."

15. W.H. Form and S. Masow, *Community and Disaster* (New York: Harper and Row, 1958).

16. Quoted by Cisin with Clark, "Disaster Research."

17. Ibid., p. 30.

18. Barton, "Emergency Social System," p. 8.

19. J.D. Thompson and R.A. Hawkes, "Disaster Community Organization and Organizational Process," in Baker and Chapman, *Man and Society*, pp. 268-303.

20. K.T. Erikson, *Everything in Its Path: Destruction of a Community in the Buffalo Creek Flood* (New York: Simon and Schuster, 1976).

21. H. Cantril, H. Gamlet, and H. Herzog, *The Invasion from Mars* (Princeton: Princeton University Press, 1940); R.W. Mack and G.W. Baker, *The Occasion Instant: The Structure of Social Response to Air-Raid Warnings*, Disaster Study no. 15 (Washington, D.C.: National Academy of Sciences, 1961).

22. Barton, *Communities in Disaster*, p. 37.

23. H.E. Moore, *Tornadoes over Texas: A Study of Waco San Angelo in Disaster* (Houston: University of Texas Press, 1958); R.W. Perry, D.E. Gillespino, and D.S. Mileti, "System Stress and the Persistence of Emergent Organization," *Sociological Inquiry* 44, no. 3 (1974): 119; B.A. Turner, "The Organizational and Inter-Organizational Development of Disasters," *Administrative Science Quarterly* 21 (1976): 378-97.

24. M. Wolfenstein, *Disaster: A Psychological Essay* (London: Routledge & Kegan Paul, 1957).

25. I.L. Janis, "Psychological Effects of Warning, " in Baker and Chapman, *Man and Society*.

26. A.F.C. Wallace, *Tornado in Worcester: An Exploratory Study of Individual and Community Behavior in an Extreme Situation*, Disaster Study no. 3 (Washington, D.C.: National Academy of Sciences, 1956).

27. See, for example, Barton ("Emergency Social System"), who summarizes the literature and the findings on this subject, or Sjoberg ("Disaster and Social

Change"), who presents this claim and notes that there is no basis for a "myth of panic," although "regressive behavior" may be noted as expressed in adherence to old patterns. He claims that such behavior occurs in those cases in which individuals believe that this is a rational response to the situation (p. 368).

28. See H. Guetzkow, "Joining Field and Laboratory Work in Disaster Research," in Baker and Chapman, *Man in Society,* pp. 337–55; and L.M. Killian, *An Introduction to Methodological Problems of Field Studies in Disaster,* Disaster Study no. 8 (Washington D.C.: National Academy of Sciences, 1956).
29. H.J. Friedson, "Older Person in Disaster," in Baker and Chapman, *Man and Society,* pp. 151-82.
30. L.M. Killian, "The Significance of Multiple Group Membership in Disasters," *American Journal of Sociology* 57 (1952): 309-14; see also Upsala University, *Disaster Studies,* no. 7.
31. O.E. Hultaker and J.E. Frost, "The Family and the Shelters," *Disaster Studies,* no. 7 (Upsala: Upsala University, 1977), p. 5.
32. R. Hill and D.A. Hauser, "Family in Disaster," in Baker and Chapman, *Man and Society,* p. 188.
33. Barton, "Emergency Social System."
34. Barton, "Emergency Social System" and *Communities in Disaster.*
35. Hill and Hauser, "Family in Disaster," p. 186.
36. L.D. Nelson, "Continuity in Helping Roles: A Comparison of Everyday and Emergency Role Performance," *Pacific Sociological Review* 20 (1977): 263-78.
37. R. Bar-Yosef and D. Padan-Eisenstark, *Men and Women in War: Change in Role System Under Stress* (The Yom-Kippur War, October 1973–April 1974), mimeographed (Jerusalem: The Labor and Welfare Research Institute, Hebrew University, 1975) (Hebrew), p. 8.
38. P.A. Sorokin, *Man and Society in Calamity* (New York: Greenwood Press, 1968) p. 50.
39. Sjoberg, "Disaster and Social Change," p. 370.
40. Hill and Hauser, "Family in Disaster," p. 193.
41. E.L. Quarantelli and R.R. Dynes, "When Disaster Strikes," *Psychology Today* 5 (1972): 67-70.
42. Bar-Yosef and Padan-Eisenstark, "Role System Under Stress," p. 11.
43. See Wallace, *Tornado in Worcester,* and Hultaker, "Evakuera."
44. The ranking of the importance of situations, activities, roles, and individuals will be determined according to their relevance to the warfare. The allocation of societal resources and rewards, including those of prestige, will be made according to this new ranking.
45. R.K. Merton, Foreword, in Barton, *Communities in Disaster,* pp. vii-xxxvi.
46. Erikson, *Destruction of a Community,* p. 208.
47. Sjoberg, "Disaster and Social Change," p. 384.
48. Barton, *Communities in Disaster,* p. 159.
49. Ibid., p. 156.
50. J.P. Gillin, "Theoretical Possibilities of Inducing Socio-Cultural Collapse," in Baker and Chapman, *Man and Society,* pp. 385-402; as well as Cisin with Clark, " Disaster Research."
51. Barton, *Communities in Disaster,* pp. 40-41.

52. R. Cahana and S. Canaan, *The Behavior of the Press in Situations of Security Tension and Its Effect on Public Support of Government* (Jerusalem: Levi Eshkol Institute for Economic, Social, and Political Research in Israel, Hebrew University, 1973), p. 60 (Hebrew).
53. See B. Kimmerling, "Anomie and Integration in Israeli Society and the Salience of the Israeli-Arab Conflict," *Studies in Comparative International Development* 9, no. 3 (fall, 1974), pp. 64-89.
54. D. Horowitz, *The Israeli Conception of National Security: The Permanent and the Changing in Israeli Strategic Thinking* (Jerusalem: Eshkol Institute, Hebrew University, 1973) (Hebrew).
55. See D. Horowitz and B. Kimmerling, "Some Social Implications of Military Service and the Reserves System in Israel," *Archives Européennes de Sociologie* 15 (1974), pp. 262-76.
56. E. Schweid, "The Endurance of Israeli Society," in A. Cohen and A. Carmon (eds.), *In the Wake of the Yom Kippur War* (Haifa: Haifa University, 1976) (Hebrew).
57. The term "directly serve" is quite problematic since a struggle may occur over the degree of relevance of various activities to the war effort and over who may determine what is or is not relevant.
58. Bar-Yosef and Padan-Eisenstark, "Role System Under Stress."
59. Sorokin, *Man and Society in Calamity,* p. 150.
60. L. Coser, *The Functions of Social Conflict* (Glencoe: Free Press, 1956), p. 144.
61. The attempt to demand housing and other benefits for soldiers who participated in the wars was indeed a subject of public debate for a short period after the wars, but it seems that nothing was actually done in this area. Institutions of higher education tended to grant advantages to student-soldiers so that they would not lose the 1973-74 academic year or the 1981-82. But aside from this there was no conversion of participation in the fulfillment of the predominant goal for resources to be used in the routine period (on this, see chapter 2). The exception to the above is the growth of protest movements based primarily on discharged soldiers and on the symbol of the "veteran." These demanded and finally considerably contributed to the resignation of the Golda Meir government. Elsewhere Sorokin shows that wars may often cause the very intensification of interclass differences and gaps: P.A. Sorokin, "Sociological Interpretation of the 'Struggle for Existence' and the Sociology of War," in *Contemporary Sociological Theories* (New York: Harper and Bros., 1928), pp. 309-56.
62. "Sex Roles in War," "Role System Under Stress."
63. A.L. Stinchcombe, "Some Empirical Consequences of the Davis-Moore Theory of Stratification," *American Sociological Review* (October 1963): 805-8.
64. The goal complementary to the predominant goal is actually a broad range of goals geared to ensuring the continuation of the system's activity during the interruption so that all its activities may be restored when the threat is withdrawn.
65. In the routine period the system develops organizations that will be able to quickly and efficiently ensure the system's continued and regular existence on the level perceived as essential without being drastically damaging to the war effort. See Chapter 2.

66. D. Horowitz, "Flexible Responsiveness and Military Strategy: The Case of the Israeli Army," *Policy Sciences* 1 (1970): 191-205.

67. Thus, an actor who in "noninterrupted" periods fulfills a role that will be relevant to the system's "upkeep" in a situation of interruption and who continues to do this in the period of interruption will be considered to be conducting routine activity. Our emphasis is not on the content of the role, but rather on its newness to the actor.

68. But this was a deviant case, since most tried to reach the front. Quite a few persons (according to our estimate, about 2-5 percent of the population subject to service of the 18-50 age group) who for various reasons were not called in the 1973 war despite the fact that their qualification and/or their self-image indicated recruitment, used "pull" to enlist or to reach the front lines. Some were given combat roles (and some even were killed in action), whereas others were annexed to headquarters units and initiated jobs for themselves. After the war some officers both complained about the pressure these volunteers had exerted on the headquarters of their units and suggested that in the future jobs be "invented" for them so that they would not disturb the fighting units. Similar phenomena are also known to us from situations of "over-volunteering" as reported in disaster studies.

69. E. Shils, "Center and Periphery," in *Center and Periphery,* pp. 3-16.

70. Ibid., p. 3.

71. See, V. Azarya, *Aristocrats Facing Change: The Fulbe in Guinea, Nigeria, and Cameroon* (Chicago: The University of Chicago Press, 1978), p. 4.

72. Here we must note that the boundaries of military status are permeable to a certain extent, and so (1) when all the factors of military status are held constant we can assume that an actor's location in the total system has an effect on the military framework as well; (2) there is a certain connection between the status a person attains in the army and his location in the whole system.

73. Such are the anti-Zionist groups, mostly from among the extremely religious (see Friedman, *Society and Religion* [Jerusalem: Yad Ben-Zvi, 1977]) or from the extreme left, such as "Matzpen," a marginal but not peripheral group (see N. Youval-David, *Matzpen,* Studies in Sociology [Jerusalem: Department of Sociology, Hebrew University, 1975] [Hebrew]). Similar tendencies toward alienation from the collectivity for quite different reasons, may be found among several segments of the Arab citizens of the country. See chapter 5 and E.T. Zureik, *The Palestinians in Israel: A Study in Internal Colonialism* (London: Routledge and Kegan Paul, 1979) or I. Lustick, *Arabs in the Jewish State* (Austin: University of Texas Press, 1980) and J.M. Landau, *The Arabs in Israel* (London: Oxford University Press, 1969).

74. Shils, "Center and Periphery," pp. 8-9.

75. See, for example, B. Kimmerling, "The Israeli Civil Guard," in L.A. Zurcher and G. Haries-Jenkins (eds.), *Supplementary Military Forces: Reserves, Militias, Auxiliaries* (Beverly Hills and London: Sage Publications, 1978), pp. 107-25.

76. B. Kimmerling, *Social Interruption and Besieged Societies* (Amherst: Council on International Studies, State University of New York at Buffalo, 1979).

77. On the general declining capacities in Israeli society and losses of its capabilities in different fields, see Shmuel N. Eisenstadt, *The Transformation of Israeli Society* (London: Weidenfeld and Nicolson, 1984). For the argument that Israel is not a modern society, see Irving Louis Horowitz, "Of Jews, Israelis, and the Third World," in id., *Israeli Ecstasies/Jewish Agonies* (New York: Oxford University Press, 1974), pp. 75-85.

2
Institutional Arrangements
of the Interruption

The central question to be examined in our study is whether in the course of about 100 years of Arab-Jewish conflict over the land of Palestine (and later, Israel)[1]—the Jewish-Israeli social system has managed to develop institutional arrangements and organizations allowing for a quick and efficient transition from a situation of "routine security tension" to one in which tension becomes much more salient until reaching the point of "active warfare."[2] Only the existence of such effective arrangements may allow a society in a situation of conflict (until now perceived as permanent) to exist not as a "society under siege"[3] but rather as an open and democratic system, which can allow itself to allocate material, intellectual, and emotional resources for the solution of problems not directly related to its immediate physical survival. It is generally accepted that Israel did indeed develop a very effective arrangement for dealing with the immediate security threat—an arrangement based on a highly developed reserves system.[4] The question is, however, whether it also developed organizations and institutions for dealing with what we referred to earlier as "the goal complementary to the predominant goal"—that is, the prevention of severe disturbances to the social system in a period in which it is mobilized for "making war," and allowing (1) for at least a minimal level of survival[5] during the period of social interruption, and (2) for the quick restoration of the situation and social processes that existed prior to the social interruption. These two questions will be dealt with in this chapter.

A glance at some social and economic indicators relevant to the years 1970–75 (Table 2.1) may lead us to conclude that on a macroeconomic (and possibly also macrosociological) level, we may note only very marginal disturbances in the activities of the economy and society, at least in the immediate time range.[6] In 1973 the gross national product continued to rise as it did in 1974, declining only slightly in 1975. Even then it was

TABLE 2.1
Selected Indicators of Economic Activity and Social Processes in Israel,
1970-1975

Indicators	1970	1971	1972	1973	1974	1975
GNP (in 1970 prices)	6,257	6,225	7,243	7,384	7,654	7,512
Gross Domestic Capital Formation (in million IL & in 1970 prices)	5,373	6,553	7,376	8,129	8,397	7,974
Private Consumption (in million IL & in 1970 prices)	3,815	3,864	4,991	4,328	4,515	4,386
Exports as % of imports	51.2	50.5	56.1	46.9	41.6	44.7
Trade Deficit (per capita in dollars)	235	292	271	480	722	657
Bankruptcies	507	n.d.	n.d.	n.d.	523	847
Crimes (registered by police, in thousands)	135	141	141	131	155	170
Suicides (per 10,000 Jews, age 15 and above)	1.09	n.d.	1.29	.94	1.08	n.d.
Unemployed (daily average)	1,595	937	744	878	844	1,000

Source: Statistical Yearbook—1976 (Jerusalem: Central Bureau of Statistics, 1977).

still higher than the GNP of the years preceding the 1973 war. This fact, of course, does not indicate anything about the possible increase or decrease in the GNP that might have occurred had there not been a war.[7] We have indicated only that despite the extensive mobilization of manpower and the partial absence of Arab labor from the conquered territories in the war's first stages, the GNP continued to rise. Similar developments can be noted in gross domestic capital formation.

The standard of living (as measured by the expenditures for private consumption) declined slightly in 1973 (relative to 1972), and did not, thereafter, return to its previous level despite the slight improvement that occurred in 1974. On the other hand, the general state of the economy as measured by exports as a percentage of imports—and primarily in the composition of the per capita deficit—deteriorated drastically. The proportion of exports declined by 10 percent from 1973 to 1972, with an additional 5 percent decline in 1974 (for 1975 an insignificant improvement may be noted). The trade deficit per capita grew from $271 in 1972 to $480 in 1973, and to $722 in 1974, thus almost tripling in this period. This great increase can be explained as follows: while Israelis continued to produce and export almost at the same level during and after the war, their economic situation deteriorated, not as a consequence of a decline in production ability, but rather because of the great increase in imports for defense purposes, to the point at which the defense budget was 40 percent of the GNP in 1974–75.

Data are not available on bankruptcies in 1972 and 1973, but in comparing 1970 and 1975 we do not note a significant increase in the rate of bankruptcies. However, a year later there was a rise of about 60 percent. Again, this does not seem to indicate an immediate effect of the war, but rather a cumulative result of the economic slowdown that took place after the war. As noted, we are studying immediate effects (which were noted simultaneously with the social interruption) and not cumulative or long-range results (in which additional reasons also intervened).

If suicide rates are indeed indicators of social anomie in the Durkheimian sense[8] and if a comparison with one previous year is valid, then we are witness to a drastic decline in social anomie in a situation of full social interruption, and this trend continued in the second year of interruption as well, but seemingly not in a partial one. The number of crimes also declined to a certain extent (or, possibly it was police reporting efficiency that declined, or, again, some potential offenders might have been recruited into the army). However, we note a steep rise later in the rate of crimes registered. Likewise, if we refer to 1972 as our base year, a rise in the rate of unemployment is indicated, but the rate does not reach the annual rates for preceding years. This rise in the unemployment rate is somewhat strange, since a larger portion of the labor force was recruited during the period 1973–74, but we shall discuss this later on.

According to preliminary estimates of the Ministry of Finance, the direct cost of the first year of the 1982 war (not including loss of days of work and the rehabilitation of the wounded) was about $2 billion. Already in the first weeks the economic system was prepared to finance this expense—primarily from internal sources. The major steps taken were the (temporary) raising of the Value Added Tax (VAT) and the imposition of a tax on every transaction in the stock market. Because of the nature of the war, most of its expenses were independent of imports (the weapons systems that were imported were almost entirely undamaged), and most of the items used were manufactured in Israel (different kinds of arms and tanks). It appears that enough locally made products can be manufactured within two years to replenish all the items used up, and this may be useful even in terms of inflation, for the government has stated it will finance the deficit by means of increasing the tax burden upon the public, and thus accomplish a double aim.

An Emergency Economy

In the sphere of the complementary goal, the "emergency economy" (or, in short, "Melah," the Hebrew abbreviation for *meshek l'sheat heyrum*—hereafter, "EE") is the functional equivalent to the reserves system in the sphere of the predominant goal. The former is an arrangement geared to meeting the system's instrumental needs and to insuring the continued and stable functioning of civilian society as much as possible in a situation of total mobilization and active combat. This arrangement is expressed in two forms. First, a small but permanent nucleus of staff (the "Supreme Committee of the EE") acts in routine periods in order to prepare the system—both in terms of food and oil supplies, and so on, and in terms of preparation of operative programs and the simulation of emergency situations. Second, in periods of emergency all government agencies and local authorities automatically become part of the EE system; each of these and all the actors who are part of them and have not been recruited continue to fulfill selectively the same functions they would normally fulfill in the routine period. Thus, for example, the Transportation Ministry continues to be responsible for transportation, the Ministry of Agriculture for the water supply, municipal authorities for education and welfare services, and so forth. The head of the EE Supreme Committee (who is responsible to the Ministry of Defense) coordinates among all these authorities, and, what is even more important, coordinates between them and the military. The system tries to attain maximum flexibility and a smooth and rapid transition from the routine period to that of social interruption by granting a dual function to all these authorities.

The doctrine on which EE is based is similar to that which guides the armed forces—to be prepared for the worst possible contingency. Here the worst possible contingency refers primarily to: (1) the existence of a very prolonged war (in Israeli terms, of several months' duration); and (2) the enemy's success in imposing a naval and air siege on the country. These two situations have not as yet come about, but an efficient staff must prepare for such possibilities by combining several measures:

(1) preparing large emergency storage areas to ensure the storage of food and oil, (2) setting aside minimum manpower so that the economy and services defined as essential may continue to function, and (3) assuring the existence of means of transport at a level that will allow for the continuation of routine life among civilians.

As an organization representing the "interests" of the complementary goal at times of social interruption and trying to fulfill the above three tasks, the EE must constantly come to terms both with other social goals in routine times and with the demands of the predominant goal in times of interruption. In a newspaper interview (*Ha'aretz*, 10 January 1977; all quotes hereafter are from *Ha'aretz* [Hebrew daily], unless otherwise stated) the head of the EE Supreme Committee said:

> I must note that in general there is alertness on this subject [the possibility of an emergency arising] and also a fairly serious attitude towards it [on the part of government vis-à-vis the EE's demands]. But when we speak of the supplies in the emergency storage houses, let us not ignore the fact that anyone who demands another supply for 3 months, in addition to that already in existence, is actually demanding that the State spend another 100 million dollars.

The above reflects the bargaining that occurs between the EE and the political center, which represents various other interests and must take these into account in addition to the allocation of resources for managing the attainment of the complementary goal. The latter is presented in a zero-sum relationship to other demands, especially those of the routine period.

Another subject for negotiation is the definition of "essential enterprises," that is, who will determine what an "essential enterprise" is and who and how many of each such enterprise's workers will be recruited into the army. In the 1973 war, about 3,500 enterprises were defined as such, and it is also in the enterprises' interest that this defining be done. For in this way they can keep their manpower, while as a result of bargaining this number had increased by a thousand by 1977. It seems that the most serious bone of contention between the representatives of the complementary and predominant goals was in regard to transportation and transport. The head of the EE Supreme Committee stated:

> Before the war, the armed forces made a written pledge to supply oil to civilians because [they were] given the right to mobilize all the tankers. But the armed forces could not meet their commitment, and on Monday, the third day of the war, we were flooded with reports that gas stations were empty. Many essential enterprises were also left without a supply of oil and the threat of their paralysis was impending. What could we do?

Demand of the armed forces that they release tankers from the front? Of course not, especially since military authorities were not prepared to commit themselves to a date on which they would do so. Since we had no other choice, we improvised the transport of oil in regular trucks on which we placed tankers. People may not know but this was the critical moment in the economy's activity in the Yom Kippur War.

The 1973 war was relatively short, and no sea or air embargo was imposed on Israel, so that the EE system's full capacity was not put to the test. Nevertheless, the social system was interrupted; and primarily as a result of the total mobilization, shortages arose, as did other constraints on the system's continued activity. In this chapter we will deal with the institutional system's reaction to these constraints and shortages and the forms of reorganization in a situation of full social interruption. We will continue to discuss the EE's activities as well.

Civil Defense and the Evacuation of Casualties

Two complementary organizations that constitute an integral part of the EE system are the Civil Defense and the Authority for the Absorption of Evacuated Populations and Evacuation Casualties ("Pesach"). But these agencies were idle during the war, and so we will not deal with them except in order to mention the following two facts: (1) they utilized some of the manpower allocations, and (2) the actors who operated in these frameworks or who were mobilized to do so could view this activity as participation in the attainment of the predominant goal.

In terms of our study, the fact that there were no civilian casualties renders the analysis of the processes of social interruption more interesting and analytically "more pure." Had the system been physically injured, we would of necessity be dealing with something more akin to a disaster situation and could not concentrate on interruption per se as a social phenomenon.

However, although there were no bombings of civilians or civilians suffering material losses (aside from several marginal incidents), there was a real threat of bombings and there were air raids. The population was requested to maintain a strict blackout and to enter the shelters during air raids. People living in houses without shelters, or for various reasons finding themselves unable to use the private shelters, were referred to public shelters.

Here we should also note that despite the long history of wars between Jews and Arabs, the vast majority of the population had never experienced (in Israel) any air bombings. The last effective bombings of civilians in Israel had occurred in 1948, and no bombing has actually occurred from the 1973 war to this point. Thus, in this matter it is difficult to speak of "past experience."

Systematic data has not been collected on the degree of adherence to the "civil defense regime" that was proclaimed and on patterns of behavior during air raids. But we do have several observations and eyewitness reports about this behavior. These observations, which were made in 1973 in a heterogeneously populated Jerusalem neighborhood,[9] allow one to draw the following conclusions: (1) peripheral populations (from poor neighborhoods, and some of the new immigrants) were characterized by "nonadaptive patterns of behavior"; (2) in all strata of the population there were various levels of a lack of basic knowledge of civil defense; (3) the manpower and equipment at the disposal of the Civil Defense seemed to be inadequate for it to fulfill its functions had it been put to the test.

This emergency revealed that there was a shortage of shelters. In the years of "peace between 1967 and 1973 the country's population had increased greatly and there was a construction "boom"—especially in the Jerusalem area. But despite the existence of legislation requiring the construction of shelters adjacent to any construction (private or public), there was still a shortage of shelters. It seems that the laws were not obeyed in full, nor was there even awareness of their existence in many instances.

A researcher from the Institute for the Study of Labor and Welfare summarized the situation:

> Most people (according to Civil Defense personnel and citizens in general with whom I spoke) are aware of the fact that there are not enough public shelters in areas in which shelters were not built in homes. We should note here that there are people who do not go down to the shelters and stay in their homes during air raids. They explained to me (and to others) that they feel the shelters have no value, either because they believe in fate or on the basis of personal experience in the past in which they saw a shelter being penetrated by a bomb. I found this approach to prevail mostly among childless people.[10]

Food Supply

Immediately at the 1973 war's beginning a shortage of food and other items perceived as essential (such as batteries for transistor radios and flashlights) developed. The shortages, which were felt to a differential degree in different areas, stemmed from three factors: (1) a buying panic spread through the population, which emptied the shelves within a short time; (2) difficulties were created in organizing means of transport; and

(3) some of the storekeepers were recruited. The buying panic ended relatively quickly, but a selective shortage of various products continued to plague the population.

On October 15 this conversation with a storekeeper was reported by the interviewers:

> The problem is a fairly great shortage in essential items such as sugar, rice, eggs, etc. The storekeeper orders these products, but is refused. The store is often closed since the storekeeper is recruited to the Civil Defense as is his partner. It opens only when the storekeeper gets a few hours leave. The storekeeper's car is also mobilized, so he can't bring products. On the other hand, claims the storekeeper, "the cooperative marketing association has power and connections, so it has no problems, while the small storekeepers and the self-employed lack power."[11]

On October 9 the press (*Yediot Achronot*) reported that in the large marketing chains there were shortages only of batteries, matches, and sugar. Tnuva—the main cooperative for the production and marketing of dairy products in Israel—began to produce and market only basic products because of a manpower shortage. However, these products were marketed in sufficient quantities. Nevertheless, an acute shortage of poultry was in evidence, and poultry is a central component of the Israeli diet, especially among the lower strata. The price of poultry increased drastically.

The shortage of eggs appeared a bit later, the result not only of a transport and manpower shortage but also of the blackout (since chicken coops are generally lit up at night in order to increase the number of eggs laid). Thus, the eggs did not reach the stores, and a black market developed.[12]

But except for the specific shortages in a number of products, it seems that obtaining goods was not a critical problem. The EE, which was in charge of coping with social interruption on the instrumental level, was aware of the connection between this level and the "morale" problems that might arise if very severe problems in the supply of essential products should develop. As noted by the EE head:

> On that very night, after Yom Kippur, we began to push large quantities of foodstuffs to all the marketing networks because we expected—and we were not "disappointed"—a large amount of hoarding. We knew that if the civilians were shocked [as a result of a shortage of products]—it would be hard to get them out of such a state.

TABLE 2.2

Shortages of Items, by Place of Residence on November 19* (according to reports of sample populations, in percent)

Item	Jerusalem	Tel-Aviv	Haifa
Eggs	57	63	75
Rice	23	19	7
Milk & Milk Products	6	3	5
Flour	3	4	2
Other	11	11	4
Total	100	100	100
	(172)	(232)	(166)

*The third week of the interruption.

Source: The Israel Institute for Applied Social Research and the Institute of Communications, *Products: Shortages and Difficulties in Obtaining Products* (Jerusalem, Hebrew University, mimeographed report submitted to the Bureau of Commerce and Industry, 27 November 1973, p. 3.

The extent to which the supply of food was not a critical problem is evidenced by the fact that the EE did not have to open even one emergency storehouse during the entire period of interruption, and the supply was taken from routine sources. Nevertheless, it seems that "shortage foci" were created as a result of the lack of efficient distribution of products, because of the shortages in means of transport and manpower and the differential organizational ability of various storekeepers. Thus, on various dates between October 16 and November 20 some 15-19 percent of those interviewed reported having to "wander" from store to store to obtain several items, and 7-14 percent reported having to do so for many items.[13]

The ability of storekeepers to mobilize help (mutual aid or help from volunteers, or both) was also a function of socioeconomic status or location on the center-periphery continuum. A storekeeper in a peripheral Jerusalem neighborhood whose store was left almost empty was asked if she received help from the neighboring vegetable store owner, inasmuch as he owned a car. She responded: "Every man for himself."[14] On the other hand, in a neighborhood of well-off old-timers an unlimited supply of volunteers was reported to have operated the local shop and transported products to it.[15]

Banking Services

The activity that perhaps typified the phenomenon of social interruption more than any other institutional one was that of the banks. Banking services constituted a potential bottleneck of the system's operation. The possibility of the disappearance of many of the means of payment within a short time reflected not only a threat to the fulfillment of the most essential complementary instrumental tasks but also a potential source of demoralization and of a sense of the loss of internal control over the situation. The partial or total paralysis of banking activity could have resulted not only from the recruitment of bank workers, but also from the fact that many of the members of families who had right of signature had also been recruited. This was particularly salient because the family bank account in Israel is often in the man's name, particularly among the lower strata.[16]

According to a report of the Institute for the Study of Labor, all bank branches opened on a regular basis from the second day of the war (the first day was Yom Kippur, and the banks were closed in any event) despite the recruitment of many of the workers. In order to overcome the manpower shortages and at the same time to adapt the bank services to the special needs of the period, the banks cut down the types of services offered to the customers and concentrated mostly on the release of cash to the public and on dealing with deposits. They also took upon themselves the collection of the "war loan."[17] To prevent panic and a shortage in money, the Bank of Israel issued 400 million Israeli pounds in addition to the regular issue. Indeed, in the first week of the war, withdrawals of cash increased by 50 percent.

On 16 and 21 October 1973 the acting manager of a Jerusalem bank was interviewed:

> The bank manager and most of the clerks have been recruited. I've been left responsible, and I also supervise what's going on in other branches. On Yom Kippur itself we found out who was recruited and who wasn't and we examined the regulations for times of emergency. On that very day we made most of the preparations. The most important thing was to prepare a lot of cash. We know that in such a situation people run to the bank and withdraw a lot of money . . . we cut down our activities to the most essential things: withdrawals and urgent activities . . . there are many "nags"—people who don't understand that in such a situation transactions in foreign currency cannot be made, nor can all sorts of questions be answered. . . . The manpower situation is very bad. We can't recruit just anyone. This is a bank! Yet we manage to conduct most of our activities.

TABLE 2.3
**Percentage of People Feeling the Need for Improvement of Public
Transportation Services, October 1973**

	October 29 Sample	Various Samples October 28-31
City public transportation in the evening	56	54
City public transportation to work	58	48
Public inter-city transportation	36	31
Transportation of children to schools	38	27

Source: Israel Bureau of Applied Social Research and the Communications Institute of the
Hebrew University, *Disturbances in Regular Civilian Services* (Jerusalem: Report
submitted to the EE committee, 4 November 1973), p. 1.

We give cash to women even if the account is only in the husband's name,
and we cash checks.[18]

Thus, we see that the banks were very flexible with their clients, and
the latter did not take undue advantage of this. The general manager of
a large Jerusalem bank indicated that most of the checks that reached
the bank during this period did not bounce."[19] Indeed, the public seems
to have been quite satisfied with banking services in this period: Between
October 16 and October 22 only 10-15 percent (on the average, 12 percent)
of the public believed that banking services required immediate improvement. Greater satisfaction was expressed here than with any other
public services (see Table 2.3). Nevertheless, the banks drew two conclusions from the experience of social interruption of 1973-74: first, that
bank employees should work in rotation so as to be familiar with all
banking tasks, and, second, that women (who generally are not recruited)
should both be promoted to higher positions and be given the right of
signature for various bank activities.

Health and Welfare Services

All patients whose conditions allowed them to be released from hospitals
were sent home with the war's outbreak. Thus, for example, 1,300 patients
remained in the Health Fund (Kupat Holim) hospitals instead of the

usual 3,200. In the Negev area, traveling medical teams were organized, and these visited patients who had been sent home from hospitals. The hospitals operated under an emergency format and accepted only those patients who were in serious condition.

The Health Fund clinics operated as usual, and used pensioners as replacements for mobilized staff. During the Sukkot holiday, the clinics were open in the afternoon as well, even though they do not generally open in the afternoons. No reports of crowding were noted in the clinics.

At the same time, in reports of the Institute for the Study of Labor and Welfare relating to the Jerusalem area, crowding was reported in both the private pharmacies and in those of the Health Fund. This was partially the result of the closing of some pharmacies because of the recruitment of their owners and the recruitment of some of the Health Fund pharmacists, and partially the result of a purchasing panic that spread through the public.[20] In one clinic, the main Health Fund clinic in Jerusalem, there was tremendous pressure of persons trying to hoard supplies of medicine, especially of medicines on which the patient depended on a day-to-day basis, such as insulin. The pharmacies reported that this panic was unjustified because a large supply existed in stock. On October 15, two observers of the Institute for the Study of Labor and Welfare made the following report, from a Health Fund branch in a long-established Jerusalem neighborhood:

> In a conversation with the head nurse, it became clear that there were no particular problems except that of the shelter—the building has no shelter, and civil defense personnel were not to be found in the area. People were generally quite tense but seemed to be overcoming their tension. The Health Fund is operating as usual: the branch clerk has been recruited but the nurse and doctors are handling everything.
>
> At the time we were there, no patients came in, and the nurse claimed that maybe this was because that was the day that the families of those who were killed in action had been notified. The branch was ready for any case in which a doctor would be summoned to a house call. Additional sedatives were brought.[21]

The mother-and-child-care clinics, which are a municipal service, operated as usual throughout this period, but there was almost no demand for their services. As a result the nurses went from house to house trying to locate women and babies needing help.[22]

The welfare offices also remained open, and here too, there was no demand for their services. In light of the situation, the social workers decided (of their own accord?) to expand the population under their care and to aid any person who turned to them for help, including financial help, even for those not defined as "welfare cases" according to the accepted criteria.[23] The workers of the Institute for the Study of Labor and Welfare found a social worker in a problematic Jerusalem neighborhood who summarized his observation as follows:

> Welfare cases who do not have relatives on the front hardly react to the war situation and complain about the same things they have always complained about. Those who have relatives who were recruited do not seem to be functioning at all: Mothers sit with other mothers all day, don't buy, don't cook, don't clean the house. I got reactions like: "Who has to eat today?" "I gave the child bread and water." When I asked them about their financial situation, they said: "Who needs money today?"[24]

Likewise, many groups organized themselves in order to offer emotional and other types of support in the wake of the difficulties the tense situation aroused. These were professional or volunteer organizations (which formed themselves ad hoc to cope with the problems that suddenly appeared or that various persons perceived as having appeared). In this framework we can only note some of them, and not in a systematic way. All other aspects of volunteering will be dealt with in chapter 4.

On October 12 a suprainstitutional body of professionals was established, including psychiatrists, psychologists, and social workers, and this body decided to grant psychological and other aid to any person in need, with the help of volunteers (not necessarily professionals). It seems that the main problem of such groups was publicizing their existence and goals (even if these were diffused). A person who was in charge of organizing the staff told us:

> At the beginning the municipal officer[25] asked us for volunteers to try and calm people who were hysterical because they had no information as to where [recruited] members of their families were. Later it was decided to send groups of volunteers to homes of persons under stress. Volunteers also went to various neighborhoods to locate problems not dealt with by existing services. . . . We also received 265 telephone calls with appeals for help. About 80 of these were requests of the staff to act as intermediaries in obtaining some sort of service.[26]

On October 14 a body already in existence began to modify its role. Many unrecruited women (and some men) researchers of the Institute for the Study of Labor and Welfare adjacent to the Sociology Department of Hebrew University announced the following decision:

> To locate some of the population's urgent needs which have not been solved by existing institutions, to deal with them ourselves or by means of one

of the bodies which has been organized for the duration of the emergency. We have decided to focus our activity on neighborhoods and to try and develop initiatives for community self-organization. At the same time we will conduct research.[27]

What characterizes this group is its thinking in terms of power, along with its desire to develop local community initiatives and its awareness of the situation of social interruption as a possible trigger of social change. The group summarized some of its first conclusions as follows:

The sociologist's job is not to do things by himself, but to indicate things which should be changed, to find ways to convey this to the appropriate institutions, and to put groups into action and then to get feedback as to how things worked out.[28]

Another organization that tried to activate its members to give community aid according to Caplan's community support method[29] was the Academic Women's Organization. In conjunction with the Jerusalem Municipality's Social Welfare Department, it decided to "enter the vacuum left by the many social workers who are now on the front."[30] About two and a half weeks after the outbreak of the war the Psychological Counseling Service of the Department of Education and Culture began to act and offered to advise psychologists and teachers how to deal with children whose family members had been recruited or had fallen in battle.[31]

Thus, there was a large supply of various types of supportive services, some of which were institutionalized and part of the system, and others of which were improvised and established by single persons or groups of persons. It is very difficult to determine to what extent the population was indeed in need of this supply, and to what extent it turned to those offering it. It is clear that such activities played a role with reference to the organizers themselves (see chapter 4).

Communications

Many of the postal workers were recruited, while the pressure on local and international mail and telephone services increased considerably. The postal services set themselves a central goal of maintaining the greatest possible connection between the front and the civilians. The minister of communications, Shimon Peres, noted that on each day of the war an average of 100,000 letters (as opposed to 60,000 in "regular" times) were sent, most of these being from soldiers, and that these "were treated as telegrams, by the minister's orders." In addition, 60,000 parcels and 10,000 telegrams were sent daily. The repair staffs of the Communications Ministry worked 24 hours a day, "so that there not be a case in which a soldier would call home and find the telephone out of order." In accordance with this policy, the Communications Ministry did not cut off telephone service of people who had not paid their bills, and 4,000 new phones were installed.

At central intersections all over the country and on the front, special telephone vans for soldiers' use were set up and were run by volunteers. Special communications centers for information on the wounded were also established adjacent to hospitals.

The personnel problem was not particularly acute in the communications field, since the postal service was an attraction for many volunteers. Already on 9 October 1973, it was announced that about 2,000 volunteers were employed in the sorting and delivery of mail. In the wake of a radio appeal, 130 ex-workers (women) of the international switchboard came to work, and the service was maintained on a regular basis. It seems that communications roles were perceived as being linked to the predominant goal.

Transportation and Transport

We have already noted several times that the most severe institutional bottleneck was the public transportation system and heavy freight transport. In public transportation the major shortage was of drivers and, to a lesser degree, of buses. Only about 25 percent of the buses in the cooperatives' possession were mobilized, but about 77 percent of the drivers were recruited. Most of the taxis and their drivers were mobilized with the war's outbreak but were released within a short time (after the transport of the reserve forces was completed). At the same time, the demand for their services was very limited.

In the first days the transportation companies combined some of their lines and canceled others. They also reduced the frequency of buses and shortened the hours of service. Workers were also transferred from administrative jobs to driving, and retired workers were called back to the job. At the same time, there was a considerable decline in the demand for transportation, for the following reasons: (1) some of the population had been recruited; (2) those who had not been recruited did not leave their homes much (see chapter 3); and (3) drivers of private cars often picked up hitchhikers. A *Ha'aretz* reporter summarized the subject as follows: "All in all, the transportation cooperatives maintained a reasonable level of service." But it seems that the public's satisfaction with transportation was somewhat more limited: Reduction of the hours of transportation (in the evenings) and the difficulties in getting to work disturbed about half those asked (see Table 2.4).

With the continuation of the state of emergency, the transportation cooperatives requested the armed forces to release about 2,000 of the recruited drivers. This request was rejected, and bargaining between the armed forces and the cooperatives ensured, resulting in the release of 460 drivers in December. But even before that, a staff composed of representatives of the Ministry of Transportation, the Ministry of Labor, and the cooperatives was set up to plan accelerated courses for training women as bus drivers by means of the cooperatives' driving schools. On 27 January 1974 a plan for combining the bus lines of the two large cooperatives was put into effect. All these actions led to a considerable improvement in public transportation, but full service was not restored until March 1974.

In contrast with public transportation, the transport system for the complementary goal almost did not operate at all. The armed forces mobilized 75-80 percent of the country's heavy vehicles, which constituted 80-90 percent of the total tonnage of civilian transport in routine periods. Some of the remaining vehicles were mobilized by the EE, which used these vehicles to transport about 18,000 tons of freight daily (mostly food and fodder), compared with the 250,000 tons transported daily in routine periods. The EE refused to supply transport vehicles to businessmen and manufacturers for transporting freight not defined by the EE as essential, and it directed consumers to the private market. At the beginning of November, Minister Peres stated in the Knesset's Economic Committee that civilian transport had at its disposal only 8-9 percent of the vehicles it needed. During the war, the only existing alternative to heavy-duty trucks—the train[32]—transported six times its usual freight tonnage, but this relief was of only minor help in the problem of freight transport.

The longer the mobilization continued, the more severe the situation became. Complaints were voiced that the armed forces had mobilized many more vehicles than necessary. The Ministry of Transportation confirmed this claim but noted that the mobilization system was constructed in a very complicated fashion and that for military reasons it could not be changed. Bitter complaints were also voiced against the EE, claiming that its transport programs were based on the assumption of a short interruption and that the programs were not equipped to cope with a state of emergency lasting more than two weeks. Likewise, complaints were made that a large percentage of the vehicles placed at the EE's disposal were unused and were kept in the vehicle centers as a reserve for an emergency, while the rest were not utilized adequately

TABLE 2.4
Percentage of Respondents Indicating That It Was "Necessary" or "Very
Necessary" to Improve Civilian Services, 20–31 October 1973 and 7 November
1973

	Necessary or very necessary to improve immediately October 30–31, 1973	Necessary or very necessary to improve immediately November 7, 1983
Mail service between you and member of family in armed forces	35	37
Telephone service	26	32
Mail service to foreign countries	--	28
Municipal public transportation in the evenings	54	64
Municipal public transportation to work	48	66
Inter-city public transportation	31	4
Transporting your children to school	27	32
Possibility of you and your family receiving medical in a hospital	20	30
Possibility of you and your family receiving medical care in infirmaries	21	30
Possibility of obtaining a doctor for you and your family	21	28
Servicemen for home repairs (electrical, plumbing)	34	37
Supply of gas to your home	39	44
Sanitation services in your neighborhood	38	30
The organization of studies in school	--	26

Source: Israeli Institute for Applied Social Research and the Communications Institute of the Hebrew University, *Public Services and Shopping* (25 October–7 November, 1973) (Jerusalem: Report submitted to the EE Supreme Committee, 12 November 1973), p. 2.

because of poor organization of the EE and because of the low productivity of mobilized drivers. Top EE workers voiced their complaints against its managers at a press conference, claiming that the latter had inaccurate conceptions of organization and were inefficient managers. They also claimed that because there was no effective supervision of the vehicles mobilized by the EE, many of the drivers undertook jobs for the private market. At a slightly later period, a columnist claimed in *Ha'aretz* (November 28): "In the midst of the war, when the system for running transportation was revealed at its worst and was on the verge of collapse, the heads of the Ministry of Transportation began to admit quietly that the system they had adopted and managed with a conspicuous lack of talent had gone bankrupt." He blamed the EE for continuing to hold vehicles even after the war was over and the whole EE system had been dismantled, alleged that its managers did so because they did not wish to yield the power they had been granted. Towards the war's end, complaints began streaming in to the EE on various aspects of transport. The chairman of the Manufacturers' Association claimed that industry was suffering because of a shortage in means of transport. The EE reacted by claiming that it could not allocate vehicles to satisfy businessmen's needs and that the latter should obtain them on their own accord in the free market. The report of the Port Authority's management indicated that exports had declined by 50 percent, one of the main reasons for this decline being cited as the lack of means of transport to the port. The situation deteriorated with the onset of the citrus season. The gas companies informed customers needing a supply of gas that they should come and take it from company storage houses because of the lack of means of transport.

EE officials were mobilized to seek solutions. On October 21 the minister of transportation announced that the means of transport in the economy would be increased: the production of vehicles in Israel could be speeded up, as would be the importation of trucks ordered from abroad before the war. A request made of the armed forces for the release of mobilized vehicles was rejected. Nevertheless, after the war was over, the armed forces agreed to place a reserves transport unit at the EE's disposal for ad hoc tasks. But this was not enough to solve the problem. The Ministry of Transport purchased 2,500 trucks of 10 tons and over. The first trucks were to arrive within several weeks; and according to the plan, all of them were to reach Israel within three months. Most or all were to become the armed forces' property, and in exchange the army was to release mobilized civilian trucks. Likewise, 30 trucks of 30 tons each were ordered from Holland along with their drivers to work in

Israel for a period of two months. These vehicles reached Israel in the middle of November 1973.

All these plans proceeded slowly. Toward the middle of November, the situation in the ports deteriorated greatly; the storage houses were not emptying out, partially because of the shortage of manpower but primarily because of a lack of means of transport. As a result, additional ships could not be unloaded. Some of the citrus exports were transferred to the port of Ashdod by train, but this tactic also failed to solve the problem. The armed forces released some of the trucks they had promised to release (650 by November 11), and most were transferred to the construction industry, which was in a very difficult position.

On November 15 the EE announced that it was incapable of coping with the problems of transportation, primarily because of the lack of a system of incentives for drivers and because of the low pay they received. According to the EE, the problem could not be solved, because it was unethical that a driver mobilized by the EE should earn more than a driver recruited by the military. The drivers took advantage of the lack of supervision of their work in order to undertake private jobs in the civilian market. Fully 2,600 EE trucks (including those which were to arrive from abroad) were placed at the disposal of 46 civilian transport offices that were declared to be essential enterprises and were to deal with the supply of vehicles in accordance with orders received. In addition, a larger number of trucks were to be attached to other essential enterprises. The chairman of the Supreme Transportation Authority, estimated on November 20 that the output of the vehicles would double in the wake of the increases in rates if they were transferred to civilian offices.

By the end of November, 600 of the 2,500 trucks that had been ordered had arrived. About 600 of these were purchased by the Council of Transport Organizations under special credit conditions. On the same date, a decision was reached on the establishment of a central transport unit, which, with the aid of 150 trucks to be placed at its disposal, would undertake tasks that had not been taken care of until that time: the transport of citrus produce and the clearing out of the ports.

It soon became apparent that transferring transport to private hands did not solve the problem. The transport capacity of the civilian economy is about 70,000 tons daily—about half the required quantity. Complaints were voiced about the fact that only 46 of more than 200 transport offices in the country received vehicles, about the priorities set for the use of these vehicles, and about instances of bribery and corruption in these offices. On December 6, Minister Peres declared that there was no immediate chance of a solution to the transport problem. The situation was particularly serious inasmuch as the military could not keep to the timetable agreed upon and did not release the trucks it had promised. The transport problem was not actually solved until the massive release of trucks from the armed forces at the end of the first quarter of 1974. Later the feeling prevailed that the need to reorganize the sphere of transport in times of emergency was the most important lesson learned from the 1973 war with reference to the civilian economy.

The Educational System

The war broke out soon after the start of the school year. Inasmuch as the vast majority of the labor and teaching force in kindergartens and elementary schools—and in a considerable portion in the high schools—is female, the mobilization should theoretically not have had seriously damaging effects on the educational system at this level. However, there were additional factors that to a certain extent made the full activation of the system difficult. First, the transportation of children whose schools were far from their homes was extremely problematic. Second, the day-care centers and elementary school teachers refused to assume responsibility for the children's safety in places where there were not shelters (or where there was not enough room in the shelters).

The Ministry of Education's policy was not only not to cut down on education at this time, but rather to expand it. The feeling was that a situation whereby children would wander in the streets in times of emergency or constitute an additional burden on parents (primarily mothers whose husbands had been mobilized) should be avoided. Thus, not only was an order issued to open the day-care centers and elementary schools (beginning on October 9), but in some cases it was decided to begin a system of an "extended school day" and even to cancel the Sukkot vacation (about eight days), which was approaching.

On October 15 an observer toured several Jerusalem kindergartens, and the following is one of her characteristic reports:

> The "Mahane Yehuda" day-care center is under the auspices of the Ministry of Education and Culture. About a year ago, it received an order to vacate, and so today it is located far from the children's homes, as the children come from the Nachlaot and Mahane Yehuda neighborhoods. The kindergarten has no shelter. One kindergarten teacher claims that she was told to go to the shelter of the tax office opposite the kindergarten in times of emergency. Civil defense personnel were to transfer them [the day-care center's children] but while yesterday 6 of the children sat near the kindergarten, today not one of them did so. It should be noted that the Tax Office knows nothing of this arrangement.[33]

Joel Shiftan, the director of the Education Department in the Jerusalem Municipality, reported that all 226 day-care centers in Jerusalem were opened on October 9 (when the fear of air attacks had declined):

There was complete attendance at the kindergartens, except for several deviant cases. There were no differences in attendance among children from the various neighborhoods. Community studies indicate that mothers from poor neighborhoods behaved less "hysterically," since they were forced to continue to function because they have many children.[34]

A somewhat different version was presented by two kindergarten teachers from a mixed neighborhood in Jerusalem:

We agree to the decision to cancel the [Sukkot] vacation. But it is annoying that the reasons for this were not explained to us by our union. What is the reason? To relieve mothers, to take children off the streets, or to reduce the tension which has built up among the children . . . it's clear to us that it helps the children. Not all the children come. Some mothers are afraid to let their children leave the house. We feel that we are doing something good, and the mothers are satisfied as well. But on the other hand, too much responsibility is given to us. We'd have to run to the shelter with the children (about 200 meters), and how could we manage that?[35]

In an October 22 report from a state religious school, the following was noted:

Most of the administrative staff, including the principal, were recruited. A teacher who generally teaches the lower classes substitutes for the principal and serves as the Civil Defense representative—something which seems to make her tense. Teachers of several subjects (especially Talmud) are absent. It is hard for the teachers to control pupils from the higher classes, because the latter don't want to stay in the classes. They would prefer to volunteer for various jobs and resent the fact that they had to come to school during the Sukkot vacation. There is a sense of a great deal of tension between pupils and teachers, and there are many disciplinary problems. The school psychologist advised the teachers to conduct many nonclassroom activities, such as sports, arts and crafts, or dealing with timely subjects, etc.[36]

These problems were even more acute in secondary schools. Their teaching forces had undergone less feminization (and so a larger portion of their teachers had been recruited). In addition, the pupils generally felt that it was not appropriate to fulfill their routine role and that at the least they should fulfill roles related to the complementary goal, if not to aid in the fulfillment of the predominant goal.

We noted such a phenomenon in an even more acute sense when we examined what happened during this period in the Ort network of vocational schools.[37] Here most of the teaching staff had been mobilized, as part of the administrative staff had been. It was nevertheless decided to keep the pupils in the school framework even if the institution's other functions would be given up on from the outset. This was done in two ways. First, hundreds of so-called paid volunteers were recruited (see chapter 4) to fulfill some of the teachers' functions:

> It was necessary to find an adult who would spend several hours with the pupils (more or less according to an improvised schedule of classes) and if possible—also teach something. Most of the volunteer teachers fulfilled the expectation of returning order to the schools, and, to a lesser degree, succeeded in transmitting material.

Second, the pupils in the higher grades, who were assumed to have already acquired considerable technical skills, were directed to work in the military industry on the initiative of the Ort network and in coordination with the defense system. Thus, the pupils not only had a sense of participation in the fulfillment of the predominant goal but also gained experience. It seems that very few pupils in other secondary schools enjoyed such privileges. However, in the Ort network even the pupils in the lower grades participated in the fulfillment of the predominant goal, in that the schools' workshops took it upon themselves to manufacture certain items for the armed forces and the military industry. This enabled the schools to operate their workshops, at least partially. In other schools as well, attempts were made to recruit pupils for volunteer jobs, but these were generally performed outside the schools. (We will discuss this topic further in chapter 4.)

At the beginning of 1974 rumors prevailed[38] to the effect that the matriculation examinations would be given early[39] in order to make it possible to recruit the pupils of the twelfth grade to the military earlier than usual. These rumors were denied by the director general of the Ministry of Education, but it was announced that changes would be introduced in the examinations (a possible lowering of the level of the examination?) in consideration of the fact that some of the teachers had been recruited for long periods of time. The matriculation examinations for external pupils (i.e., those not studying within the public school system),[40] which were to have taken place in October 1973, were postponed to December and were held in a greater number of centers than usual in order to make it easier for recruited examinees to attend them. It was also announced that "the examinations would be graded while taking the situation into consideration."

The opening of the universities engendered difficulties on a different level. Because of the heavy burden borne by Israel's citizens both in routine periods and in periods of active warfare, the entire system is based on a delicate system of a "fair sharing of the burden."[41] In the 1973 war, as well as in the 1982 war, there were frequent complaints that the distribution of the burden was unfair and that the war's main burdens fell on the shoulders of a relatively narrow stratum of the population. The opening of the institutions of higher education in 1973 was directly relevant to this delicate matter. About 60 percent of the student population was not mobilized—mostly females, older students, the disabled, foreign students, and Arab students. The remaining 40 percent bore most of the burden of attaining the predominant goal. At stake was not only the potential absence from classes and even from an entire academic year, but also the risk of one's life. Nevertheless, the government (in a decision made on the cabinet level!) decided that the institutions of higher education should be opened, and thereby symbolize the continuation of normal life as much as possible even in the midst of war.

On their past, the institutions of higher education (which also exerted pressure to begin the academic year) promised to make every effort to help recruited students, primarily by (1) sending lecture summaries to all soldier-students in all required courses (2) setting additional and flexible examination dates for students who had been recruited, and (3) opening an additional session of studies (in March 1974) for students who would return from the front. In addition, a controversy erupted over whether every potential student who had served on the front and met certain minimum requirements (of having a recognized matriculation certificate) should be accepted at an institution of higher education for the 1974-75 academic year. This controversy resulted in a victory for those who argued against "lowering standards." Nevertheless, it was decided that when all other conditions for acceptance were equal—that is, matriculation grades and grades on entrance examinations to institutions of higher learning—released soldiers would receive priority over those who were not soldiers.

Likewise, students who were released soldiers were granted a tuition exemption for one academic year, a monthly allotment of about $95 (for up to six months) and priority in obtaining low-interest loans to be repaid at the end of their studies.

The above constitutes a specific case within the framework of a more general problem with which the system had to cope: Should those who bore the burden of the predominant goal in the period of interruption be "repaid" (for loss of time and money and the physical risk of injury and loss of life involved therein)?[42] From the time that military service became universal and armies became citizen-armies, there has developed a tendency to "reward" released soldiers, particularly in the wake of a severe battle (in which the system is not totally defeated). In Israel as well there has been such a tendency all along, but never have there crystallized unequivocal norms about whether participation in the attainment of the predominant goal should be converted to material resources, and if so, to what extent and in which spheres. This problem was left unsolved, primarily for two reasons, though it was the subject of public discussion and controversy (in the wake of each of the wars). First, the scope of participation in the attainment of the predominant goal is relatively great (because of the combination of the system's needs and the institutional solutions that were arrived at to fulfill these needs). Thus, when participation tends to be universal, there is little significance in rewards given for fulfullment of tasks for which such large portions of the population are involved. Second, it goes without saying, a powerful norm exists that claims that participation in the attainment of the predominant goal is natural and routine; thus, the main (although not exclusive) reward for it is the very fact of participation. The situation becomes problematic when the feeling arises that the burden was not divided in an egalitarian manner.

However, we must distinguish between rewards for participation in attainment of the predominant goal and the prevention of losses as a result of this participation. The feeling is that an individual and his family who contribute to the fulfillment of the central goal should not incur severe losses as a result. These losses cannot be prevented but should be kept to a minimum. This conception is rooted in and strongly connected to the approach indicating that at times of social interruption an attempt should be made to insure that the situation and order existing prior to the interruption be restored as quickly as possible. One result of this approach was the establishment of a loan fund for the self-employed whose businesses had suffered as a result of the mobilization (see below, in the section on manufacturing and commerce).

The Equalization Fund

The underlying concept of the equalization fund is that a minimum income should be guaranteed to each recruited individual and to his family. For this purpose, there were two types of payments. First, there were "family payments," which the armed forces transferred directly to the soldier's family (or to the soldier himself) in accordance with his marital status and the number of his children. Second, there was a mechanism built into the system (i.e., an equalization fund) that guaranteed income up to a certain level (in 1973-74, the ceiling was 1,800 Israeli pounds for those in the army, which was remitted to employees by their employers and to the self-employed by means of the National Insurance Institute. This fund is an integral part of the Israeli social security system, and the monies to finance it are collected as a small percentage of income during routine periods (similar to union strike funds, for example). Students and pupils in Yeshivot also benefit from this arrangement when they are mobilized. This arrangement operates both in wartime and in routine periods when a soldier in the reserves is called for his annual service.

Thus, we have before us an additional institutional arrangement that allows the system to enter periods of social interruption and to end such interruption in an almost routine manner, without the system and the individuals within it incurring severe losses.

The Main Branches of Manufacturing and Commerce

As noted above, there were three main problems faced by industry, the various branches of manufacturing, and commerce during and after the war in 1973, but to some extent also in 1982.

First were the manpower problems. According to the data of the EE planning committee, the military mobilized 25-30 percent of the civilian labor force. This number was not divided proportionately among the various civilian branches. In addition, when attempting to evaluate the effect of mobilization we must remember that except for enterprises defined as essential, the only consideration taken into account in re-cruitment was the military one. (In December-January and later, with the continuation of the state of emergency, many complaints were voiced against the armed forces, claiming that they held on to people with key roles in the economy but with military roles of secondary importance.) In addition, most, if not all, the Arab workers were absent from work during the war. By November 4 only about 40 percent of the Arab workers from the occupied territories had returned to their jobs.

The gradual release of soldiers began soon after the cease-fire and ended around May-June 1974. This process proceeded along two lines. First, there was the release of a large number of persons according to military considerations. Many of those recruited were thus released by mid-December 1973. According to the Director General of the Ministry of Labor, 85 percent of the employees who had been mobilized were already at their jobs by this time. On March 6 the head of the armed forces Manpower Branch noted that more than half of those mobilized had already been released. The second channel consisted of the requests of institutions and various bodies for the release of key persons in the economy. The armed forces responded to these requests only partially, and sometimes after a relatively long period had elapsed. Thus, for example, on December 12 the military agreed to release 900 bus drivers of the 2,500 the transportation companies had requested (see the section on transport). In the end, only 460 of them were released. Up to this date the armed forces had agreed to the release of 600 key men of the 3,000 for whose release requests had been made.

Along with the shortage of workers in certain branches, certain indications of unemployment could be noted at the beginning of this period. In the wake of the mobilization and the decline in orders, many workers were dismissed, especially in the construction trade, commerce, tourism, entertainment, and so on. In the first 10 days of November, an average of 2,100 to 2,400 persons registered daily in the Employment Bureaus, compared with a daily average of 700 in the period prior to the war. In the same 10 days a total of 10,000 people registered, in contrast with a monthly average of 19,000 before the war. Nevertheless, a decline in the demand for employment was noted in December, and the director of the Employment Service noted that the number of requests not fulfilled in this month was the same as that of September, and that no longer were any signs of unemployment in evidence. Toward the end of the month there was even an increase in the demand for workers over that of the period prior to the war.

The second-most-important problem faced by the production system was that of transport. The situation in this sphere was summarized earlier, in the section on transportation and transport.

The third problem lay in raw materials and credit. Actually, almost no real shortage of raw materials, whether imported or Israeli-produced, occurred in any branch. Perhaps the most conspicuous shortage was that of cement—the result of the cutback in production in the Nesher factory because of manpower and transport problems. On the other hand, many branches suffered from a reduction of credit by the suppliers of raw materials. Suppliers of raw materials for industry demanded payment in cash, instead of credit for three months as was generally accepted; and this new practice imposed severe difficulties on industry. Another severe problem was the wave of price increases in November, December, and January and the period following these months, including the increase of prices of raw materials and gasoline. The limitations placed on consumption of electricity and water also presented problems. We should also add to this picture the sharp decline in sales in most stores, particularly in the first part of the period.

We shall now present a more detailed survey of some of the sectors particularly affected in 1973-74 by the situation.

Industry

With the outbreak of the war, production declined to 40 percent of its usual rate. By mid-November the economy had recovered somewhat and production reached 70 percent of the usual level, according to data submitted by the minister of commerce and industry, Haim Bar-Lev, to the Emergency Advisory Council. Five days later it was announced that the economy's output had declined by 34 percent in comparison with the period prior to the war and that 27 percent of the industrial workers were still mobilized (*Ha'aretz,* November 20). In December data was published indicating that industrial output had reached 75 percent of the normal level.

During the war it had already become clear that a boom would ensue in those branches working for the defense industry, primarily in the metal, electronics, electric, and vehicle sectors. The rise in the volume of orders from these branches on the part of the defense system as a result of the war was estimated at $238 million (October 20). The immediate problems faced by these branches were the shortage in means of transport and in trained manpower, and the mobilization of a large portion of key personnel. This problem plagued industry for several months. At the end of December the general chief of staff promised the chairman of the Manufacturers' Association that he would release 900 key persons in industry.

In addition to the problem described above, industry geared for export also suffered from severe difficulties in transferring goods abroad, primarily because Israel's ports were almost totally blocked by the mobilization of the dock workers and the lack of means of transport to clear the storage houses (see also the section on transportation and transport). In the report of the Port Authority management, a decline of 50 percent in exports was noted because of the reduction of output and the lack of means of transport to the port. The food industry suffered from the difficulties noted above but continued to operate both for the needs of the military and for those of the civilian market, while receiving as much aid from volunteers as possible. The diamond industry suffered particularly from a shortage of manpower. With the war's outbreak, 50 percent of the workers in this branch were recruited.

Particularly difficult was the situation of small enterprises and work-shops, most of which did not receive orders from the defense system and found their business suffering greatly in the wake of mobilization. According to a survey conducted by the Labor Productivity Institute, a quarter of the small industrial enterprises were not operating in November. At the end of November the Craftsmen's Union demanded government loans for the rehabilitation of 2,000 craftsmen who were on the verge of bankruptcy as a result of the situation. The situation of the self-employed was perceived as so severe that the government announced the establishment of a fund for rehabilitating businesses, and discussions of this matter were held in the Knesset.

The situation in garages is perhaps indicative of the situation in small businesses and workshops. In a report at the beginning of November, it was noted that about half of the 7,000 workers in this sector had been mobilized. In spite of this, the 100 largest garages in the country worked at full capacity for the private market with most of the jobs filled by Arab workers. (The same source indicated that the large garages refused to work for the EE, because the pay received for such work was lower than that received on the free market.) Most of the other garages closed down because their owners had been recruited. In January, 40 percent of the garages were still closed, while in the rest only a quarter of the manpower was present, with the prediction that the release of workers could not be expected in the near future.

In agriculture as well, problems were focused primarily around the shortage of manpower and the means of transport. About a third of the Kibbutz members were recruited. The problem of manpower was solved by the extension of the working hours of the remaining members. The situation in the Moshavim was more severe. The farms of those who had been mobilized were on the verge of collapse because of manpower and transport problems. Here, too, frameworks for mutual aid were put into action. The representative of the Farmers' Union in the EE Supreme Committee reported that the sector had not adequately organized itself before the war for EE activities, and now this was being felt, primarily in the spheres of transport and the harvest.

It should be noted that the supply of agricultural produce to the cities was not affected, and in the report of directors general of government ministries in the EE Supreme Committee it was noted that the agricultural sector was producing at its usual rate. With the beginning of the citrus harvest season, though, the two principal problems—manpower and transport—became more severe. At one point there was talk of transporting citrus produce to Ashdod port by train. Likewise, programs were prepared for the expansion of secondary school pupils' national service in order to aid farms. Volunteers were directed to agricultural work, primarily during the harvest and packing times. In addition to the problems noted above, the export of citrus produce also suffered from bottlenecks at the ports. When, at the end of November, it was decided to establish a central transport unit to deal with tasks that could not be coped with until this time, its main tasks were the clearing of the ports and transporting citrus produce for export.

Despite the efforts made, in March the collapse of thousands of farmsteads whose owners had been recruited was noted, and the government decided to aid the owners by granting them loans.

The construction sector suffered perhaps more than any other. A large portion of the Jewish workers were recruited; and because most of the Arabs from the country as well as from the occupied territories did not come to work during the war, there was a severe shortage of means of transport and of heavy equipment, and at a later stage there was also a shortage of raw materials, particularly of cement. In addition, there were sharp increases in prices, sales came almost to a complete standstill for several months, and predictions (which later failed to materialize) were made to the effect that immigration to Israel would decline following the war. In his report to the Emergency Advisory Council, Minister Bar-Lev indicated that during the war the construction industry had declined to 20 percent of its usual activity; by mid-November activity reached 40 percent of the usual level. The situation was in accordance with the prediction of the Ministry of Commerce and Industry, which estimated that the construction sector would be one of the hardest hit as a result of the war. In November, several measures were taken aimed at saving that sector from collapse. In order to ease the problem of transport, it was decided that the construction industry would receive 750 of the first 2,000 trucks the army had promised to release; 500 additional trucks were promised to this sector from among the trucks that had been ordered from abroad, and about 250 additional trucks from the transport companies to which vehicles had been transferred by the EE. All these measures were aimed at allocating to the construction industry 1,500 trucks, compared with 3,000 trucks generally employed by it. But the army did not keep to this timetable, and instead of releasing the 750 trucks within a week as promised, had released only about 120 of them by December. The imported trucks also were delayed for longer than had been expected. In mid-November it was announced that the armed forces would release 1,500 key persons in the construction sector, but the implementation of this decision also was delayed.

Another serious problem with which the construction sector had to cope was the shortage of heavy mechanical equipment. In January 1974, 60 percent of this sector's equipment was still mobilized. Equipment owners claimed that simply releasing the equipment was not enough to solve the problem, because a large portion of the equipment was damaged owing to poor maintenance and operating conditions in the armed forces. The military denied these claims but announced that it would not be able to release significant numbers of heavy mechanical equipment.

In the middle of November the government decided to reactivate the construction sector by encouraging initiatives by private contractors, and announced that the volume of government construction jobs would not decline in 1974-75. In the wake of government incentives and the first releases from the armed forces, the construction trade began to recover; and at the beginning of December was employing 60 percent of the number employed before the war. Nevertheless, there was still fear of serious unemployment in this sector, primarily because of the delay in releasing vehicles from the military.

In light of the slowdown in construction, the Ministry of Housing announced that in the future it would tend to offer young couples financial aid rather than flats.

During the 1982 war the armed forces apparently were inflexible in not releasing those workers who were classified by their places of employment as essential, possibly just because there was only a partial mobilization. In the first month, 3,000 essential workers were released, a number that represented 27 percent of the requests. Eighty percent of the requests were put in by industry, and the rest by agriculture, construction, and the various branches of the services. Industrial sources complained that even after the committees involved had authorized soldiers to be released, they were still kept mobilized for some time thereafter (about five days after the decision) or were not released at all because of the opposition of the officers in the field, who themselves defined the men as essential for the furthering of the war effort. The problems appeared likely to become more severe, since there is a certain coalition between the functional importance of a person in the armed forces and his importance in his occupation. Most of the managers and production foremen occupied important technical positions in the military, and administrative managers were engaged in either combat or technical leadership roles in the armed forces.

Thus, for example, in a large factory for manufacturing pipes, the director general and a large number of the workers were mobilized. The others agreed to work 12-hour shifts (from 6 A.M. to 6 P.M.), but their productivity soon declined because of exhaustion. In another company (the Harsa tile company), 40 percent of the workers were mobilized, but productivity only declined by 15 percent as a result of longer shifts and the moving of workers. In yet another large company, this one involved in electronics (Telrad), 20 percent of all the males were drafted, but this included almost all the foremen and engineers.

Tourism

In the forecasts of the Ministry of Commerce and Industry, tourism—along with the construction trade—was at the top of the list of sectors of the economy likely to suffer because of the 1973 war. When the war broke out, the tourists left the country. On October 17 the last foreign airlines—Air France and Alitalia—stopped their flights to Israel, and foreign passenger ships also stopped arriving in Israel. Tourism was totally paralyzed until the end of the war.

After the cease-fire, this sector recovered quickly, partly because of the approach of the pilgrim season in December. Indeed, in December 1973, 47,000 tourists visited Israel, only 8.4 percent less than the number for the same month in 1972.

Movie Houses, Catering Halls, and Restaurants

Movie houses were closed for the three weeks of the war; and when they were reopened, they drew only 10-30 percent of their normal occupancy. On December 3 owners of movie houses held an emergency meeting at which they claimed that their sector was facing collapse because of a 50 percent decline in clients. The main reason for the decline in moviegoing, besides the mass mobilization and the atmosphere of a state of emergency, was the fact that public transportation to the suburbs stopped operating at 8 P.M., and to the city at 10 P.M. Thus, it was impossible to return home via public transportation after a movie.

From an article published in the *Ha'aretz* daily, we learn that catering halls were completely shut down, and a similar situation existed in high-class restaurants. On the other hand, the cheaper restaurants operated almost as usual.

Commerce

Except for essential commodities, trade came to a virtual standstill with the outbreak of the war. Merchants were not interested in sales because of the rise in prices, the cutbacks in production, and the loss of credit. The decline of revenues, in turn, caused a reduction of orders from importers abroad.

Toward the end of November 1973 a decline of 50 percent in automobile sales was noted, as was an almost total standstill—continuing into December—in the sales of luxury items, as well as a decline of 25-30 percent in gasoline sales.

At about the same time, the slump in trade reached serious proportions because of the rise in taxes and prices, and because of inflation. Merchants were forced to reduce the prices of furniture, jewelry, clothing, materials, and so forth. Despite this, at the beginning of December there was still talk of a paralysis of sales, and real estate sales had also come to a standstill.

At the beginning of 1974 trade began to recover, primarily because the public feared a decline in the value of the currency. A rise in sales of electrical appliances was noted, and automobile importers reported that their sales in December totaled 80 percent of their volume in the parallel period in the year, mostly because of rumors both of price increases and of a currency devaluation. Likewise, an increase in demand for basic products became evident during this period.

Immigration

Immigration to Israel was halted during the 1973 war but recovered quickly afterwards. According to reports published on 1 January 1974, the annual balance showed only a slight decline from previous years' number of immigrants.

Several things should be said about the immigrants who arrived in Israel shortly before the war. Some were transferred to their apartments before the war's outbreak. Surveys by the Institute for the Study of Labor and Welfare indicate that in several of Jerusalem's new neighborhoods— especially Neve Yaakov (reports dated October 15 and October 31) and Gilo (report dated October 21)—large concentrations of immigrants could be found whose situation during the war was difficult. In some cases, their apartments had not been completed, and in the period of emergency their completion was postponed. Neighborhood services such as kinder- gartens, schools, and the like were not yet operating smoothly. The decrease in public transportation led to a partial detachment from the city. Nor was there coordination among the various bodies dealing with these neighborhoods. However, according to the institute's reports, the most serious problem was the immigrants' sense of detachment, brought about primarily by the fact that their new country was still strange to them and the language caused them difficulties.

This problem of detachment also characterized the situation of the 800 immigrants in the Absorption Center in Mevasseret Zion. Most were professionals, and some were in vital professions. The majority attempted to volunteer, but no one utilized their services—something that led to a sense of helplessness.[43]

Summary

There is no doubt that, particularly because of the total surprise and suddenness of the transition to a state of active warfare, we have been able to demonstrate that there were mechanisms and institutional arrangements built into the system that were put into effect immediately to deal with both the predominant goal (which we are not analyzing here) and with the complementary goal. These arrangements can be understood only by reference to the previous experience of the system (and of some of the actors in it) both with a "routine" conflictual situation, which is a permanent factor in the system, and with sudden increases, in the past, in the salience and intensity of the Jewish-Arab conflict. A process of social interruption cannot be conceived of without experiences of this nature.

However, it appears that the arrangement did not encompass all the institutional spheres; the institutional arrangements did not all operate with the same degree of efficiency, nor was there the same degree of readiness to accept the interruption for the entire length of time in all spheres. For example, from data of the Israeli Institute for Applied Social Research (see Table 2.4) we may note that even if the supply of public services improved with time, the degree of tolerance toward difficulties— or toward the interruption—declined steadily. This trend was particularly evident with regard to public transportation. It seems that the period of full social interruption may be divided into two periods: (1) that of active warfare, and (2) that immediately following the war, in which the immediate physical threat was removed, but in which the system remained almost totally mobilized. The desire for quick restoration of the system was an integral part of the state of interruption.

But the previous "experiences" (i.e., the earlier wars) did not always contribute to the effective functioning of the system in 1973, both in the sphere of the predominant goal and in that of the complementary goal. This was because the earlier experiences, with their shorter interruptions, created expectations inappropriate to the situation. These two previous wars (in 1956 and 1967) had been shorter and had demanded mobilization—and thus, social interruption—for a shorter period of time. The duration of mobilization—of manpower and of means of transport, for example—is not only a quantitative variable but also a qualitative one. Thus, institutional arrangements geared to a given length of time are not necessarily suitable when this period is extended.

The situation becomes particularly difficult when the demands of the predominant goal are presented in a zero-sum situation vis-à-vis those of the complementary goal, as in the case of total and long-term mobilization of transportation equipment. In this context the combination of an unexpected duration of mobilization with a zero-sum situation challenged the institutional arrangements that should have existed. On the other hand, it seems that these arrangements operated with reasonable efficiency in the sphere of banking and at a "reasonable" level in public transportation.

The most conspicuous sphere in which institutional arrangements did not fulfill the "needs" (although arrangements began to be made in the midst of the period of interruption) was the creation of an encounter between the large supply of manpower (skilled, semiskilled, and unskilled) and the demand for manpower in many and varied spheres. With considerable justice, groups of women (4 December 1973) claimed that this fault of the social organization stemmed from the fact that some of the roles (not only in the zone of the predominant goal but also in that of the complementary goal) were perceived as being "masculine" roles, thus depriving women of access to them.[44] However, this was just one of the symptoms of the fact that the institutional arrangements were not complete. Therefore, perhaps we should view the model of social interruption presented above as a Weberian ideal type and examine the social reality in terms of the distance from the ideal type. Let us now examine the situation with reference to the fulfillment of routine roles of individual actors not mobilized for the attainment of the predominant goal.

Notes

1. See B. Kimmerling, *Zionism and Territory: The Socio-Territorial Dimension of Zionist Politics* (Berkeley: Institute of International Studies, University of California, 1983).
2. The Israeli experience until now indicates that this movement is quite sudden. Two wars broke out with no warning at all (from an institutional point of view)—those of 1956 and 1973—and the 1967 war with a relatively short warning (on May 15 an intelligence warning about mobilization of forces and movement of Egyptian forces was noted; the Israeli mobilization began several days later). The 1947-48 war was "deviant" in terms of the Israeli system. First, it developed in stages; second, it continued for a relatively long period of time; and third, it involved considerable injury among the civilian population. This was the war that most resembled the patterns of war "familiar" to other modern nations.
3. Concerning the examination of the differential degree of state of siege of Israeli society at different times and in various spheres, see B. Kimmerling, *Social Interruption and Besieged Societies* (Amherst: Council on International Studies, State University of New York at Buffalo, 1979).

4. See D. Horowitz and B. Kimmerling, "Some Social Implications of Military Service and the Reserves System in Israel," *Archives Européennes de Sociologie* 15 (1974):262-76.
5. The concept of "minimal existence" is of course relative and depends both on the perceived degree of the security situation's severity and on other psychosociological factors.
6. This does not imply that in the long run there were no severe disturbances or damages in additional spheres.
7. The planned yearly increase in gross national product was to be 6.8 percent. Not only was this increase not maintained, but an opposite trend of decline began to be noted. See *Israel Economic Development: Past Progress and Plan for the Future* (Jerusalem: Economic Planning Authority, 1968), p. 45.
8. We refer here to a social situation in which norms that were previously valid lose their validity and the individual does not know what society and complementary actors expect of him. Durkheim predicts that in a situation of war (against an external army) the rates of anomie in the system will decline. See E. Durkheim, *Suicide: A Study in Sociology,* trans. J. A. Spaulding and G. Simpson (Glencoe: Free Press, 1951).
9. Y. Levi, Reports from 15 October and 31 October 1973, the Institute for Research on Labor and Welfare (hereafter IRLW).
10. Y. Levi, report of October 15.
11. Z. Levi and R. Hollander, report of October 15, IRLW.
12. On November 12-13 between 41 percent of the respondents (in Haifa) and 49 percent (in Jerusalem) complained of price boosting. On November 19 and 20, the percentages of those who complained were: in Tel Aviv, 34 percent; in Haifa, 59 percent; and in Jerusalem, 58 percent. The figures are from data of the Israel Institute for Applied Social Research and the Communications Institute (Hebrew University) available in *Products: Shortages and Problems in Attaining Them* (Jerusalem: submitted to the Ministry of Commerce and Industry, 27 November 1973), p. 7.
13. Ibid., pp. 5-6.
14. G. Schild and J. Varsher, 14 October 1973, IRLW.
15. Z. Levi and R. Hollander, 15 October 1973, IRLW.
16. In recent years the National Security Institute began to struggle against this partially by refusing to transfer payments for children (and other payments meant for the wife) to any bank account for which the woman did not have the right of signature.
17. Already in the war's first days, a spontaneous movement for financial contributions to the war effort began to develop. This was an additional attempt on the part of those who had not been mobilized for the attainment of the predominant goal to participate in some way in its attainment. Implicitly there was also probably a sense of paying "ransom" in the form of money by those who felt "guilty" for not endangering their lives as the soldiers on the front did. On November 19-20, 55 percent of the respondents indicated that they had already purchased war bonds, 14 percent committed themselves to such a purchase, 7 percent indicated that they "would certainly purchase them," and 24 percent that they "might purchase" or "would not purchase" the bonds.
18. Y. Levi, IRLW.

19. Interview conducted in January 1975 with M. Yonovsky, head manager of a large Jerusalem bank.
20. N. Toren and M. Negri, 15 October 1973, IRLW.
21. Z. Levi and R. Hollander, 15 October 1973, IRLW.
22. G. Schild and J. Varsher, 15 October 1973, IRLW.
23. Ibid.
24. Ibid.
25. The "municipal officer" is an officer located in all large settlements, whose job it is to care for soldiers arriving in town for vacations (food, lodging, entertainment, etc.). In certain cases—primarily in times of large-scale mobilization for war—he serves as the link between soldiers and their families.
26. The interview was conducted in January 1975.
27. Institute for Research on Labor and Welfare, *Summary Discussion on Our Activities in Ten Days of War,* mimeographed (25 October 1973).
28. Ibid., p. 2.
29. G. Caplan, *Support Systems and Community Mental Health* (New York: Behavioral Publications, 1974).
30. Interview with Ms. A. Katzir, February 1975.
31. Interview with Ms. C. Pollack, Bureau for Mental Health, Jerusalem, January 1975.
32. The train system is not at all developed in Israel. Actually there are only two main railway lines (Tel Aviv/Haifa, and Tel Aviv/Jerusalem). In 1972 the trains transported about 3 million tons of freight; in 1973, 3.5 million; in 1974, 3.6 million.
33. N. Toren, *Day-Care Centers and Kindergartens,* IRLW, 15 October 1973.
34. Interview, February 1975. On the other hand, Ms. Ben-Schach, the person in charge of municipal kindergartens, reported that several were not operating. Anita Griffel, October 15-21, IRLW.
35. Y. Levi, "Kiryat-Yovel—Borochov Street," IRLW, 15 October 1973.
36. A. Griffel, "The Area of Ramot Eshkol and Shmuel Hanavi," IRLW, 22 October 1973.
37. Based on interviews with Mr. Posner (the spokesman for the Ort network of schools), Ms. Bareli (a psychologist and adviser to the network), and Mr. Kimmelman (the school principal), February 1975.
38. As in any situation of intense pressure on the one hand and scarcity of information on the other, the system was characterized by the spread of a great number of rumors. For example, Yael Levi listed a tremendous number of rumors, most of which later proved to be false. Y. Levi, "Summary of Rumors and Reactions in the First Week of the War in Kiryat Yovel," IRLW, 15 October 1973.
39. The matriculation exams are a set of exams given to graduates of secondary schools by the Ministry of Education and Culture and are very similar to the French *baccalauréat.* They are supposed to measure the achievements of the educational system as a whole and those of each school and to predict the pupil's ability to continue to study for higher degrees. Today the matriculation certificate constitutes a necessary but not sufficient condition (until 1963 it was sufficient) for acceptance to an institution of higher education in Israel.
40. Pupils who studied for the exams on their own or in private schools not recognized by the Ministry of Education.

41. See Horowitz and Kimmerling, "Some Social Implications of Military Service."
42. Released soldiers in 1973-74 as well as in 1982 had the right to a limited number of privileges in spheres outside that of education. First, for instance, there was a moratorium of a month from the day of release on payment of debts (their own and those of their families) to both private and public institutions. In general, the enactment of any contract signed by a soldier was postponed up to a month after his release. At the same time, soldiers were advised not to take advantage of this privilege unnecessarily. Second, the state promised priority to released soldiers in receiving housing (besides an increase of 15 percent to their mortgages). Third, it was forbidden to dismiss a soldier from his job while he was in service and for a month following his release.
43. Z. Levi and R. Hollander, "Summary of Problems," 15 October 1973, IRLW.
44. This point is focused on in the article by R. Bar-Yosef and D. Padan-Eisenstark, "Women and Men in War," *Megamot* 22 (November 1975: 36-50. But the women's position constitutes only a special case of the general problem of incompatibility between supply and demand during the period of interruption, although it is possible that the problem of women was emphasized more because of the rear/front differentiation, which was clearly determined through sexual classification.

3

Performance of Routine Activities

After presenting the processes of social interruption on the institutional level, we turn now to the analysis of the reactions of individuals within the interrupted system. As we saw in chapter 1, these activities can be divided into two basic forms: the continuation or interruption (or any other change) of routine activities engaged in by the individual during routine periods (i.e., periods in which, according to our definition, the system is not interrupted), and "new" activities stemming from the situation of social interruption. This chapter will focus on activites of the former type.

In order to examine the changes in the level of performance of these activities, we presented our respondents (see the Methodological Appendix) with a list of 18 different activities (see Table 3.1), some of which are very specific and independent of others (such as smoking), while others are a part of social roles that may constitute indices of the degree of an individual's performance (i.e., regular attendance at work). The respondents were asked to assign a score indicating the frequency with which each activity was performed, first during "regular times" and then "during the war" (the 1973 war).[1] Table 3.1 presents the frequency of the performance of each of the activities in a routine situation as opposed to the situation of social interruption for the entire sample population, and the rates and directions of changes in these frequencies. A first glance at the table reveals great variance in the frequencies of performance of various activities (for example, in reference to taking medication there is a change of 0.5 percent between the two periods, as compared with a gross change of 32.0 percent in reading of books—with the net change possibly being even greater).[2]

In principle, all these activities were exposed to two main types of pressures: (1) psychological pressures and various anxieties (as noted in chapter 1) and (2) pressures and constraints as a result of the situation of social interruption (as depicted in chapter 2). Without entering into the question of which individuals were more exposed to each of the two

TABLE 3.1
Frequency of Performance of Various Activities in Routine Situations
Compared with Situations of Active Warfare and the Differences between
Them (in percent)

The activity	Performance "most of the time" or often		Rate and direction of change
	In "regular times"	In wartime	
Care for personal cleanliness	97.9	90.0	- 7.9
Sleep	29.7	16.8	-12.9
Listening to news	89.3	98.0	+ 8.7
Absence from work	6.0	24.6	+18.6
Regular eating	75.1	43.6	-31.5
Staying home	77.7	79.3	+ 1.6
Meeting friends	66.6	36.61	-30.0
Cleaning one's home	83.5	59.0	-24.5
Prayer	13.4	20.4	+ 7.0
Studying	26.9	9.8	-17.1
Handicrafts	40.0	23.7	-16.3
Taking medication	21.5	22.0	+ 0.5
Travelling	38.2	26.1	-12.1
Care for personal appearance	79.1	51.4	-27.7
Visits to doctor	18.7	11.8	- 6.9
Smoking	34.0	39.3	+ 5.3
Reading the newspaper	83.0	88.0	+ 5.0
Reading books	59.2	27.0	-32.2

types of pressures and with reference to which activities, it seems fruitful
to classify the activities according to the potential *degree of control* that
the individual was able to exert as to whether or not he would perform
them, or, alternatively, which activities can be viewed objectively as
subject to the influence of environmental constraints (of the institutional
system or of actors fulfilling complementary roles).

TABLE 3.2

Levels of Significance of the Associations (p) between the Frequency of Performance of Various Activities and Ethnic Origin in Routine Periods and in Periods of Social Interruption*

Activity	In routine periods	During social interruption
Travelling	.0005	.0238
Meeting friends	.0030	.0015
Reading newspaper	.0000	.0000
Reading books	.0000	.0000
Regular eating	.0095	.0000
Taking medication	.0178	.0162
Prayer	.0009	.0000
Absence from work	.0250	--
Studying	.0001	--
Cleaning home	.0160	--
Care for personal cleanliness	--	.0010
Care for personal appearance	--	.0052
Smoking	--	.0133

*The significance of association was obtained as a by-product of the *chi* square test. The categories of the father's ethnic origin were: Asia-Africa, Israel, Europe-America.

However, there is no doubt that a large portion of the activities or the perception of their frequency, both in routine times and in periods of social interruption, are culturally conditioned or determined. Support for this may be found in Table 3.2, which presents the associations between the ethnic origin of the respondent's father[3] and the declared frequency of the performance of various activities. Seven of the activities listed are to a large extent determined culturally, both in routine times and in periods of interruption, and an additional six in one of these two periods. This pattern of association between ethnic origin and the mode of performance of activities has additional far-reaching implications, which we will deal with below.

We also noted a tendency to significant associations between the level of performance of activities and other background variables (such as religiosity, education, and occupation), and this lends support to the hypothesis that the performance patterns of most activities are culturally conditioned, and/or depend on an individual's location in the system.

It should be emphasized that we cannot make any predictions about the frequency of the performance of the various activities either in routine times or in periods of social interruption—but these matters are not of interest to us, primarily because most of the activities are not inherently significant. We are focusing on changes in levels of activity, so that we may utilize the level of performance of activities in routine periods as a base line and examine the rates and the directions of change from the base line we created.

Had we satisfied ourselves with the descriptive data presented in Table 3.1, we could conclude too hastily that very few changes occurred in the frequency of the performance of the activities studied in our sample. This conclusion would be reached because, according to the data of this table, the most drastic changes occurred in reading habits (32 percent less reading in wartime), in regular eating (a decline of 31.5 percent in frequency), in meetings with friends, and in care for personal appearance. With reference to all the other activities, there were only moderate changes, some of which did not exceed 10 percent. In the taking of medication, for example, we can note an increase in only about 0.5 percent of the sample. However, the changes in this table express very general trends that might possibly reflect the norm in the system, but do not in any way present a picture of patterns of change in each of the activities. In chapter 1 we noted that every individual performing any kind of routine activity has three basic possibilities: to maintain his performance level as in routine times, to raise his level of performance, or to lower it. Thus, we must reexamine each activity according to the proportion of the sample population continuing to perform at the same level during the period of interruption as in the routine period, the proportion who raised the level of their performance, and the proportion lowering their level of performance. By doing so we will be able to compare activities and rank them according to their degree of stability (with the most stable activity referenced to the sample population that made the smallest changes in its level of performance), and according to the dominant (and subordinate) direction of the changes in frequency of activity—a rise or decline in the frequency of performance. It is also interesting to examine the question of the relationships between the trends of change: Was there an unequivocal trend, or were the two trends of change—that in the direction of increased frequency of performance (which will be noted as "+"), and that in the direction of declining frequency of performance (which will be noted as "−")—more or less balanced, without a predominant trend being indicated?

Table 3.3 presents the patterns of changes in each of the 18 types of activities examined. A first glance at this table leads to several immediate conclusions. First, the degree of stability (or lack of change in frequency of performance) of the activities, when analyzed in a more refined fashion, is much lower than one might have concluded on the basis of the data in Table 3.1. Only with reference to three types of activity—care for personal cleanliness, smoking, and praying—was a high degree of stability maintained. That is, more than 77 percent of the sample population did not change (increase or decrease) its frequency of performance of these activities. As for the next six activities, about 40 percent of the sample population reported changes in the frequency of their performance. About half the population reported changes in the performance of the next six activities, while with reference to the last three activities, between 60 and 66 percent reported changes in their frequency of performance. If some or all of these activities indeed constitute indicators for the performance of routine roles during periods of social interruption, then it seems fairly far-reaching changes occurred in the behavior of individuals between the two periods. To what extent these changes were the result of situational constraints, psychological anxiety, and/or perceived social norms will be a question dealt with later in this chapter.

Second, most of the major changes (14 in number) were in the direction of lowering the frequency of activity.[4] Actually, there is no activity that can constitute an indicator of the performance of routine roles (except for the consumption of information) in which the major change that occurred was in the direction of increased frequency of performance or increased level of performance. At least at first glance, the conclusion that suggests itself is that the changes in the system were in the direction of reduced frequency (and possibly also a reduced level) of routine activities. However, this is not an unequivocal conclusion, inasmuch as with reference to most activities there was a minority of actors (whose identity we shall try to determine later) who actually *increased* the frequency of their performance of the activities investigated here. Also, the average of all the activities had a stability coefficient of 56.7. Furthermore, in the activity that seems to us to be central in this context—going to work—along with the 21 percent who lowered their level of performance of this role, there were 17 percent (i.e., only 4 percent less) who reported increased frequency of performance. But except for this case (and possibly also the activity of "leaving the house"), there is a fairly decisive trend as to the direction of change. This leads us to

TABLE 3.3
Rates of Stability and of Major and Minor Changes in Various Activities and Their Direction between Routine Situations and Those of Social Interruption
(in percent)

Activity	Rate of Stability of Activity	Rate of Major Change	Rate of Minor Change	Relationship Between the Changes*
Care for personal cleanliness	77.7	−19.4	+ 2.9	.85
Smoking	77.6	+16.7	− 5.7	.66
Prayer	77.5	+16.1	− 6.4	.60
Taking of medication	62.5	−25.6	+11.9	.54
Absence from work	62.0	+21.0	−17.0	.19
Reading the newspaper	61.9	+31.3	− 6.8	.88
Studying	60.9	−35.6	+ 3.5	.90
Sleeping a great deal	59.6	−32.0	+ 8.4	.74
Staying home	52.6	+29.7	−17.7	.40
Listening to news	51.1	+47.0	− 1.9	.96
Care for personal appearance	50.8	−43.4	+ 5.8	.87
Handicrafts	49.4	−38.0	+12.6	.67
Cleaning house	48.7	−44.7	+ 6.6	.85
Visits to doctor	48.5	−46.0	+ 5.5	.88
Regular eating	48.3	−46.6	+ 5.1	.89
Reading books	39.3	−54.7	+ 5.4	.90
Meeting friends	36.1	−49.1	+14.8	.70
Travelling	34.0	−56.8	+ 9.2	.86
Average rate of stability	56.7			

*The relationship between the changes was computed according to the formula:

$$\frac{1\text{-Proportion of minor change}}{\text{Proportion of major change}}$$

conclude that a consensus, or a more or less crystallized normative imperative, exists for most of the patterns of behavior that we studied in a situation of social interruption and/or the pressures accompanying it as a result of the existence of an anxiety-generating situation of war.

Below we shall analyze each activity separately and thereafter different groups of activities, classified according to the degree of control that the individual has over its performance, independently of external constraints or of the demands of complementary actors. Despite the hypothesis presented at the beginning of the chapter, we do not expect that each such group will be homogeneous in terms of the changes in frequency of performance of the roles in routine periods and in periods of social interruption, because of the existence of other factors that determine such changes and that are difficult to isolate.

Situationally Dependent Activities

This group includes several activities that have no clear substantial connection, but are all dependent to a very great extent on factors *outside* the actor's control, with the nature of their performance dictated to a large extent by the situation of social interruption and the institutional constraints described in the previous chapter. Regardless of the evaluative and psychological predispositions of individuals, the frequency and level of performance of these activities must decline, and if the major change is not in the direction of decline or if the trend is not unequivocal, we should see it as an unusual phenomenon and attempt to analyze its causes.

Travelling

About 38 percent of the respondents in our sample reported that in routine times they travel "most of the time" or "often." The more educated the respondents and the higher their occupational status, in addition to being of European-American origin, the more they travel. Thus, we can assume that the more central an individual's location in the system, the more he travels. These findings are more or less compatible with those of Katz and Gurevitch[5] as to patterns of activity outside the home.

During the war, there was a decline of almost a third in the proportion of travellers as compared with routine times. This sharp decline must first be viewed as a result of the situation of social interruption on the institutional level. As noted above (in chapter 2), public transportation was almost completely paralyzed and even some private vehicles were mobilized. Also, persons who generally served as the "family driver" were mobilized as well.[6] In addition, it is clear that leisure activities involving travel, such as hikes, entertainment shows, etc., were almost completely brought to a standstill. It seems that the decline in travelling during the period of social interruption characterized all strata of the population we examined (see Table 3.2); those who travelled more during routine times travelled more than others in the period of interruption as well, even though on an absolute level they travelled less.

Absence from Work

There is no doubt that situational factors may have a decisive effect on the rates of absenteeism from work during a period of social interruption. Some places of employment were completely shut down during this time and whole economic sectors were partially or totally paralyzed (as described in chapter 2). The lack of public transportation made it considerably more difficult to reach work. We would therefore expect not only low stability in the frequency of arrival at work, but also a major tendency in the direction of lowering the level of activity (that is, an increase in absences from work). However, it emerges that going to work was one of the most relatively stable activities, and only about 38 percent of the employed changed their frequency of performance of this activity. Furthermore, only 21 percent reduced the frequency of their attendance at work, while 17 percent attended work even more frequently than in routine periods. Inasmuch as this is the most routine type of activity on the list that may be perceived as contributing to the system's continued smooth functioning, we should view this finding as supporting one of our central hypotheses—the one claiming the existence of normative pressures within the system, besides the institutional arrangements, aimed at maintaining the system on an optimal level. In the present case, the actor who was under the cross-pressures of constraints and the normative demands of the interrupted system to continue to fulfill his routine roles, which supported the collectivity's continued operation, would in many cases (more precisely, in 79 percent of the sample) tend to respond to the normative demands to continue to function at least as in the routine period, in order to fulfill the complementary goal.

Of the background variables, we found that absence from work in routine periods was primarily associated with ethnic origin and occupational status. Sons of the Israeli-born tended to be absent more than sons of the Asian-African born, while the latter tended to be absent more than sons of the European-American born. The higher the occupational status, the less the tendency to be absent from work. During the period of social interruption, the association between ethnic origin and the tendency to be absent from work (or to go to work more often) was eliminated. It seems that the impact of social interruption overcame cultural differences, and possibly overcame differences in location in the system.

But let us not forget that taking a moratorium from routine activities may be no less a demonstration of identification with the collectivity than is the performance of roles that support the continuation of the order that prevailed before the interruption (see chapter 1). Echoes of this ambivalent normative message can possibly be found not only in the low coefficient of association between the major and minor changes in this activity (see Table 3.3), but also in three additional findings presented in Table 3.4. The first is that indicating that respondents who had family members mobilized tended to show greater changes in the level of absences (both increases and decreases) than did respondents who did not have members of their family recruited. We should note here that almost certainly the implication of having a mobilized relative in the context of social interruption was not only greater exposure to psychological anxieties and pressures, but also somewhat of a feeling of personal "contribution" to the fulfillment of the predominant goal. This granted the individual a more central place in the system, which also meant greater exposure to normative messages.

Another finding in support of this approach is that the Israeli born (and we are speaking here of at least second-generation Israelis), who are generally perceived as centrally located in the system, tended to change the level of their activity (upwards or downwards) in this sphere, and that men tended to greater instability in this area than did women. No connection was found between opinions and attitudes and the degree of stability or instability in this behavior, which implies that what is important here is the person's objective location in the system, rather than his perceived location.

Visits to the Doctor

We classified this activity in the category of "dependent on circumstances," not because of its content in routine times, but because of the transformation of the significance of the general medical sphere in a period of social interruption. The "circumstances" in this case were not only the institutional constraints (as described in the previous chapter) but also the total social significance of the interruption as analyzed in chapter 1. In this sense, the entire medical sphere constitutes a miniature case study in and of itself.

Our main claim is that during a period of interruption, the entire medical sphere is perceived as belonging to the zone of the fulfillment of the predominant goal. This was so in this case for several reasons:

TABLE 3.4
Changes in Tendency to Be Absent from Work during the War Compared with Routine Times, by Sex, Ethnic Origin, and Recruitment or Nonrecruitment of Family Members (in percent)

Direction of Change	Sex			Origin				Recruited Family Members		
	Male	Female	Total	Asia-Africa	Israel	Europe-America	Total	Yes	No	Total
Decline	6.9	10.0	16.9	3.0	6.5	7.5	17.0	14.0	8.3	22.3
No change	16.5	45.6	62.1	17.0	21.7	22.2	61.9	26.0	21.7	47.7
Increase	8.6	12.4	21.0	3.9	10.7	6.5	21.0	22.0	8.0	30.0
Total	68.0	32.0	100.0	23.9	38.9	37.2	100.0	62.0	38.0	100.0
N	490			494				300		
x^2	10.71			11.628				8.293		
p	.0047			.0203				.0158		

Immediately upon the outbreak of the war, most of the medical manpower was mobilized, many patients were discharged from hospitals, and most of the hospitals began to operate on an emergency schedule (see chapter 2). In practice, the medical system did not collapse, and health authorities operated at least partial medical services for the general civilian population. But this service was almost not utilized by the civilian population, and in chapter 2 we saw reports of empty health clinics. On the other hand (see chapter 4), hospitals served as a central focus of attraction for volunteers for performing roles perceived as relevant to the situation of interruption or as connected with the fulfillment of the central goal (caring for soldiers wounded on the front). The emptying of medical clinics was totally consonant with our finding that 46 percent of the sample population reported a decline in the frequency of their visits to the doctor (see Table 3.3). It follows that we can almost completely reject an alternative hypothesis to the effect that a visit to the doctor constitutes a tension-reducing activity. (Below we shall see that consumption of medicines also did not seem to serve such a function.)

It is also possible that people tended to impose a moratorium on the solution of "personal problems" while a severe collective problem had to be dealt with. We do not have direct data to support this hypothesis, but we have reports of similar reactions, of persons who refrained from turning to services less urgent than medical services (for example, the Welfare Office) since, "In such times, who thinks of things?" (see chapter 2). The image of a medical service paralyzed (or mobilized to fulfill roles connected with the predominant goal) along with the objective difficulty of lack of public transportation, no doubt also added to the decline in the frequency of appeals for medical services.

Very few associations were found for routine periods between socio-economic and cultural background variables and the frequency of visits to the doctor. Nevertheless, there are statistically inverse relations between the frequency of visits and education or occupation. (When any statistical association is mentioned hereafter, it will be assumed that this will not be less than the $p<.05$ level of significance, as measured by the chi-square test.) During periods of social interruption, these associations were eliminated, and the total sample population tended to a low frequency of only 12 percent of visits to the doctor (see Table 3.1) and this was one of the least frequent activities relative to all the others examined in our study.

Consumption of Information

In this category we included various aspects of consumption of information via the mass media, but did not include patterns of information transmission by means of interpersonal contact (such as conversations with friends and acquaintances).[7] In addition, we did not deal with consumption of information via the theater, movies, and other shows that were not held anyway (see chapter 2). Information was classified into two functional types: information relevant to the situation of the war and social interruption (such as listening to news on the radio[8] and reading newspapers), and information not relevant to the interrupted situation or not up-to-date even when perceived as being relevant (the conspicuous example being reading books).

While in chapter 1, in which we presented and analyzed the situation of social interruption, we did not explicitly deal with the dimension of communications consumption, it is clear that in a situation of interruption there will be a steep increase in the demand for information. This included four types in the present case: (1) information as to the course of the war or the management of the predominant goal;[9] (2) instrumental information and emotional messages connected with the fulfillment of the complementary goal (such as notices on the supply of products, changes in public transportation); (3) maintaining a connection between the front and the "home" (thus, for example, the popular daily radio program for women changed its name to "Here at Home"), by transmitting "personal" messages from area to area, with the main content focused on the temporariness of the situation of interruption; and (4) the "entertainment" functions of tension-reduction[10] as substitute for entertainment shows that had been cancelled.

Consumption of Up-to-Date Information

In examining the data as to the consumption of news in routine times, we note a high rate of performance of this activity. More than 89 percent of the sample population listen to or watch the news ("most of the time" and "often"), and 83 percent often read the newspaper (Table 3.1). This trend is compatible with the claim made by Katz and Gurevitch to the effect that "Israel is a country hungry for news. The news broadcasts, both on radio and on television, have the largest audience of any program."[11] They also found that 86 percent of the total Israeli adult population (in 1970) read at least one daily newspaper. We found a significant association between the reading of a newspaper and education, but not between listening to the news and education—probably because of the very high rate of listening or watching the news among all strata of the population. In addition, it appears that the population of Western origin, which is more educated, of higher occupational status, and secular, reads newspapers more than do other groups in the population.

As expected, we found an increase in the reading of newspapers during the period of interruption, with 31 percent of our sample reporting an increase in the performance of this activity, but almost 7 percent reporting a decline. This increase was associated directly and significantly with ethnic origin, education, and occupational status in a similar way to the direction of the associations in routine periods between reading habits and background variables. The association with the attitude towards religion was found to be eliminated in times of interruption, seemingly because in such a period even people who defined themselves as religious consumed as much information as did the nonreligious.

The increase in listening to the news during the period of social interruption was even more marked than the increase in newspaper reading. This seems to be explained by the advantages of electronic media (the speed, immediacy, and directness of transmission of information). Ninety-eight percent reported that they listened to the news "generally" or "often" (Table 3.1) and 47 percent reported increased activity in this sphere as compared with the routine period, while less than two percent (which may well constitute the standard error) reported a lowering of the level of activity. We can learn of the function fulfilled by the electronic media during the period of social interruption most of all from the fact that no significant associations were found between the level of listening to the news and all the socioeconomic background variables, but that such an association was found between the level of listening and the mobilization of family members (see Table 3.5).

Consumption of Noncurrent Information

Learning represents for us a clear example of consumption of noncurrent information, of a structured and organized nature. Katz and Gurevich found that "about one-third (28 percent) of the sample population are engaged in some kind of studies," a finding which almost recurs in our sample population, in which 26.9 percent studied "most of the time" or "often." Nevertheless, our findings are not compatible with those of Katz and Gurevich when we attempt to characterize those who studied. Katz and Gurevich claimed that study should be viewed as a "traditional Jewish occupation," and noted the positive association between religiosity and allocation of time to studies. In addition, they found that "the factor of ethnic origin does not affect the degree of learning activity,"[12] and that the tendency to study increases with education. In contrast with this picture, we found a strong association between studying and ethnic origin, with respondents of European-American origin tending to study more than the Israeli-born, while the latter group tended to study more than those of Asian-African origin. In addition, we found an association

TABLE 3.5

Changes in the Proportion of Respondents Listening to the News in Routine vs. Interrupted Periods, by Recruitment or Nonrecruitment of Family Members (in percent)

Direction of Change in Performance of Activity	Family Members Recruited		
	Yes	No	Total
Decline	1.6	0.2	1.8
No Change	30.4	21.2	51.6
Increase	35.1	11.4	46.5
Total	67.1	32.9	100.0

N	490
x^2	10.846
P	.0002

between level of education and studying and between occupational status and studying. No significant association was found between religiosity and studying, and the tendency that emerged was one of an inverse relationship to that found by Katz and Gurevich.

Over half (59.2 percent) of our sample population noted that they read books "most of the time" or "often." It is difficult to compare these data with the parallel data of Katz and Gurevich because they used very different definitions ("whoever reads at least one book a month"). Nevertheless, our data are compatible with theirs as to the background variables that explain or predict the differences in levels of reading among the various groups of the population. Katz and Gurevich conclude that the main variable explaining the level of reading is the level of education, and we found such an association as well. In addition, associations were found between the level of reading, ethnic origin, and occupational status. This is not surprising in light of the characteristics of Israeli society, in which these variables exist as a cluster.

According to McLuhan's[13] well-known claim, reading books is an individual activity that isolates a person from his external environment even more than does the reading of newspapers, watching television, and listening to the radio, because the variety of contents to which the book-reader is exposed is vast, compared with the much more limited contents presented by radio and television. According to McLuhan, the result is the reduction of the common denominator among book-readers and the expansion of the common denominator among newspaper readers, television spectators, and radio listeners.

The activity of book reading (on the assumption that there are no "Guides to Behavior in Wartime") may be viewed as the activity least relevant to the interrupted situation among the list of activities that we studied. Nevertheless, the *continued* reading of books on the level at which the individual was accustomed reflects an attempt to maintain the individual's private "world order," something that is one of the system's messages as to behavioral norms in periods of interruption. Still, 27 percent of our population (Table 3.1) read "most of the time" or "often" during the war, while 5.4 percent even increased their reading of books. We tend to interpret increased reading, and possibly also continued reading, as an appeal for a moratorium from the fulfillment of roles connected with both the predominant and complementary goals. However, in comparing the two periods being studied, the most prominent characteristic of this activity was the drastic decline of 54.7 percent in its performance in the period of interruption (see Table 3.3). An examination of the rates of reading in the period of interruption reveals the same pattern of associations as in routine times, and only the association between reading books and occupational status was eliminated. It seems that the performance of the occupational role was more dominant during the time of interruption on *all* levels of occupational status than were the other background variables.

Social Contacts

In this group we will include two activities having a significant component of connections with other people within them. The assumption is that in such cases—despite the existence of the institutional constraints of the period of interruption—the individual has partial control of his level of performance and frequency of the activity. The partial control stems from the necessary (though certainly not sufficient) condition of the response of the complementary side to the maintenance of the interaction. But the assumption is that when the individual is predisposed to maintain social ties, it is generally possible to find persons who will respond to initiatives of contact (of at least some of the available partners). If, nevertheless, the frequency of such activities declined significantly, our tendency was to attribute this to two aspects of social interruption: the institutional constraints and the normative messages. The alternative hypothesis is the spirit of Louis Coser,[14] to the effect that external pressure (war) will increase the integration of the collectivity, which may be expressed in the strengthening of interpersonal ties among its members and an increase in the frequency of interaction. But on the level of the collectivity as a whole, the increase in cohesiveness and identification with the collectivity as a whole is not necessarily expressed in an increase in the frequency of interpersonal contacts. It is more reasonable to assume that in the zone of the complementary goal (as opposed to the front, where intensive collective action, interdependence, and trust are demanded among the fulfillers of the common goal), the cohesiveness will be expressed more in a strengthening of the direct ties between the individual and the center, primarily via the mass media. (One of the prominent expressions of the interrupted situation was the great willingness of drivers to take strangers in their cars, and sometimes even to go out of their way to take them to their destinations. Thus, the driver would respond to the demand of the interrupted normative system, and serve as a substitute for public transportation. However, it is erroneous to attribute this phenomenon to the strengthening of social ties. The opposite is the case: taking a passenger without distinction is an apersonal and collectivistic action. It constitutes service to the collectivity rather than to the passenger [from the point of view of the driver].) Furthermore, in every society there are various expressions of identification with the collectivity that are also culturally conditioned. These vary from society to society and from one social stratum to another within a given society. Thus, expressions of general social solidarity will be expressed in the degree of interpersonal ties. Let us now analyze the major types of social contacts.

Staying at Home

In routine times, "staying at home" (which in Israeli culture expresses, to a large extent, the focus of leisure activity around the home, as opposed to social activity and/or entertainment focused outside the home) is significantly associated with religiosity, with the tendency for staying at home being greater among the religious and those of a traditional background[15] than among those who define themselves as secular. Significant associations were also found with education and occupational status[16] with the tendency to stay at home declining. This finding contradicts that of Katz and Gurevich, who claim that, "In general, those with higher education tend to greater activity within the home."[17]

During the war there was an increase in the tendency to stay at home. The change across the entire population was relatively small and was a modest increase of only 1.6 percent (Table 3.1). But when we examine the net movement *within* the sample population (Table 3.3), it becomes apparent that only about 30 percent changed their staying-at-home habits in the direction of staying at home more, while almost 18 percent stayed at home *less* in the interrupted period than in the routine periods. The relation coefficient between the major and minor changes is very low relative to the other changes (.40) and is among the lowest in the list of activities.

In examining the changes in the level of activity, we found that women tended to change their behavior in this sphere more than men, in the direction of a greater frequency of staying at home in the period of interruption as opposed to routine periods. This finding can be explained both on the basis of the constraints that stemmed from the interruption on the institutional level (for example, educational institutions did not operate in the first days of the war, so that many mothers were forced to stay at home) and also on the basis of the conception of the woman's traditional role in Israeli society, and on the fact that women are generally more dependent than men on public transportation (which is a com- bination of the situational constraint with the conception of the woman's role—some women do not drive a car even when they have one at their disposal).

An interesting find is the association between religiosity and the change in the level of activity. Here (as opposed to the situation in routine times) we note a tendency among religious persons to show a decline in staying at home, while the nonreligious tended to stay at home more in interrupted times (see Table 3.6). It is possible that this phenomenon is connected with the tendency of religious groups, particularly in the Jerusalem area (in which our sample was selected—see the Methodological Appendix), to be concentrated geographically, so that the network of social interaction was less spread out and less dependent on situational constraints. If this explanation is indeed correct, then it seems that these constraints played a more decisive role in the decline of "leaving the house."

We have already hinted above that the alternatives to "staying at home" were reduced drastically in the period of interruption. Some places of employment and entertainment closed down, and there were very few places to go. But a new alternative, unique to the period of interruption, was created; i.e., volunteering to support the fulfillment of the predominant goal, and primarily that of the complementary goal. We shall deal with this subject at length in the next chapter, but in this context we should note the finding that those who indeed went out more than others in the period of interruption were more involved in volunteering than those who went out less (Table 3.6).

TABLE 3.6

Changes in the Tendency to Stay at Home between Routine and Interrupted Periods, by Self-Definition in Regard to Religion and Readiness to Volunteer in the Interrupted Periods (in percent)

Direction of Change in Performance of Activity	Religious Identification			Volunteer Activity		
	Secular	Religious	Total	Did not volunteer or did not succeed in finding volunteer job	Volunteered	Total
Decline	5.9	11.6	17.5	13.5	7.2	20.7
No change	24.1	28.8	52.9	43.7	8.5	52.2
Increase	18.0	11.6	29.6	22.6	4.5	27.1
Total	48.0	52.0	100.0	79.8	20.2	100.0
N		510			531	
χ^2		18.039			17.578	
P		.0001			.0001	

Meeting with Friends

Katz and Gurevitch note that "it seems Israelis maintain an active social life." In response to the question, "How important is it to you to spend time with friends?", 55 percent of the respondents indicated that this was very important to them. And almost 70 percent of the population reported meeting friends almost every week.[18] In our study, 66.5 percent of the respondents indicated that in routine periods they "generally" or "often" met with their friends (Table 3.1). An examination of the associations with background variables indicates that the nonreligious had more frequent meetings with their friends than did religious persons, those of European-American origin more so than those of Asian-African origin, and the better educated more so than the less educated. These patterns tended to be maintained in the period of interruption as well. In comparing this activity in the two periods studied, we note that this activity was among the lowest in stability (36.1 percent), and the major change was a sharp tendency towards a decline in the frequency of performance, with this decline reaching 49.1 percent (see Table 3.3). It is interesting to note the existence of an association here with ethnic origin, with the tendency for the frequency of the activity to decline during a period of interruption among those of Western origin, while a moderate increase was noted among those of Eastern origin. A partial explanation for this finding may be found in the study's findings, which indicate that among those of Asian-African origin there was role impingement among the roles of "neighbor," "relative," and "friend."[19] As a result, it is possible for that part of the sample population that the term "friends" represented a more geographically centralized group (when compared to other groups) and, thus, it was less affected in its contacts by the institutional constraints of the interrupted system. Thus, the patterns of social contacts tended to be affected primarily by the situational constraints of the interrupted situation and were brought about by predispositions stemming from cultural and class differences and the location of the individual in the system as a whole.

Management of Time

On the continuum that we suggested between circumstantially dependent activities over which the individual has very limited or no control and those over which the individual has potentially complete control, the activities presented until now have had a predominant component of dependence on circumstances (particularly on the constraints of the situation of social interruption). In activities connected with the management of the home, there seems to be a predominance of components over which the individual has relatively great control. In contrast with going out to work, travelling, and even meetings with friends, for example, activities connected with the management of the home and household are much less affected (objectively) by the constraints of the institutional system, such as difficulties in transportation and the partial paralysis of other public services. Certain difficulties might have been caused as a result of shortages in specific products on the market (see previous chapter), but not to an extent that would disturb the smooth functioning of the household. Nor was the severe financial hardship among a minority of families of self-employed businessmen who had been mobilized (or possibly also among those who had not been mobilized but whose businesses suffered as a result of the interrupted situation) a cause for disturbing the smooth functioning of the home. The fact is that the very continuation of the existence of the family framework creates a commitment and pressure on each member of the family to continue to fulfill his roles, at least on the minimal level that allows the framework to continue to exist. This pressure indeed differs from the institutional constraints that we discussed above, but there is no doubt that it too limits the degree of control or voluntarism of the performance of activities connected with the management of the home, especially if actors, in addition to the respondent, remain at home.

Regular Eating

In routine times this activity was characterized by a high degree of performance, so that most of our sample population (75.1 percent) ate regular meals "most of the time" or "often." The background variable with the great effect on this activity was ethnic origin, with those of European-American origin taking the greatest care to eat regularly, while sons of the Israeli-born took the least care to do so. In times of interruption, activity appeared to be unstable (that is, only about 48 percent of the sample population maintained the same level of activity during the interruption as in routine times), and there was a clear trend to a decline in the level of performance and the relationship between the major and minor changes being among the highest of all the activities examined (see Table 3.3). Despite the lack of stability of behavior in the transition from the routine to the interrupted period, the association between performance of the activity and ethnic origin was maintained. However, what is more interesting is that women tended to reduce their performance of the activity more than did men (see Table 3.8).

Intuitively we would say that we are dealing here with a pattern of activity connected with the existence of a stable and "orderly" family life, the latter having been shaken to a considerable extent with the mobilization of one or more family members. But the findings do not support such an explanation. No connection was found between the decline in eating regularly and the fact of having family members mobilized. On the other hand, if we return to our analysis in chapter 1, we may remember the hypothesis that in a situation of social interruption, the individual is subject to cross-pressures in the zone of the complementary goal, between performing roles that will support the continued existence of a "cosmic order" and an appeal for a moratorium from all activities or from a specific activity. The decision in this case (especially among the female members of the sample) was in the direction of an appeal for a moratorium, seemingly because eating regularly was perceived as marginal to the entire set of activities for the maintenance of the system and the "cosmic order." If we compare this to the role of "going out to work," we may categorize the latter as more central (and possibly most central) among the activities for the maintenance of the "cosmic order" until the end of the interruption. We are thus suggesting the introduction of an additional component (besides those appearing in chapter 1) that may determine whether there will be a tendency to appeal for a moratorium from the performance of a given activity during the period of social interruption: the *degree* to which the activity is perceived as supporting the continued existence of the order that existed before the interruption or its supporting of the system's maintenance during

TABLE 3.7
Changes in Frequency of Meeting with Friends between Routine and Interrupted Periods, by Father's Ethnic Origin (in percent)

Father's Continent of birth	Direction of Changes in the Performance of Activity			
	Decline	No Change	Increase	Total
Europe-America	26.6	21.9	5.9	54.2
Israel	6.0	3.3	2.3	11.7
Asia-Africa	16.5	10.9	6.8	34.2
Total	49.1	36.1	14.8	100.0

N	515
x^2	11.3
P	.0229

TABLE 3.8
Changes in Regular Eating Habits between Routine and Interrupted Periods, by Sex (in percent)

Direction of Change in Performance of Activity	Sex		
	Male	Female	Total
Decline	12.2	34.3	46.5
No change	17.4	31.0	48.4
Increase	2.2	2.9	5.1
Total	31.8	68.2	100.0

N	510
x^2	6.843
P	.0327

the period of interruption. In such a case, even if an individual has the resources and opportunities to perform an activity, if it is perceived to be marginal (or possibly, irrelevant) to the complementary goal there will be a general tendency to appeal for a moratorium from its performance.

Order and Cleanliness at Home

To the extent that the hypothesis presented above is correct, we should apply it to the activity of maintaining order and cleanliness at home. Indeed, we find a high rate of respondents claiming that in "usual" times they performed such activities often (see Table 3.1), compared to a sharp decline in the proportion of respondents claiming to have performed such activities often in the period of interruption as well. Indeed, the rate of stability of this activity was 48.7 percent, and it is located in the lowest quartile (i.e., this activity showed much less stability than most other activities). As expected from our hypothesis, here too there was a clear and definite trend to an appeal for a moratorium, with 44.7 percent of the respondents having lowered the level of their activity in this sphere during the period of social interruption (see Table 3.3). However, there was also a small but significant group of respondents who increased their level of activity during this period (6.6 percent).

Despite the general trend represented by these two "household" activities in the interrupted period, it seems that they differ in their sociocultural significance. While no association was found with socioeconomic background variables except for ethnic origins in regard to eating patterns, care for order and cleanliness of the home was found to be significantly associated with all the background variables we examined. Furthermore, while regular eating habits characterized those of European-American origin, care for order and cleanliness was more characteristic of those of Asian-African origin, those with less education, the more traditional, and those with lower occupational status. Most of these associations were eliminated during periods of social interruption, and since the general level of activity declined, it seems that the decline (that is, the appeal for a moratorium) was sharper among those strata located in more peripheral social zones. This conclusion is also compatible with the findings in Table 3.9, which indicate that the changes in the level of activity between the two periods under study are correlated with religiosity and ethnic origin (father's origin), with the sharpest decline occurring among religious persons and those of Asian-African origin. It is perhaps interesting to note that no association was found between the respondent's sex and the change in the level of activity between the periods, and that women did not appeal for a moratorium more than did men in this activity.

The Management of the Self

In dealing with activities connected with the management of the home, we claimed that these activities were almost independent of the conditions of social interruption that resulted from the 1973 war—on circumstances external to the actors but still could be derived from the pressures and role commitments of the members of the household toward one another. In activities belonging to the sphere of "management of the self," we

TABLE 3.9

**Changes in the Tendency to Care for Order and Cleanliness in the Home
between Routine and Interrupted Periods, by Father's Ethnic Origin and
Attitude toward Religion (in percent)**

Direction of Change in Performance of Activity	Ethnic Origin				Religious Attitudes		
	Euorpe-America	Israel	Asia-Africa	Total	Secu-lar	Reli-gous	Total
Decline	21.2	4.3	19.2	44.7	17.6	26.9	44.5
No change	29.5	5.6	13.6	48.7	26.5	22.5	49.0
Increase	3.5	1.7	1.4	6.6	3.9	2.5	6.5
Total	54.2	11.6	34.2	100.0	48.0	52.0	100.0
N	515				510		
X^2	21.153				12.050		
P	.003				.0024		

can hypothesize that these factors would be much less exposed to changes,
since we are dealing here with activities which are at least partially
perceived as a private matter of the individual.

Care for Personal Appearance

Most of our respondents (79 percent) reported that in routine times
they generally or often took care of their personal appearance. In comparison between the two periods, two phenomena are worthy of note:
the first is that there was a tendency to greater decline in care for personal
appearance among women (see Table 3.10), possibly because for them
care for personal appearance may be interpreted as "getting dressed
up"—something not appropriate for a situation of emergency. We also
found that among respondents who had members of their family mobilized,
there was an even greater tendency to decline in this pattern of behavior
(Table 3.10), this too possibly for the same reason. Additional support
for this hypothesis was found in the correlation we found between
responses regarding care for personal appearance and those expressing
agreement with the statement that "when soldiers are falling at the front,
there's no point in doing anything at home" (see Table 3.10).

This statement, which was aimed at examining the respondents'
readiness to grant themselves a moratorium from most activities, did
not succeed in predicting behavior with reference to most of the activities,

TABLE 3.10

Changes in the Proportion of Respondents Caring for Personal Appearance between Routine and Interrupted Periods, by Agreement with the Attitude That "when soldiers are falling on the front, there's no point in doing anything at home" (in percent)

Direction of Change in Performance of Activity	Do not agree	Agree somewhat	Agree to a great extent	Agree completely	Total
Decline	30.8	4.5	4.1	5.0	44.4
No change	41.1	3.3	3.3	3.7	51.4
Increase	2.7	1.2	0.0	0.2	4.1
Total	74.6	9.1	7.4	8.9	100.0

N	486
χ^2	19.072
P	.0040

possibly because of the low variance in the distribution of those who responded to the question (74.6 percent of the sample did not agree with claims that "when soldiers are falling on the front, there's no point in doing anything at home," and only 16.3 percent agreed with it completely or expressed agreement with some reservations). Thus, if this attitude indeed predicts a tendency to take a general moratorium during the period of the social interruption (as a result of the overemphasis of the predominant goal), it becomes clear that only a small portion of the population showed such a tendency. However, it should be emphasized that this does not mean to imply that there was no tendency to take a moratorium from *specific roles,* as we saw in the case of care for personal appearance.

Care for Personal Cleanliness

This activity was characterized by two prominent features from which its other traits were derived as well. First, this was the activity with the highest rate of performance in routine times (97.9 percent generally or often took such care).[20] In the period of the war and the social interruption as well, the rate of decline was only about 8 percent and thus this continued to be an activity which, according to the respondents' reports, was performed at the highest rate of frequency (90 percent; see Table

3.1). From this we also derive the second characteristic; that is, that this was the activity least affected (that is most stable) by changes occurring in the system from one period to another—77.7 percent of the respondents reported maintenance of the previous (generally high) level of performance, more than 19 percent lowered their level of performance, and almost 3 percent actually increased it. Thus, the major change is also very clear (.85 was the rate of the relationship between the major and minor changes; see Table 3.3). In routine times there was no association between the background variables we examined and this particular activity, inasmuch as the level of performance was very high among all strata of the population. But during the period of interruption, the picture tended to change somewhat, and an association was created between ethnic origin and education and performance of this activity. Thus, those of Western origin showed a greater tendency to take care of their personal cleanliness than did those of Eastern origin, and those of Asian-African origin tended to appeal for a moratorium to a significantly greater extent than did those of European-American origin. The association between the level of performance of this activity and education is clearly significant. But in general and despite these associations, care for personal hygiene was perceived as an essential activity that was unaffected (among most groups) by the interruption of the system, and this interruption (including the war) could not grant legitimacy to an appeal for a moratorium from such activity.

Activities to Reduce Tension

In terms of their content we could have continued to classify most of the next five activities—work in handicrafts, smoking, sleeping, consumption of medicines, and prayer—in the category of management of self. This is so inasmuch as most of these activities (except for prayer, which sometimes has clear apects of social interaction) are by the individual and solely for himself. But inasmuch as such activities were generally perceived by professionals as well as by the lay population as a whole as activities that reduced and/or expressed tensions and anxieties, we decided to analyze these behaviors separately, particularly since the existence of tensions and anxieties—as a direct result of the war and indirectly because of the constraints of the interrupted system—was a variable that was part of our conceptual framework (see chapter 1).[21]

Before beginning a detailed discussion of each of the tension symptoms that we examined, it should be noted that even these activities are not pure and may include at least two dimensions that are difficult to distinguish empirically: (1) the activity itself as a sign of the individual's being in a state of stress and anxiety or the attempt to reduce tension by means of specific behaviour, and (2) the perception of the "accepted" rate of tension at such a time and its demonstration (sometimes as a sign of identification with the collectivity), and the accepted way of demonstrating and/or reducing tension.

Excessive Sleep

This can be interpreted as an activity to escape a difficult reality that arouses anxieties and worries. Of the respondents in our sample, 29.7 percent reported that in routine times they generally or often slept a great deal.

But contrary to the "psychologistic predictions" on the one hand, and the circumstances on the other, both of which would predict a rise in the level of frequency of this activity, we can present other good reasons that should lead to opposite predictions. Thus, for example, lack of sleep may be caused by states of tension and anxiety, while the high level of social mobilization (very similar to the term used by Karl Deutsch),[22] which characterizes the system in a period of high exposure to media (a finding noted in the section of this chapter headed "Consumption of Information"), turns the members of the population into information "addicts"—both on the level of the collectivity as a whole and on the personal level as well, and thus has them involved in an activity that may be at the expense of the time generally allocated to sleeping. We can find some support for the hypothesis in this direction in the existence of a correlation between having family members who were mobilized and changes in sleep frequency. If to choose between the alternative hypotheses—an increase or decline in the frequency of this behavior between the two periods—it seems that the "functionalist" consideration would be decisive: lack of sleep would be a more legitimate expression of tension than would sleeping a great deal, the latter being perceived as an escape and as lack of identification with the collectivity and its goals by the actors themselves. Indeed, the proportion of respondents reporting much sleep during the period of interruption declined to 16.8 percent (Table 3.1). When we examine the changes in this behavior (Table 3.3), we indeed see that among 32 percent of the total sample population, the frequency of this behavior declined, and only among slightly more than 8 percent did it increase.

Handicrafts

In terms of its content, it is possible that this activity belongs to the zone of activities connected with management of the household, but we tend to include it in the present category both because it is generally free of circumstantial constraints connected with the situation of the interruption, and primarily because it is customary to view such an activity as tension-reducing. This seems to be a culturally conditioned activity, since in the routine period it is connected with most of the background variables and is more frequent in more peripheral social zones. Traditional persons (a variable connected with ethnic origin; see note 3) tended to engage in such an activity more than did secular persons, and the latter more than the religious, the less educated more than the better educated, and those with lower occupational status more than those with higher status. The association with ethnic origin reveals a similar tendency, but this is not significant.

A clear decline in handicraft work appeared among respondents who had members of their family recruited (Table 3.2). In fact, respondents who reported that their workload increased in the period of social interruption were more stable in the performance of handicrafts than were respondents who reported that their workload was reduced. That is, in terms of allocation of time (and fatigue), these two activities were not mutually exclusive or in a zero-sum situation vis-à-vis one another. It seems, therefore, that this activity (in contrast with smoking, for example—see below) might be perceived as basically instrumental, and not as a tension-reducing or tension-expressing activity.[23] Alternatively, it is possible that this activity had different implications among different strata. While in the more peripheral strata engaging in handicrafts is perceived in an instrumental fashion (i.e., fixing a door, knitting a dress), in more central strata it is possible that handicrafts are perceived as hobbies that are felt to be restful and tension-reducing activities. Comparisons of the changes that occurred in this type of behavior in the two periods studied in different populations seem to support this hypothesis. Therefore, our results should be explained in the following manner: In strata in which these activities are perceived as instrumental, there is a tendency to request a moratorium on them. However, in strata in which these activities are perceived as hobbies there will be a tendency to at least preserve the level of these activities during the interruption period.

Medicine Consumption

In this section we are primarily concerned with the use of all types of tranquilizers. However, we avoided direct questions concerning tranquilizers because in some of our pretests the received responses seemed to indicate that these questions threatened the respondents. Furthermore, the consumption of other types of medicine may also express tension. One fifth (21.5 percent) of the sample population reported that in normal periods they used medicine "most of the time" or "often" (see Table 3.1). Westerners reported a greater tendency to use medicine than Easterners did, while both reported more use than the Israeli native-born population. Other background variables were found to have no effect on the use of medicines, which indicates that medicine intake is culturally dependent and not dependent on the position of an individual in the social system.

In the general sample there was no change in the use of medicines between the two periods (Table 3.1). However, when this behavior is broken down, we discover that over 25 percent of the population reported that they used less medicine as opposed to 12 percent that reported they used more. It is possible that this phenomenon is directly or indirectly related to the removal of health-related activities from routine activities and from the complementary activities. However, it is clear that despite the relative stability of this behavior (see Table 3.3), there was not a high degree of fitness between the tendencies of the changes that did occur. In addition, the ratio between the major change and the minor change was only 0.54. The differences between the ethnic groups in the consumption of medicines were preserved in the period of interruption as well. What is surprising is that the background variables we examined did not delineate the groups that increased or decreased their consumption of medicines, and there seems to be a variable of which we are not aware of that caused these differences. At any rate, we cannot say that there was a large and unequivocal increase in the consumption of medicines in this anxiety-producing period of the war and social interruption.

Smoking

This is a behavior that tends to cut across socioeconomic groups. In routine times, 34 percent of the respondents report that they "generally or often smoked" (Table 3.1). This behavior was significantly associated with education, with the better educated tending to smoke less than the poorly educated. But a connection with religiosity also existed, with the secular smoking more than the traditional and the religious. Thus, in contrast to the tendency among most of the activities, in which we generally found a fixed cluster of characteristics, with individuals who were religious (or traditional), poorly educated, of Asian-African origin, and of low occupational status being on one side, in the analysis of smokers we found two groups with background variables that were different from the usual pattern. We shall return to this finding in the discussion of the next item since, as we shall see below, it is possible that these may complement one another.

Smoking is a very stable behavior relative to other activities, and 77.6 percent of the sample population maintained the same level of smoking during the two periods. But among the 22.4 percent where there was a change, the direction of the change was not as clear as one might have expected: 16.7 percent increased the frequency of their smoking (we have no data on those who began smoking during the period of the interruption), but 5.7 percent reduced their smoking (and again, we have no data on how many stopped totally, or for the period of the interruption). While the direction of the major change, that of increased smoking, is easily explained in terms of efforts aimed at the reduction of tension or its demonstration in ways perceived as socially legitimate, it is very difficult for us to explain those for whom there was a decline in the frequency of smoking.[24]

Prayer

There is no doubt that the habits of prayer are above all an integral part of a way of life and a world view. In this sense we would expect stable behavior in the face of situations of tension and anxiety, and that an individual who did change the frequency of this behavior would do so in the direction of increased frequency; that is, a major change in the "plus" direction. But while the first component of this prediction was indeed fulfilled, the second appears problematic.

In the period of routine activity, 13.4 percent of the respondents generally or often prayed; in the period of war and social interruption, the rate of those who prayed in the population as a whole increased by 7 percent (Table 3.1). The behavior was indeed very stable and 77.5 percent of the total sample population did not pray more or pray less than "usual" in the period of interruption. But when we decompose the proportions of change, we note that 16.1 percent of the population increased the frequency of their prayer, while 6.4 percent decreased it (Table 3.3).

Despite the fact that we are dealing with a behavior that is part of a broader style of life and that includes almost all spheres of human activity and behavior, we can view changes in the frequency of prayer during the war and the period of social interruption as possible signs of tension and anxiety, and possibly also as symptoms of more far-reaching social phenomena. We find support for this claim in the significant association found between changes in prayer patterns and the respondents' agreement with two attitudes—one which may express anomie and the other, the aspiration to appeal for a moratorium from any activity that is not connected with the predominant goal (see Table 3.1). First, we found a significant association between agreement with the claim that "in such times you can't be sure what your closest friends will do"[25] and the tendency to pray a great deal during the war and the period of interruption. Second, we found an association between prayer and agreement with the claim that "When soldiers are falling on the front, there's no point in doing anything at home." It is important to note that this was the only behavior of the 18 activities examined that was associated with these two tendencies.[26] We therefore hypothesize that individuals who are more exposed to an anomic situation will tend to pray more as will those who appeal for a *general* (not selective) moratorium from the performance of activities during the interruption, and for whom prayer is probably perceived as a vicarious activity, which is possibly more relevant and functional than other activities. But it should be emphasized that no association was revealed between the tendency to anomie and the appeal for a moratorium during the interruption, so that each of the two variables operated separately. An additional finding that may clarify this picture is the association found between the tendency to pray a great deal and the presence of mobilized family members in the household (see Table 3.12).

Prayer (as opposed possibly to sleeping a great deal, consuming medicines, etc.)[27] is to a certain extent similar to smoking as a mechanism that is perceived as being legitimate for reducing tension, and is certainly not regarded as detaching the individual from the collectivity. It is very likely that this was the only activity serving as an outlet for tension that we examined that had not only expressive, but also instrumental, significance (at least in the eyes of the religious and traditional respondents). This is so, since prayer may be directed—among other things—to nullification of the stern Divine decree. In this sense, our findings are compatible with the hypothesis that the frequency of various activities for the reduction of tension depends on the differential degree to which they are perceived as not contradictory to the commitment to the collectivity or as "dysfunctional."

Summary

The activities analyzed in this chapter constitute a sample of routine activities in most of the spheres of performance of social roles in Israel at times of noninterruption, or routine activities that may also express anxiety and tension. In times of social interruption, most of the activities (except for going to work and prayer) became marginal—even in terms of the complementary goal—and indeed there was a general tendency in the system to appeal for a moratorium (to a differential extent) from the fulfillment of various routine roles, which indeed aided in maintaining

TABLE 3.11
Changes in Prayer Habits between Routine and Interrupted Periods, by the Existence of a Sense of Anomie* and the Desire for a Moratorium in the Period of Interruption** (in percent)

Direction of Change in Performance of Activity	No Sense of Anomie	Sense of Anomie	Total	No Desire for a Moratorium	Desire for a Moratorium	Total
Decline	4.4	1.9	6.3	5.2	0.8	6.0
No change	57.1	21.2	78.3	67.9	10.2	78.1
Increase	8.4	6.9	15.3	10.9	5.0	15.9
Total	69.9	30.0	99.9	84.0	16.0	100.0
N	462			486		
x^2	17.155			21.221		
p***	.0087			.0017		

*The sense of anomie was examined by the degree of agreement with the statement: "In such times you can't be sure what your best friend will do."

**Desire for a moratorium was examined by the degree of agreement with the attitude "When soldiers are falling on the front, there's no point in doing anything at home."

***The original test was done according to a scale of agreement/nonagreement with 4 levels, and thus the number of degrees of freedom in each of the two tests is 6.

TABLE 3.12
Changes in Prayer Habits between Routine and Interrupted Periods, by Recruitment or Nonrecruitment of Family Members (in percent)

Direction of Change in Performance of Activity	Recruitment of Family Members		
	Yes	No	Total
Decline	4.3	2.1	6.4
No change	50.6	27.2	77.8
Increase	12.8	3.0	15.8
Total	67.7	32.3	100.0
N		486	
x^2		6.974	
P		.0306	

the individual's "cosmic order," but whose contribution to the system's upkeep seems to have been perceived as marginal (and this is in contrast with the types of roles that will be analyzed in the next chapter). However, we have not succeeded in discovering a uniform pattern of an appeal for a moratorium nor an actual general moratorium (despite the fact that such attitudes existed in the system), probably because some of the social roles of a considerable portion of the sample population were too rigid to permit an appeal for, or receipt of, a moratorium. The social roles had to continue to be fulfilled, although the level of their performance might have been lowered (for example, one still had to cook for children— but possibly less regularly).

The contradictory messages that the system gave forth—and that were to a large extent linked to the internal dialectics of the concept of interruption (that is, to continue the smooth functioning of the system while at the same time interrupting it)—were primarily expressed in the fact that there were very few behaviors in which unequivocal changes occurred, and there was almost always at least a small but significant group that changed its behavior in a direction opposite to that of the major change. However, as we noted, the more the activity was perceived as relevant to the "situation" (that is, to the attainment of the predominant or complementary goals), the greater was the tendency not to lower the level of performance, even in the face of the constraints and shortages that appeared in the interrupted system.

Finally, we found hints to the effect that the more central the social location of a group, the more it would display a tendency to include a broader spectrum of activities in the sphere of the complementary goal, and the less it would tend to appeal for a moratorium on these activities.

Notes

1. We can relate to this series of questions in two ways: We can view the questions as examining the respondents' actual behavior, since they were asked about their actual behavior. A second means of observation is to view the questions as measuring a norm—that is, how the respondent perceived either the actual behavior in the situation described to him or what desirable behavior should be. Whatever the interpretation of the validity of this series of 36 questions, what was more interesting to the researchers was the differences between the two periods involved (the routine and the interrupted) as elicited by means of the questions; thus, the problem of their validity (in the above context) became marginal. The problem does not exist at all if we assume a high correlation between attitude and behavior, or if we view an attitude as a certain type of behavior. Nevertheless, the reader should be aware that the interpretation of the findings presented in this chapter is problematical to a certain degree. The researchers themselves did not tend to attribute

importance to this problem of validity of the data, but they acknowledge the legitimacy of its presentation.

2. As will become clear below, there are two clearly different types of quantitative changes. Those which we refer to as *gross changes* are changes occurring in the sample population as a whole and are not refined enough to measure the fluctuations that occur in each direction, since the minor changes can cancel out major ones, and the "real" volume of changes may not be reflected in this kind of data. Thus, we developed a measure for examining the *net changes,* which takes into account all the changes in the population, with these differences being compared with the part of the population that remained *stable* and did not change its behavior in either direction.

3. When referring below to cultural differences between members of the population studied, we refer to ethnic origin (in this case the origin of the respondent's father) because this is the only variable that was found to predict a certain behavior or activity. When, along with origin, other socioeconomic variables—education, occupational status, and in many cases also religiosity, are discussed—we shall relate to all these variables (when they operate together in the same direction) as to a single one, indicating the individual's location in the system. As in every contemporary society, these variables tend to form fairly fixed clusters, so that in general any of them constitutes a good predictor of the others. These clusters are also good predictors of the individual's location in the stratification system and less successful predictors of the individual's place on the center-periphery continuum (see chapters 1 and 2), since a high location on the stratification ladder is not a sufficient—and sometimes not even a necessary—condition for an actor's location in a central societal zone. This is so since access to sources of information, some sense of participation in the collectivity and participation in the attainment of its central goals, are not always accompanied by a high class position, particularly not in a society that tends to egalitarianism and collectivism, as Israeli society does.

4. For some of the activities, the definition in the questionnaire was negative, as in "absence from work"; and in such a case the "plus" sign also designates a decline in the frequency.

5. E. Katz and M. Gurevich, *The Culture of Leisure in Israel* (Tel Aviv: Am Oved, 1973). The quotations hereafter are from the Hebrew edition. For an English-language version see *The Secularization of Leisure* (London: Faber and Faber, 1976).

6. In most families in Israel it is still customary that only the male has a driver's licence. Thus, when the male is mobilized, the family car is not used.

7. Despite the fact that in Israel, as a small and intensive society, there is a special significance of the transmission of information via informal channels. Sometimes, an individual's location in the system depends to a great degree on his location in the transmission network of informal communication. This will be mentioned again in chapter 4, in a different context.

8. In the questionnaire, we asked about listening to the news (on the radio), but during the course of the interviews it became clear that the respondents did not tend to distinguish between listening to the news on the radio and watching the news on television.

9. From the first day of the 1967 war, the Israeli radio (which is state-controlled) began to broadcast the news every hour (whereas previously there had been only about seven editions of the news daily). Since then, this pattern has become institutionalized; and when, because of a labor dispute, the night broadcasts were stopped, the military radio station took the place of the larger civilian stations by broadcasting hourly newsbreaks.

10. In the period of interruption, the television station began to telecast 16 hours a day, with most of the programs including suspense and adventure movies and entertainment (some imported and some recorded in the armed forces bases).

11. Katz and Gurevich, *Culture of Leisure,* p. 185.

12. Ibid., p. 154.

13. M. McLuhan, *Understanding Media: The Extension of Man* (New York: McGraw-Hill, 1965), passim.

14. L. Coser, *The Functions of Social Conflict* (Glencoe: Free Press, 1956).

15. In Israeli culture the concept of "traditional" has a dual significance. First, it constitutes an intermediate rung on the ladder of the degree of religiosity, in terms of fulfillment of religious precepts, frequency of visits to synagogue, adherence to the dietary ("Kashruth") and Shabbat laws, etc. Second, it is similar to the original sociological concept of an individual whose culture is the antithesis of the so-called modern culture and also includes within itself the component of strong attachment to religion. Generally when an individual of Western origin defines himself as "traditional," he refers to the first meaning of the concept. Thus, in our study we tend to combine the categories of "traditional" and "religious," despite the fact that they are separate in the original questionnaire. When we nevertheless use the concept in the presentation of the data, we refer to the second meaning.

16. Our respondents ranked the occupational status according to prior instructions on a scale of 16 categories.

17. Katz and Gurevich, *Culture of Leisure,* p. 100.

18. Ibid., p. 163.

19. M. Chazani and A. Yishaya, *Social Changes in the Wake of Rehabilitation of Poor Neighborhoods: Institutionalized versus Spontaneous Rehabilitation* (Haifa: Technion Institute for Research and Development, 1971).

20. But here we have to take into particular consideration the dimension of social desirability the respondent wished to present to the interviewer. But even though some of the respondents to the question of personal hygiene responded in a way aimed at impressing the interviewer, the results are still significant, because we are measuring the perceived gaps and their directions between the two periods.

21. There has been too great an emphasis in the so-called professional literature on psychological pressures and anxieties stemming from them as a variable central to the understanding of social behavior during the war. The salience of "pathological" and extreme phenomena that appeared during and after the wars, at the front and at the rear, is understood; but we believe that it distorts the prevalent patterns of reaction, of both the system and the individuals within it. Some of these studies are noted in note 34 of chapter 1, and an example of overemphasis of the "psychological point of view" and pathological phenomena may be found in Amia Liblich, *Tin Soldiers on Jerusalem Beach* (New York: Pantheon, 1979).

22. K. W. Deutsch, "Social Mobilization and Political Development," *American Political Science Review* 55 (September 1961).
23. But the two "functions" are not necessarily mutually exclusive.
24. We cannot ignore the fact that at various stages of the interruption there were local and temporary shortages in cigarettes, but generally a smoker could find an alternative to his regular brand. In the first days of the war there were also some air raids (although as noted there was almost no bombing of civilian population), and sometimes it was somewhat difficult to go shopping. But this still cannot be viewed as an explanation for the decline in smoking among almost six percent of the sample population.
25. The phrase "such times" can be understood as about six months after the end of the period of interruption and about a year after the outbreak of the war. In this sense the "regular times" are those *after* the war and the precedent interruption, and it is possible that they differ from the "regular times" before the interruption.
26. All the associations among all the variables were examined. Most were analyzed and presented here to the extent that they were relevant to the discussion.
27. American colleagues asked us why we did not ask about drinking alcoholic beverages, and we had to explain that alcoholism is not a traditional Jewish behavior pattern and is possibly the only trait we in Israel "inherited" from the Diaspora Jews.

4
The Volunteers

In this chapter we will examine how various actors acted in their new roles perceived as relevant to the situation of social interruption, which of them occupied new roles and in what way, and what—if any—were the patterns of coordination among these actors and the interrupted institutional system as described in chapter 2. Within the interrupted institutional system these actors were referred to as "volunteers," and this term applied even to actors who obtained rewards (financial or other) in exchange for their work. Thus, participation in the attainment of the complementary goal of maintenance of the system's continued functioning was perceived as an activity subject to a large extent to the free choice of the member of the collectivity, as opposed to the compulsory selective-participation in the realization of the predominant goal. However, we can assume that the concept of "volunteering" included another component besides that of voluntary participation—that is, action demanding a great degree of initiative in a social situation not entirely structured. This initiative was of two types: first, the attainment of *access* to new roles, more relevant to the situation of social interruption; second, the development or building of new societal roles not provided for by the system. In accordance with our approach (as presented in chapter 1), we shall hypothesize that the more central the location of the actor, the more he would tend to voluntary activity and the more his volunteering would take on the character of the construction of new roles.

In this chapter as well, we shall not differentiate in the analysis of the findings between volunteer roles perceived as relevant to the pre-dominant goal and those perceived as relevant to the complementary goal, because of two basic assumptions noted earlier: (1) the entire area of activity analyzed is located in the zone of the complementary goal, and (2) the actors themselves did not tend to differentiate between activity in these two zones (and our differentiation is only for analytical purposes).

119

Institutionalization of Volunteering

With the outbreak of the 1973 war, many persons turned to what they perceived to be the main centers of volunteering: Magen David Adom (the Israeli Red Cross), hospitals, post offices, municipalities, etc. These bodies were flooded with volunteers beyond their needs or their abilities to absorb chiefly unskilled manpower. For example, about 7,000 volunteers turned to the Hadassah Hospital in Jerusalem, but only about 1,500 of them were employed in some manner, these contributing a total of about 9,000 days of work.[1] About 2,000 volunteers were employed in the post offices in the sorting and distribution of mail (*Ha'aretz*, 2 November 1973). Within several days, a volunteer network was organized, which had several main foci:

Volunteering for Pay

The system of paid volunteer work was put into effect by the Ministry of Labor via the existing employment offices. On October 12 notices appeared in the press announcing the opening of registration offices for paid volunteer work, starting from October 14. Already on the first day, 5,000 people responded, of whom 2,000 were immediately placed in jobs. The target population of the volunteer campaign was primarily composed of those not mobilized, such as pensioners, women, and youth. The Ministry of Industry and Commerce estimated that the mobilization of the economy for a prolonged state of emergency would call for the recruitment of at least 10,000 volunteers. A spokesman of the Employment Service noted that at the beginning of the war a system of paid volunteers was put into effect according to a program drawn up in advance and aimed at supplying suitable manpower for essential enterprises (see chapter 2). After the warfare per se (but not the differential degree of social interruption) was over, the Employment Service directed volunteers to sanitation, transportation, and public services, in which a serious manpower shortage arose as well as to nonessential enterprises. The main difficulty in fulfilling the need for manpower stemmed from the fact that most of the enterprises were primarily in need of skilled workers, while the supply offered by the employment offices was mainly made up of unskilled manpower. At this stage about 14,000 people turned to employment offices, of whom 8,000 were actually placed in jobs in October. The spokesman of the Employment Service noted that in contrast to the first stage of activity of paid volunteering services that was put into effect according to a plan prepared in advance, the second stage (from October onward) was put into effect without any prior preparation.

TABLE 4.1
Volunteers Registered through the Employment Service of the Ministry of
Labor for Paid Jobs, by Month (October 1973-March 1974)

Month	No. of those requesting jobs
October	14,500
November	22,250
December	18,000
January	16,500
February	15,500
March	14,000

Source: Spokesman Bureau, the Employment Service, Ministry of Labor, May 1975.

From December 1973 to March 1974 there was a continuous decline in the number of volunteers (see Table 4.1). The main reason for this decline was that the offices could supply jobs only to some of the persons who requested them, and thus most of them (according to the spokesman) felt a sense of frustration. At the beginning of January 1974 the third stage of paid volunteering began. Special departments in the offices devoted their main efforts to locating women who were not working, workers laid off their jobs, and those requesting skilled work. The goal was to fulfill the economy's needs for skilled workers in the metallurgical industry, and unskilled workers in other industries and in the collection and packing of the citrus crop.

The main conclusions drawn by the Ministry of Labor from the above efforts were as follows: (1) patterns of action must be planned for times of emergency, (2) the definition of "essential enterprises," for the purpose of supplying volunteers, should be broadened (to include export industries, for example), and (3) substitutes should be prepared for key personnel in industry and the services (see chapter 2).[2]

Volunteering through the Volunteers' Bureau

This bureau was established in the framework of the Office of the Prime Minister before the 1973 social interruption, and it registers and directs volunteers to unpaid jobs. During the interruption the system contained three foci: the emergency centers of the municipalities, to which many volunteers turned and which directed them to the Volunteers'

Bureau; the Employment Office, which received requests from enterprises and organizations in need of volunteers and which directed all or most of them to the Volunteers' Bureau; and the Volunteers' Bureau itself, which directed people to places of employment. Those placed through the Volunteers' Bureau did not receive pay, but were insured during their work.[3] In a report of the Institute for the Study of Labor and Welfare, it was noted that the Volunteers' Bureau apparently functioned well, but severe tension among the various volunteer services was noted as well.[4]

The volunteers were directed to jobs in bakeries, in food packing, in factories manufacturing clothing for the armed forces, in transporting soldiers, in care and aid to families of recruited soldiers, in aid to bereaved families, in snack bars at hitchhiking stations, in baking cakes, etc. In addition, the volunteers of the Jerusalem Bureau aided new immigrants who had arrived a short time before the war and needed help in getting organized.[5] The bureau dealt with a total of 909 volunteers during the period of the social interruption of 1973-74.

Youth Volunteering through Gadna

During the interruption, the Gadna (a pre-military youth corps, organized and commanded by the armed forces) established a volunteer framework aimed at offering service to families of mobilized persons. The idea was to send Gadna volunteers to families in order to help children prepare their homework and to allow mothers of small children to leave the house by offering them babysitting services, etc. The response of the Gadna members was disappointing, especially in Tel Aviv. On the other hand, the rate of requests for such services was also low. The Gadna command explained this fact by noting that a population not defined as "needy" in the usual sense was involved here, and this population did not tend to accept aid because of the negative connotations that seemingly accompany such requests for aid. The negative image of such requests also explains the low responsiveness of Gadna members. At the end of February about 2,000 persons were activated in connection with this project, each of whom devoted two or three hours twice or three times a week to these activities. It is noteworthy that other bodies that dealt with giving aid to the families of the recruited faced a similar problem. The Ministry of Welfare initiated a program of service for families of mobilized persons. By February not more than 2,800 persons from all over the country had requested such help. A staff that tried to establish a neighborhood service in Jerusalem to deal with those problems of the residents that were derived from the situation of the social interruption, was also faced with an absence of requests for aid on the part of the population.[6]

The Ministry of Education announced that it would expand the National Service (a two-week duty for high school students) for aid to agricultural farmsteads (January 28), and a short time later (February 6) a proposal for a law made by a Parliament member (U. Feinerman) was noted, to the effect that National Service should be declared compulsory for any adult not required to give military service.

In addition to these three main frameworks, a wave of volunteers was noted during the first weeks of the social interruption and these volunteers approached institutions and organizations that had advertised their need for volunteers in the newspapers and the other mass media. The organizations involved were perceived as being particularly significant in the situation of social interruption, being connected to the predominant or complementary societal goals (e.g., hospitals, Magen David Adom, municipal emergency staffs, industrial plants, and schools). Most of those who volunteered in this way were rejected by these institutions, inasmuch as the latter were swamped with volunteers and did not have the capacity to absorb such numbers.

As the interruption continued, a wave of public resentment arose as to the unjust division of the burden (mainly between the military and civilian sectors). One of the implications of this phenomenon was the tendency to view volunteering (according to our definition) as the fulfillment of a civilian *duty*, which should be also imposed on the "dodgers" (see the above-mentioned proposal of the member of Parliament for compulsory National Service). A similar tendency had been noted two months earlier, when, in the Institute for the Study of Labor and Welfare, a staff was established in order to plan a "Women's Reserves Service" to take over jobs in the economy that had suffered from the mobilization of males.

Women

We should perhaps deal in brief with the subject of women volunteers. As Dorit Padan-Eisenstark noted (*Ma'ariv*, December 6), "women constitute the most stable labor force [during social interruptions]." She added that "it would be worthwhile to base the entire plan for the organization of the civilian economy in times of emergency primarily on female labor."

However, little was actually done in this connection. On December 6 a daily (*Ma'ariv*) noted the establishment of the so-called Women's Reserve Service, with female teachers from the various universities participating along with the heads of women's organizations. In its report, the new established group noted that the female labor forces were not taken advantage of during the war, and this had many ramifications both for the civilian economy, which suffered from a shortage of workers, and for morale among the civilians. (The group's four main recommendations were: the expansion of women's vocational training and know-how to spheres that until then were mostly or exclusively reserved for men; the placement of women in all levels of management during "normal" times; the formulation of a plan for "reserves service for non-recruited civilian population"—first and foremost for women; and the construction of day-care centers starting from infancy and adjacent to women's workplaces.[7] Here is an example of an attempt to create social change in the Israeli society, for "normal" times, that could improve the system's capabilities in the period of social interruption.)

The actual activity in the direction of training women for jobs vital to the economy in the course of social interruption was very limited. One of the few things done was the establishment of a committee to deal with the training of female bus drivers, with the purpose of filling in for the thousands of bus drivers who had been mobilized (see chapter 2). Another example can be noted in the words of the general director of a big bank in Jerusalem, who noted that the bank continued to function during the interruption thanks to the efforts of its female workers. He claimed that one of the lessons learned from this period was that women should be promoted to top-level positions in the bank and be granted the right of signature.[8] However, in general, no serious attempt was noted to integrate women in the framework of volunteer and work programs during the period of social interruption.

Profiles of Volunteers

We will now deal with the question of *who* volunteered or, in other words, we shall try to delineate variables by means of which we can characterize the volunteer population as opposed to nonvolunteers. The first question to be posed is whether socioeconomic variables account for different degrees of volunteering or attempts to volunteer among the population of the sample (see the methodological appendix). Some of the answers may be supplied by the findings in Table 4.2.

Sex

As we may note from the table, a statistically significant trend existed among males to volunteer, or to attempt to volunteer, as compared to females. This finding can be explained by the fact that men may have important skills for fulfilling interruptive roles (such as a driver's licence for heavy vehicles, experience in production jobs, possession of technical

TABLE 4.2

Population of the Sample, by Volunteering and Selected Background Variables (in percent)

Variable	Categories	Volunteering			total	N	p*
		Did not volunteer	Attempted to volunteer but did not find a job	Volunteered			
Sex	Male	48.1	26.8	25.1	100.0	331	.0041
	Female	62.2	20.9	16.9	100.0	183	
Father's birth contin.	Europe-America	54.4	23.5	22.1	100.0	272	.0081
	Israel	64.2	15.1	20.7	100.0	53	
	Asia-Africa	68.2	21.8	10.0	100.0	170	
Occupation	Not employed or lacking a vocation (students, housewives, etc)	62.9	20.2	16.9	100.0	183	
	Manual workers & low-level administrative positons	58.4	28.5	13.1	100.0	214	.0012
	Professions & high level administrative positions	52.2	17.7	30.1	100.0	113	
Age	0-25 years	39.9	31.8	28.8	100.0	66	.0030
	26-35 "	69.9	19.9	11.1	100.0	126	
	36-45 "	63.1	22.3	14.6	100.0	130	
	46 years +	59.0	20.2	20.8	100.0	173	
Education	0-8 years schooling	74.4	18.3	7.3	100.0	66	.0001
	9-12 "	56.0	27.7	16.3	100.0	209	
	Matriculation certificate +	53.2	19.2	27.6	100.0	156	

*Level of significance measured by *chi* square.

know-how, etc.). Men may also have had priority in access to the places for volunteering (i.e., via their jobs; see below). Again, this tendency may be connected with the greater rigidity of women's roles in the system. The Israeli normative system also demanded greater participation from males—in case of war—in the attainment of the predominant or at least the complementary societal goal, than it did from females.

Ethnic Origin

As indicated in Table 4.2., a significant association was found between volunteering and one's father's country of birth. We find the highest proportion of volunteers among respondents born to fathers born in the Occident (i.e., Europe, America, and Australia), with the proportion of volunteers among sons of Israeli-born fathers approaching that proportion, while among those born to fathers from Oriental countries (i.e., Asia and Africa) the proportion of volunteers was much lower. The picture becomes more complex when we examine the association between ethnic origin and *attempts* to volunteer: we note the highest rate of attempts to volunteer among sons of Asian-African born fathers, a lower rate among those of Occidental origin, and an even lower rate among respondents whose fathers were born in Israel. In other words, prima facie an almost inverse picture emerges when we compare actual volunteering and attempts to volunteer. Thus, the crucial factor seems not to be the predisposition to volunteering, but the *capability* of finding volunteer jobs. But this conclusion must be limited because the rate of those responding that they did not attempt to volunteer at all was very high among sons of Oriental-born fathers, was less among sons of those born in Israel, and was lowest among respondents whose fathers were born in the Occident.

In analyzing these data, several factors that may be relevant should be taken into account. First, in each family the head of the household at the time of the social interruption (described in the questionnaire as the "war period") was interviewed. Thus, in the light of extensive mobilization, the majority of the respondents in our sample (68.2 percent) were women. If we recall the higher birth rate prevailing among those of Asian-African origin, it is possible that the objective difficulties—or what we called "role constraints" in chapter 1—in volunteering were greater among members of this subsample, and thus the higher rate of respondents who did not attempt to volunteer at all.

The higher rate among those of Oriental origin or those who attempted to volunteer and were unsuccessful, may perhaps be connected with the fact that because of the pressure on the volunteer foci, those persons possessing skills and connections (with which sons of Occidental and

Israeli-born fathers were more equipped) were given priority. In support of this point it is worthwhile noting that in response to the question asked of the volunteer subsample, "How did you arrive at your volunteer job?" only 16 percent responded that they were approached and asked to help. However, 84 percent needed their own initiative and social contacts to obtain their volunteer jobs. Of those that were asked to volunteer, the majority (62.5 percent) were sons of Israeli-born fathers, 25 percent were sons of European-American born fathers, and only 12.5 percent of these respondents had fathers born in Asia-Africa. Thus, in this channel of volunteering, which was based almost entirely on skill and/or social contacts, we may note a clear priority given to the first two origin groups.

Occupation

The whole occupation spectrum, for the sake of methodological convenience, was grouped into three categories: nonworking, manual workers, and professionals.[9] The association between one's occupational position and his tendency to volunteer was found to be significant. Professionals volunteered more than manual workers and those without a vocation, while manual workers responded that they attempted to volunteer more than the nonworking and more than professionals. When we examined those respondents who indicated that they did not try to volunteer at all, we noted a greater tendency for this among those lacking a job than among the manual workers and the professionals.

These findings and the findings noted above as to ethnic origin can be explained in accordance with our approach. One's occupation might be one of the indicators as well as a determinant of one's centrality in the system. Thus, those higher in the occupational structure (i.e., more centrally located in the system) volunteered to a greater extent. Manual workers, though, reported more attempts to volunteer; this was because their chances of obtaining volunteer jobs were smaller than those of persons more centrally located in the system. On the other hand, their desire to participate in the system expressed itself in their claims of having tried to volunteer. Those not working were characterized by a lesser degree of volunteering and lesser claims of having volunteered, because of their great distance from the central zone of the system and their relatively low exposure to the center's demands. These trends are indeed supported by the data (although we should note that the category of the nonworking included a large number of housewives—a population whose routine roles were almost unchanged during the interruption, and which might possibly even have been expanded).

Income

No association was found between a household's net monthly income and volunteering. It should be noted that the association between income and other stratification characteristics was relatively weak and also that generally there is a problem of the reliability of the reportage in this area.

Age

As noted in the table, a significant association was found between the respondent's age and his tendency to volunteer. Examination of the data reveals that there was one differentiated group—those of 25 and below—that showed a considerable rate of volunteering as well as attempts at volunteering. In the other three age groups, there was almost a uniform rate of attempts to volunteer, while in actual volunteering there was an increase among the older group of respondents, age 46 and over. This can be explained by noting that young people are characterized by a fairly low rigidity of routine roles (see chapters 1 and 3) and even those roles (for examples, students, bachelors, married persons without children) tend to be disturbed during an interruption time. Thus, the younger age groups having few routine roles may be characterized as a group of whom there were strong expectations of volunteering together with pressures that encouraged volunteering (or at least encouraged members of the group to report having attempted to volunteer). Most of the members of this group did not have skills that were particularly in demand, nor did they have personal connections that could aid in obtaining volunteer roles, and thus they found it difficult to obtain volunteer jobs.

The older age group can be characterized by its persistent struggle for its place within the system. If we accept the claim that volunteering in times of interruption can be somewhat of a source of legitimation for the claim of belonging, it is clear that this group would show a relatively strong inclination to volunteer. If we add to this the fact that we are dealing with persons whose routine roles were few, and some of whom had both professional and social skills (e.g., personal connections and know-how, as well as access to such roles), it is clear that this group would be more powerfully motivated to seek volunteer roles and would be at an advantage in attaining them.

Education

A significant direct association was found between volunteering and level of education—the higher the education, the higher the rate of volunteers and those attempting to volunteer within the group. The only exception was the higher than expected percentage of volunteers and those attempting to volunteer among the respondents who had 9-12 years of schooling. The explanation offered above as to the relatively high concentration of attempts to volunteer among individuals defined as intermediate in terms of their occupation status is probably applicable here as well—the attempt to volunteer reflected an aspiration for greater participation in the system.

In sum, among the background variables examined, a signficant association was found between volunteering and sex, ethnic origin, age, education, and occupational status. If most of these variables may be perceived as indices of the actor's location in the system, the findings supported our hypothesis about the role of centrality in the determination of behavior in the case of social interruption. In almost every case a higher rate of volunteering was associated with a higher stratificational position and a more central location in the system, while a higher rate of attempted volunteering was associated with an intermediate stratificational position and, seemingly, expressed greater motivation to participate in the collectivity. The high proportion of respondents who did not try to volunteer at all was probably an expression of their distance from the central societal zone. Even the deviants from this principle— the youngest and oldest age groups—can be explained in the spirit of this claim.

The Cost of Volunteering

It is generally assumed that different groups in the population suffered different economic losses as a result of the social interruption (see chapter 2). We may assume that the severity of these losses incurred by an individual would affect his ability or desire to volunteer. At the outset we examined the association between the employment status of the head of the household and the volunteering of the respondent, who was, as noted, the head of the household during the interruption. Three of the four response categories as to the employment status of the main breadwinner—employee, pensioner, and welfare recipient—corresponded to groups in the population whose economic situation did not deteriorate severely as a result of the interruption and the prolonged mobilization. In the fourth category—the self-employed—the possibility of such a deterioration did exist. No association was found between the status of the main breadwinner and the respondent's volunteering. In another question, respondents were asked to indicate whether the family's economic situation deteriorated during the war. We found that most respondents (71.2 percent) indicated no change had occurred, 20.9 percent indicated a slight change for the worse, and only 7.9 percent of the respondents indicated that the family's financial situation deteriorated markedly during the war. In this variable as well, no association was found between the deterioration of the financial situation and the inclination to volunteer. The volunteers were asked whether they had continued to receive their salaries from their regular places of employment during the period in which they had volunteered. Of 101 respondents to the question, 30.7 percent had not been employed and so, of course, had not received a salary;[10] however, more than half the volunteers (53.5 percent) had continued to receive their full salaries during the period in which they volunteered, so that they did not incur material losses (and possibly even profited if they received pay for their volunteer work). Four percent received partial salaries, while 11.9 percent did not receive salaries from their usual place of work while volunteering. Thus, the family's economic situation, the material loss it incurred during the interruption, and the loss incurred by the volunteer himself did not predict the individual's volunteering or not volunteering.

Another aspect of the cost of volunteering that was examined was the cost of volunteering in terms of alternative employment. Almost two-thirds of the volunteers indicated that had they not volunteered, they would not have had other jobs outside their homes during the war.[11]

All of the respondents were asked whether the demands made on them during the war in their regular jobs were greater or lesser than "usual." A statistically significant association was found between the variables (see Table 4.3): 66 (20.7 percent) of those individuals of whom greater demands were made on the job, volunteered. If we combine the categories of "volunteered" and "attempted to volunteer," this enlarged group included 47.3 percent of the total of the respondents of whom greater demands were made, as compared with 47.1 percent of those who reported no change in the demands made on them, and only 32.4 percent of the respondents whose workload lessened during the period.

At first glance, this finding is surprising when we relate it in terms of the investment of time and effort demanded of the individual in alternative jobs. The individuals of whom greater demands were made tended to invest additional effort in volunteer activities, while those of whom less demands were made tended to volunteer less. To explain this seeming anomaly, we will attempt to relate to these findings in terms of our argument. We must remember that the various vocations were subject to reclassification according to the degree of their relevance to the predominant and complementary goals. Those occupations in which greater demands were made during the interruption were also those more relevant to the situation of social interruption, and thus these occupations

TABLE 4.3
The Sample Population, by Volunteering and Workload during the War
(in percent)

		Workload		
Volunteering	total	lessened	did not change	grew
Total	100.00	27.3	12.8	59.9
Did not volunteer	56.8	18.4	6.8	31.6
Attempted to volunteer but did not find a job	23.8	5.3	2.6	15.9
Volunteered	19.4	3.6	3.4	12.4

$$N = 532$$

$$x^2 = 14.657$$

$$p = .0192$$

also granted a greater reward; i.e., a sense of participation and centrality in the collectivity for those persons employed within them. This sense of participation and centrality led to greater exposure to the normative system stemming from the center and to obedience to the prevalent norm—that of volunteering. This interruption is capable of explaining why the very persons who bore a heavier workload during the interruption were more inclined to volunteer.

Some additional support for this interruption can be found in the responses obtained as to political party affiliation (see Table 4.4). A significant association was found between party membership and volunteering. Thus, of those who were active in a political party, or at least registered as members, about 36 percent volunteered, as opposed to only 17.2 percent of those who were not members. If indeed there is validity in the interpretation indicating that a central location led to a greater tendency to volunteer, this can also explain the present finding, with party membership serving as a criterion for a sense of centrality. Nevertheless, we cannot ignore the fact that party membership can also fulfill an additional function in connection with volunteering. If we compare the percentages of the respondents reporting that they attempted to volunteer but did not obtain jobs, we see that they constituted about 22

TABLE 4.4
The Sample Population, by Volunteering and Political Party Membership
(in percent)

| Volunteering | total | Party Membership | | |
		active	registered	not a member
Total	100.00	2.4	12.7	84.9
Did not volunteer	56.2	1.1	5.2	49.9
Attempted to volunteer but did not find a job	23.7	.4	3.0	20.4
Volunteered	20.0	.9	4.5	14.6

N = 539

x^2 = 15.764

p = .0034

percent of the party members as opposed to 24 percent of those who were not party members. As such, it is possible that the party also served as a channel for recruiting individuals and granting greater opportunities to its members who volunteered during the interruption period, by means of a network of personal connections with persons holding key positions in the volunteering system.

Some Constraints

At this point we should examine an additional question: Are there categories in the population with respect to which volunteering is more difficult because of role constraints as compared with the rest of the population? Several factors that may be potential obstacles to volunteering were examined.

Child-Care

It is quite likely that the presence of children (particularly small children) at home will make it difficult for the person directly responsible for their care to volunteer. Thus, we can assume the existence of an

TABLE 4.5
Women, by Volunteering and the Age of the Youngest Child in the Household
(in percent)

Volunteering	Total	Age				
		0–5	6–15	16–19	20+	no children
Total	100.00	37.4	17.8	8.6	11.1	25.4
Did not volunteer	62.2	30.2	12.1	3.6	5.7	10.6
Attempted to volunteer but did not find a job	20.8	4.5	2.7	3.3	2.4	7.9
Volunteered	16.9	2.7	3.0	1.2	3.0	6.9

$$N = 331$$

$$x^2 = 44.105$$

$$p = .0000$$

association between the age of the youngest child in the family and volunteering by women. Such an association was indeed found (see Table 4.5), but more unexpectedly another association was found as well—one between the age of the youngest child and volunteering by men. Is the responsibility for child-care shared among the women and the men in Israeli society? That is hard to believe. Possibly the existence of small children in the family occupied most of the cognitive and emotional resources of the entire family, even more than the social interruption.

Mobilization of Family Members

The mobilization of family members who constitute part of the household necessarily creates a vacuum in the system of division of roles in the family. We may hypothesize that some of these roles would be neglected for the duration of the interruption because in many spheres the norms as to the level of functioning in this period changed (see chapter 1). Nevertheless, we can expect that at least some of the roles would have been filled by members of the family remaining in the civilian sector (compare with the findings in the previous chapter). Thus, we can hypothesize that the demands made on families of recruited persons, in terms of their family functioning, increased relative to those made on people who did not have members of their families recruited, and thus it is possible that the ability of the former group to volunteer would have been impaired. Claims to this effect can be found in the report of the Institute for the Study of Labor and Welfare[12] dealing with severe impairment of functioning in the families of some of the recruited men.[13]

Finally, it is interesting to note that there was a greater tendency among females to respond that they had not volunteered or attempted to volunteer (65.4 percent as opposed to 56.7 percent of the males). This was probably because the fulfillment of routine roles was one of the role sets emphasized by the system. Women's routine roles probably suffered less (see chapter 3), and thus these roles still could serve as a source of legitimation for the activities in the interrupted system.

Competition for Volunteer Roles

Until now we have tried to locate groups in the population for whom volunteering was more difficult than for others. We will now deal with the complementary question: Were there groups in the population for whom it was easier to volunteer? "Ease" here refers to greater access to volunteer roles. It should be borne in mind that at least in the months of October and November 1973 most of the organizations absorbing volunteers found themselves in a situation whereby the number of persons offering their services far exceeded the necessary manpower. In such a situation with an excess of demand (for volunteer jobs) over supply, we must examine to what extent a particular group had resources at its disposal that placed it at an advantage in the competition for volunteer jobs.

We shall begin this examination by ascertaining the channels through which volunteers arrived at the places that they volunteered (see Table 4.6). At first glance it seems that the main characteristic demanded of an individual was initiative and not necessarily personal connections or particular skills. Nevertheless, two points should be noted. With reference to personal connections, we should take into account the fact that even if a person approached an organization "on his own initiative," it is not clear to what extent his chances of being accepted for volunteer work were affected directly or indirectly by the fact that he had "friends in the right places," or that he knew where to apply by relying on these friends. In addition, it is clear that persons who responded that they were approached and asked to help, or who volunteered at their place of employment, or on the initiative of friends or acquaintances (a total of 35 percent), certainly exhibited some component of personal connections. The importance of personal and vocational skills and qualifications

TABLE 4.6
Volunteers, by the Way in Which They Obtained Their Volunteer Jobs

The Way	Percent
On personal initiative	58
Approached by others	16
Via mass media	3
Via workplace	10
Through friends or acquaintances	9
Other	4
Total	100

TABLE 4.7
Volunteers, by the Connection between Their Volunteer Work and Their Usual Professions (in percent)

Worked in same profession	25.2
Indirectly connected to job	3.9
Used some knowledge acquired in past	8.7
No connection with present or past jobs	53.4
Did not have profession	8.7
N	103

for volunteering was examined separately (see Table 4.7). The most salient finding was that more than 61 percent of the volunteers either worked at jobs that had no connection with their profession or had no profession at all (housewives?). We thus concluded that vocational skills were significant, since almost 40 percent worked at jobs that utilized these skills, but as in the case of personal connections, it still seems that the most important factor determining an individual's chance of finding a volunteer job was the degree of initiative he developed.

Another possible channel for volunteering was by means of membership in voluntary organizations (including the political parties discussed earlier).

Most of these associations were in some way connected with the volunteering system during the social interruption. Thus, there was a convenient channel for volunteering open to individuals who had been members of such organizations, even prior to the interruption period. Of course, it is possible that there are sociological and/or psychological traits characterizing people who tend to volunteer, and that the existence of such characteristics in certain individuals led them to membership in voluntary associations and would also have led them to volunteering during the period of the social interruption. But at this stage we are interested in these organizations only as a *channel of access* to the volunteer roles. We indeed found that members of voluntary associations displayed a signficantly greater tendency to volunteer during the interruption, compared with those who were not members in such associations, which would seem to corroborate this hypothesis.

In dealing with the individual's possession of resources that could have made it easier for him to volunteer during the period of social interruption, we should include at least one additional resource that was very important in the conditions of the interruption (and was mentioned several times previously, but in different contexts)—ownership of a car.

It can be argued that ownership of a car in Israel is an indicator of level of income of an individual (and the SES variables associated with the income—see note 2). However, there is one consideration that makes ownership of a car crucial when we examine the differential capabilities for volunteering among various groups of the population. To a large extent, ownership of a car determined the degree to which an individual could be mobile (see chapters 2 and 3), and thus also affected his ability to reach volunteer centers, the chance that he would attempt to volunteer, and/or his success in doing so.

To consolidate this point, it is worthwhile citing again the example of the Hadassah Hospital. The hospital, located several miles outside of Jerusalem, was a central focus for volunteering. As noted previously, during the interruption period about 7,000 volunteers registered at the volunteer center of the hospital. There were only two ways of reaching the hospital at this period—by hitchhiking or by private vehicle. That is, the fact that a person owned a car had a major effect—in this and other cases—on the possibilities of his volunteering. In addition, the vehicle in and of itself constituted a resource that increased an individual's chance of being able to volunteer, because it opened the door to a large number of roles connected with transportation and transport, roles that desperately needed to be filled, inasmuch as the transport system was the Achilles heel of the entire economy (see chapter 2).

TABLE 4.8
Volunteers by Possession of a Private Vehicle by the Respondent (in percent)

	total	no	yes
		Possession of a vehicle	
Total	100.00	76.0	24.0
Did not plan to volunteer	59.9	47.4	12.5
Attempted but did not succeed	22.3	18.4	3.9
Volunteered	17.8	10.2	7.6
N	489		

Thus, we found (as predicted) a significant association between owning a car and volunteering. Persons owning a car volunteered more than those not owning one, while among the latter group the proportion of persons trying to volunteer but not being successful was somewhat higher (see Table 4.8). If we subscribe to the above explanation, we may note that those persons not owning a car could reach only some of the volunteer centers and also lacked an important resource (the car), and thus they were rejected more often. This was what created the slightly higher proportion of persons without cars reporting that they had attempted to volunteer but had not managed to do so, relative to the proportion reporting this among car owners.

In sum, the attempt to locate groups in the population with relatively easy access to volunteer jobs indicated that the tendency to volunteer cannot be explained by having members of the family mobilized (contrary to the impact of this factor on performing several "routine" activities; see chapter 3). On the other hand, we found that men tended to volunteer more than women, and an association was found between the tendency to volunteer and the age of the youngest child both among women and men. A large number of the volunteers reported that individual initiative was what led them to volunteer, and for most of them there was no connection between the job they did as volunteers and specific skills they possessed. Nevertheless, it seems that such skills played a part in receiving jobs in about one third of the cases. Personal connections—

and possibly access to information, as in "whom to turn to"—were also significant. About one third of the volunteers obtained volunteer roles in ways that did not require personal initiative. Membership in voluntary associations was also found to be linked with volunteering, although this association can be interpreted in several ways. Likewise we found that car owners tended to volunteer and also seemed to have had better chances of receiving volunteer jobs relative to persons not owning cars.

Volunteering Outputs

Until now we have attempted to discover background variables for predicting volunteering; next we shall examine the types of the outputs that were produced by the volunteers in their jobs. It is important to note that the possible outputs presented here are not mutually exclusive, and since the respondents were presented with close-ended questions, we must add that we do not claim that the list is all inclusive (see Table 4.9).

We wish to emphasize that we are using the term "outputs" and not "rewards" or "gratification," because the latter two terms rest on an implicit assumption of the existence of a need that the behavior serves to fulfill. We limited ourselves by citing a list of possible outputs of volunteer work, and attempted to determine to what extent the volunteers felt that they received these outputs from their jobs.

The outputs were classified into three major groups: first, the altruistic instrumental category of outputs that stem from a sense of contribution to the collectivity. An example of this output category was perception of the volunteer's contribution as "important to the country." More than 77 percent of the volunteers felt that their volunteering was important to the country to a very great or a great extent, while only 2 percent felt that it was not important at all. It is interesting to note that no differences were found among the respondents to this question according to ethnic origin (of their father).

In the second type we include egoistic-instrumental outputs that yield tangible benefit to the individual volunteer. We will examine, as an example of this group, the chance to meet new people—43.8 percent of the respondents noted that volunteering enabled them to do so to a very great or great extent. The association between this output and the father's country of birth was found to be statistically significant. Only a third of the respondents of European-American origin felt that volunteering offered them chances to meet new people, as opposed to 54.6 percent among the respondents born in Israel and 72.7 percent of those of Asian-African origin.

TABLE 4.9
Volunteers, by Outputs of Their Volunteer Work (in percent)

Output	Type	The Perceived Importance of the Volunteer Work*					
		to a very great extent	to a great extent	to a small extent	not at all	total	N
Important for the country	altruistic-instrumental	31.7	45.5	20.8	2.0	100.0	101
Important for those helped	"	43.3	41.3	12.5	2.9	100.0	104
Contributes to the war effort	"	29.8	39.4	20.0	5.8	100.0	104
Gives an opportunity to meet new people	egoistic-instrumental	15.2	28.6	28.5	27.6	100.0	105
Is appreciated by the employer	"	26.0	34.0	21.0	19.0	100.0	100
Helps reduce tension	egoistic-expressive	26.9	34.6	25.0	13.5	100.0	104
Helps reduce loneliness	"	21.8	20.8	25.7	32.7	100.0	102
Causes sense of satisfaction	"	41.9	37.1	14.3	6.7	100.0	105

*The series of questions asked was: "To what extent did you feel that your volunteer work was . . . important for the country," ". . . important for those helped," etc.

In the third type we include egoistic-expressive outputs, and as an example of this type we will examine the output of tension reduction. In this category we found that for 61.5 percent of the respondents, volunteering aided in reducing loneliness to a very great or great extent, while 38.5 percent claimed that volunteering helped in this manner to a small or very small extent. When we examined the responses to this question according to the respondent's (father's) origin, we found that those of Asian-African origin tended to view volunteering as tension-reducing to a greater extent than did those of European-American origin. Eighty-one percent of the Asian-African respondents said that volunteering reduced tension to a great or very great extent, while no one claimed that volunteering did not reduce tension at all, as compared to 58.3 percent of those of European-American origin and 35 percent of those of Israeli-born (father's) origin who claimed that volunteering helped to reduce tension to a great or very great extent. The association between ethnic origin and the tendency to view volunteering as tension reducing was found to be significant. A similar picture emerged with reference to the second category of this output type: the relief of loneliness—66.7 percent of those of Oriental origin felt that volunteering helped them to relive loneliness, as opposed to 50 percent of the Israeli-born (father's origin) and only 33.8 percent of those of Occidental origin.

Thus, we see (Table 4.9) that the most predominant type of output was the altruistic-instrumental. For example, the volunteers felt that their work was important for the country (77.2 percent) or at least for those they helped (84.6 percent), and this gave them a sense of satisfaction (79 percent). The volunteering also helped reduce tension in a smaller proportion of our sample population (61.5 percent), or helped reduce loneliness in 42.6 percent. The only output that did not make a significant difference between the ethnic origin group was "importance [of the volunteering] to the country."

The respondents were also asked to what extent they received each specific category of output from their volunteer work. This does not indicate, at least not directly, the relative weights of the different categories and types of outputs in the actual decision to volunteer. Nevertheless, the findings support our claim that the greatest significance of volunteering lay in the fact that it represented the realization of the second most salient expectation of the normative system of the members of the collectivity during the interruption period—to maintain the system. The findings in this area of the social activities are also consistent with our hypothesis on the diverse orientations of differentially located collectivity members toward the performance of social roles in such a period. Thus, the egoistic-expressive types of outputs of the volunteer activity seem to be emphasized by the Asian-African origin group, because most of the membership of this group was concentrated in the more peripheral societal zone. Thus, even when they volunteered, individualistic considerations were more salient among this group than among origin groups that located their members in a more central zone.

Conclusions

In this chapter we attempted to analyze the encounter between the interrupted socio-institutional system and the actors within it who tried or did not try or who succeeded or did not succeed in fulfilling new roles that were relevant to the social interruption. We have already described and analyzed the functioning of the institutional system in chapter 2. Here we turned to the question of how this system responded to a specific problem—that is, giving individual actors the opportunity to be mobilized for activities perceived as voluntary.

Difficulty arises in the very encounter, inasmuch as the institutional activity is structured, specific, tends to professionalization, and is essentially paternalistic; while the very existence of volunteer activity is random, diffuse, tends to amateurishness, and demands initiatives that may be somewhat opposed to paternalism.[14] Here there was a two-sided expectation for such an encounter: many of the volunteers expected the system to supply them with opportunities to act and an institutionalized framework to provide access to the volunteer roles. On the other hand, the extensions of the political center (i.e., the bureaucracy) expected that a large pool of volunteers would be created that could be mobilized and operated *unconditionally* to maintain the interrupted system and minimize the interruption. In the main, there was an expectation for skilled manpower that could fulfill specific roles. As for the rest of the volunteers—and these seemed to be the majority—the institutional system did not know what to do with nor how to utilize them effectively. Thus, the roles in demand were scarce, and very few volunteers could fulfill roles perceived as relevant to the interruption.

Finally, we must note, and emphasize, that we found no pattern of relationship between previously examined routine activities (see chapter 3) and actual volunteering or attempts to volunteer during the period of social interruption. The two spheres of activities seem to be unrelated to each other. However, the major hypothesis about the relationship between the actor's location on the center-periphery continuum and his tendency to obtain a moratorium, perform his routine role, and activate new roles (i.e., volunteering) seems to be generally supported by the data. The greater centrality of various actors in the system thus played a double role: (1) the more central the location of an actor, the greater his predisposition to act in the framework of the interrupted system; and (2) because of the relative scarcity of roles relevant to the interruption, the more central an actor's location, the greater his access to such roles.

Notes

1. The data are based on an interview conducted with the person in charge of volunteering in the Manpower Branch of Hadassah Hospital, April 1975.
2. The data are based on an interview conducted with Zalman Chen, the spokesman of the Employment Service in the Ministry of Labor, May 1975.
3. An interview with Chava Yaari, the manager of the Volunteers' Bureau, April 1975.
4. N. Toren and P. Nigri, report of the Labor and Welfare Research Institute, Jerusalem, 15 October 1973.
5. Labor and Welfare Research Institute, *Activity in the Period of Emergency,* Summary of Discussion no. 2 (Jerusalem: Hebrew University, 13 October 1973). According to this report there was in fact a lack of services in Neve Yaacov (a "new immigrant" neighborhood).
6. D. Padan-Eisenstark, O. Horowitz, and I. Schelach, *Report on Service Bureaus in Kiriyat Moshe, Beit Hakerem, and Yeffe Nof* (Jerusalem: Labor and Welfare Research Institute, Hebrew University, 14 October 1973).
7. D. Padan-Eisenstark, D. Amir, A. Hertzberg, and Y. Levi, *Report of the Planning Staff of "Reserves Duty for Women" for the Civilian Labor Force* (Jerusalem: Labor and Welfare Research Institute, Hebrew University, November 1974).
8. Based on an interview with Ms. M. Yanovski, the Director of *Bank Leumi* Ltd., Jerusalem, April 1975.
9. The category of nonworking included those lacking a vocation, housewives, students who were not working, and pensioners. The category of manual workers included unskilled and skilled workers, small tradesmen, low- and intermediate-level clerks, and semi-professionals. The third category, the professionals, included professionals, top-level administrative workers, artists, etc.
10. This proportion is more or less equivalent to the proportion of respondents not working in the sample as a whole—35.9 percent.
11. It is very likely that the respondents understood the question as if it related to work on their regular job when they spoke of "work outside the home."
12. A. Griefel, *The Ramoth Eschkol and Shmuel Hanavi Area* (Jerusalem: Institute of Labor and Welfare Research, Hebrew University, 22 October 1973).
13. We wish to emphasize that we are dealing here with an analysis of the constraints and functional difficulties in volunteering. It is possible that our claim would be different if we examined the volunteering of families of recruited men in terms of the motivational or normative aspects. We have not done so, because we did not find an association between the recruitment of family members belonging to the household and volunteering. Thus, there is no justification for viewing this group as a separate sample.

14. An analysis of a case study illustrating the tensions between the paternalistic approach of the bureaucracy and its claims for volunteering may be found in B. Kimmerling, "The Israeli Civil Guard," in L.A. Zurcher and G. Harries-Jenkins (eds.), *Supplementary Military Forces, Reserves, Militias, Auxiliaries,* Sage Research Progress Series on War, Revolution and Peacekeeping (Beverly Hills and London: Sage, 1978), pp. 107–25.

PART TWO

5

The Routine: Cumulative Influences of the Conflict upon the Civilian System

The major aim of this study is to present and analyze a civilian social system in a war situation. This war is a unique one, in that it is but part of a continuing conflict and but one of the ways this conflict was expressed. Elsewhere (chapter 1) we defined this situation, in terminology borrowed from medicine or psychiatry, as the acute eruption of a chronic condition. However, to present the system as merely in its "acute stage" will be only partially correct, and may possibly present a distorted picture of the situation. In addition, there is no way to understand some of the phenomena of the social interruption without analyzing all the cumulative influences of the Jewish-Arab conflict upon Israeli society, where the interruptions represent a part of these accumulated influences. It is the aim of this chapter to present and to analyze the cumulative influences of this conflict upon the Israeli civilian social system.

However, we must immediately stress that the presentation and analysis that will appear in this chapter will to a large extent be speculative and fragmentary for two major reasons. The first is that to this time no comprehensive and full study has been undertaken as to the total influences of the conflict upon Israeli society. In reality, we are not aware of a single comprehensive study in the social sciences that examines the influence of a prolonged conflict upon any society. The second reason, which may be a partial explanation for the first, is that methodologically it was impossible to undertake a rigorous study of such a subject, for it is almost impossible to isolate the influence of the variables related to the conflict from the influence of other variables that are not related to or do not stem from the conflict. In other words, the fact that we do not have a control society (i.e., a society identical to Israeli society but without an external conflict) poses a problem in analyzing the situation presented here.

Nevertheless, as we will show in this chapter, we do have some of the parts of this exciting puzzle. We will attempt to find other parts by means of various hypotheses, or will leave these to the reader's imagination. In any event, the additional aim of this chapter will be to raise a series of further questions for future studies that should be undertaken in this area

A Cost-Benefit Analysis of the Conflict

It appears that the major salient characteristic of the Israeli civilian social system is not necessarily the fact that it is a society involved in an extended conflict with its surroundings, but that it is an immigration society in which, during the course of a very limited period of time,[1] immigrants from developed and extremely developed countries (Eastern Europe, Western Europe, and the American continent) met immigrants from developing countries (in Asia and Africa) upon a common religio-traditional basis.[2] The differences in country of origin became relatively quite pronounced in Israeli society, where at least to a certain extent they became part of the stratificational structure and where the societal occupational division was to some degree based on country of origin,[3] and thereafter on a national basis.[4] It follows from this that in terms of Israel's central aims—which include a wide range of social goals relating to welfare (such as education, health, etc.)—the Israeli society has an additional goal to the one dealing with the Jewish-Arab conflict[5] and which can compete with it. This goal of "the integration of the different exiles," or of decreasing the social gap and conflicts (both in terms of the allocation of resources and of eliminating them on the conscious level), has been defined repeatedly in negative terms. In other words, it deals with the problem of the internal conflict (as opposed to and/or together with the external conflict), which has threatened to unravel, or at least cause great damage, to the Israeli society. These two major goals are sometimes regarded as being in a zero-sum situation in regard to one another (primarily when there are debates about the allocation of the society's material resources), and sometimes as complementing one another—primarily in the area of their successful management. This complementarity between the two goals is understood to go both ways: in order to deal with the external conflict successfully, there is a need to solve, or at least to limit or to localize the internal conflict. The reverse direction is not agreed upon, neither in regard to the existence of a causal relationship nor as to its nature: there is an attitude that in order to arrive at a solution to the internal Israeli problems, there is a need to allocate financial and manpower resources, which are not in a condition of contending with the extended conflict (we may remember Dayan's comment that it is impossible to carry two bans at the same time; see chapter 1), therefore a radical solution of the social problems in Israel is dependent on a solution (or at least a great deescalation) of the Jewish-Arab conflict.[6] An opposite position—which is supported by parts of sociological theory—is that the external conflict has a "positive function" internally, for as long as the external conflict exists it is likely to prevent a marked escalation in the internal conflict.[7] Incidentally, these possibilities of causal relationships between the two central societal goals do not exclude one another, and during the course of our deliberations one should relate to each as a hypothesis that should be stated and examined.

The generalization of these hypotheses brings us to the question of the "costs and benefits," of the "price," of the conflict. Costs and benefits can be examined at the individual level and at that of the collectivity as a whole (as well as for specific subgroups within the collectivity). Profits and losses can be either objective or subjective—and here it is interesting to examine the discrepancy between the two, and what can be concluded from this discrepancy in different areas. It would appear that this is also a convenient framework for surveying, analyzing, and summarizing at least some of the cumulative influences upon the Israeli social system.

Individual Risks and Danger to the
Very Existence of the Collectivity

In any war, be it major or minor, there are casualties: the wounded and dead. From the time that the relationship between the Jews and Arabs in Palestine turned into one of a political conflict—at first one between two nationalisms, and later between the Arab states and the state of Israel—there were constantly casualties on both sides.[8] In this chapter, we will deal only with the period beginning with the war of 1947-48, which included the achievement of Jewish sovereignty over part of the territory of Palestine, and, of course, we will deal only with the Israeli side.

As can be ascertained from Table 5.1, the Jewish collectivity suffered mortal casualties, in differing proportions, throughout this time. The highest rate of casualties that the Jewish collectivity paid in a short period of time was the 1947-48 war, in which one percent of the population was killed—and here we do not distinguish between civilian and military

TABLE 5.1

Fatalities in Israel as a Result of the Jewish-Arab Conflict (Wars and Guerrilla Actions), by Periods and Percentage of the Total Jewish Population, 1947-1983

Wars and Periods	No. Killed (absolute)	Percentage of Population
1947-8 war	6,023	1.0000
From 1948-1956	1,176	0.0830 (*)
1956 war	177	0.0106
Between 1956-1967	795	0.0433 (*)
1967 war	893	0.0367
Between 1967-1973	738	0.0281 (*)
1973 war	2,636	0.0930
1982 war	550 (**)	0.0103
Total	12,988	0.6382 (*)

*Based on average population during those years.

**Through the end of 1983.

casualties. In the later wars, the percentage decreased markedly, to fractions of a percent, and the same was true between the wars, when there were only minor confrontations. In total, cumulatively and using the average of the total population during the years, Israel has suffered approximately 0.6 percent mortalities in both its military and civilian sectors combined, as a result of the conflict in all its forms. This is comparatively a very low percentage. In World War I, France lost 7.7 percent of its population between 1914 and 1918 (3.4 percent military casualties), while Germany lost 5 percent of its population (3 percent military). In World War II, the Soviet Union lost about 10 percent of its population, and the same was true for Yugoslavia. Germany lost 7 percent, and Poland (even disregarding the Jews who were killed as a result of the Nazi genocide) lost 5 percent (including the Jews, this added up to 15 percent of its population). Great Britain lost 265,000 men of its military forces—these having been composed of members of all the countries of the British Empire (as compared to 3 million German military personnel), as well as approximately 63,000 civilians on the British Isles. The latter represented a relatively low percentage (in spite of the repeated bombings of Great Britain). Both in absolute and in relative terms, the United States lost far fewer people, with its losses totalling about 250,000.[9]

However, it would appear that from our point of view, there is greater importance to the way the losses are perceived than to the absolute number or the percentage of losses. It would appear that Israelis regard the conflict as costly, both at the level of the collectivity and as a potential danger and threat to the individual. When, in 1978, we asked a sample of students regarding the degree of actual danger they might be in of being injured as a result of the conflict (both as soldiers and as civilians), we received very high percentages (see Table 5.2). The average subjective chance of being injured was 23.8 percent and the median was about 10 percent. When we compare this to the data in Table 5.1, the gap between the objective and the subjective probability can be seen to be extremely large.

It is very difficult to calculate the danger of any individual being injured in war. We know that (primarily in the wars up to and including 1967) the higher a person was on the socioeconomic scale, the more likely he was to be in one of the front-line units, and to be of a higher rank. And since there is a strong correlation between the degree of danger and one's role and rank, the more centrally a person was located in Israeli society (i.e., male, young, of Western ethnic origin, of higher educational level) the greater the danger of his being injured.[10] From this point of view, part of our sample population certainly had greater chances of being injured than did the average member in the population. However when we divided our sample population into those who had served and would serve in the army, as compared to those who had not and would not serve in it, or when we divided it into those who had served in front-line units (and who would in all likelihood serve in them again under war conditions), we did not find any significant differences in the individual's estimation of their degree of danger.

From this one can arrive at our first conclusion, which is that at the individual level the conflictual situation is perceived as most threatening by sizable parts of the population. One can attribute this phenomenon as a perception of one of the prices that one pays for belonging to the Israeli collectivity, a price that stems from the conflict. As opposed to this, when he relates to the perceived "objective situation," General Binyamin Peled (res.) claims:

> When we say that we are fighting all the time—how many consecutive days have we fought? Thirty years? A total lie! The days in which everyone was mobilized [i.e., social interruption]—that is war. All the rest have been quite normal days. . . . Do you believe that we sacrificed many losses?

TABLE 5.2
Subjective Evaluation of the Probability of Being Killed as a Result of the Israeli-Arab Conflict Compared to the Subjective Evaluation of Being Killed in a Car Accident (in percent)

Subjective evaluation of the probability	of being killed as the result of the conflict *	of being killed as the result of a traffic accident **
No danger	12.6	13.7
0.1-1	11.9	13.8
2-10	26.7	24.0
11-49	21.0	18.3
50	19.1	23.7
51-75	3.5	1.9
76-100	5.3	4.6
Total	100.0	100.0
n	262	262
mean	23.8	24.4
mode	50.0	50.0
median	10.04	10.03
variance	623.34	650.50

*The question was phrased as follows: "As you know, life is full of opportunities and dangers. We would like to ask you to evaluate and write down in percentage points (or fractions of a percentage point) the chances that the following will happen to you." The event here was defined as "your chances of being mortally wounded as a result of hostile acts stemming from the Israeli-Arab conflict, in the coming five years."

**The event here was described as "your chances of being killed in a car accident, in the coming five years."

Our sacrifices until now are not considered a considerable investment according to world criteria in struggles for much less serious goals.[11]

Table 5.2 is an indicator that a large number of Israelis do not share his opinion that the price of the conflict has been minimal.

However, it is worth our while not to exaggerate this finding, for, in that same table, in the following column, the respondents were asked to estimate their chances of being killed in a car accident. And here we find an almost identical distribution, with a slightly higher probability of being killed in a car accident.[12] At the same time, it is clear that the two events are not perceived as being equivalent in terms of their societal significance, or, as expressed by the head of the Bereaved Parents' Association, an organization of parents of sons who had fallen in war: "No person would dream of setting aside a day to remember those who had been killed in car accidents."[13]

However, it appears that a more significant and far-reaching cost than the danger to the individual is the danger to the very existence of the collectivity. As a result of the extended conflict, Israel is among the few nations in the world (together with Taiwan and South Africa) where there is (1) questioning of the very legitimation of its existence, and (2) a permanent and declared threat of physical destruction. Here we are not referring to threats to this or that internal regime, but to a threat of its very existence as a social and political entity with its own independent identity.[14] We thus asked our sample population what the chances are of the Arabs realizing their aims of destroying Israel in the foreseeable future (within 20 years) and at some time in the more distant future (see Table 5.3). This question was asked five years after the trauma of the 1973 war, but before the Egyptian peace initiative. It appears that as far as the foreseeable future is concerned, only 34 percent see this as totally impossible, while 39 percent see this as having a probability of between 0.1 to 10 percent, 7 percent see this as an even chance, and 4.6 percent see the chances as more than even. The average of our sample population here was close to a 13 percent chance of the nation being destroyed. In addition, our sample population believed that time was working on the side of the Arabs, and the chances of the nation being destroyed some time in the future averaged about 17 percent according to the responses given. When one compares the two evaluations (the near future and the distant future) one can see consistency within the "optimists" and the "pessimists." The optimists believe that time is working in favor of Israel, and that the probability of the state being destroyed will decline in the future, while the pessimists believe that as time passes, the chances of the collectivity being destroyed increase. There is no doubt that one must pay a heavy price to build one's life and family in a collectivity that one is not even sure will survive, even though one cannot be sure that people are conscious of this in their day-to-day life.[15] Another price, which is connected to the lack of confidence in the existence of the collectivity and its social structure, is the awareness of the problem of the legitimation of the existence of the collectivity.

The problem of legitimation, or the absence of the right of the Jews to maintain a political and social entity, which is perceived as coming at the expense of the parallel right of the Palestinian Arabs—two rights

TABLE 5.3
Subjective Evaluation of the Probability of the Arabs Being Able to Defeat Israel (in percent)

Subjective evaluation	In the coming twenty years (*)	In the distant (undefined) future (**)
No danger	34.4	29.4
0.1–10	38.8	34.3
11–49	14.9	19.5
50	7.3	8.4
51–75	1.5	3.8
76–100	3.1	4.6
Total	100.0	100.0
n	262	262
mean	12.8	17.0
mode	0.0	0.0
median	19.9	50.0
variance	440.42	576.20

*The event was defined as "the danger that within the coming twenty years the Arabs will vanquish Israel and will bring about the dismemberment of the State."

**The event was defined as the "danger that at some time the Arabs will vanquish Israel and will bring about the dismemberment of the State."

that both sides are accustomed to seeing as mutually exclusive—has been one that has accompanied the Zionist settlement in Palestine almost from the beginning, and especially from the time that it became a political conflict between two national movements, starting with the British Mandate in Palestine.[16] This conflict did not always remain at the same level of intensity, nor did it include all the strata of the population, but the problem of the right of the collectivity to exist was a built-in existentialist problem within the system, and the latter had to create mechanisms to provide answers to the problem of "the right to the land." One can mention many such mechanisms (beginning with the

Hebrew-Zionist terminology and going through collective symbols and the use of both the distant and recent history, and especially using the concept of the Holocaust as a symbol of legitimation),[17] but it appears that the most important and salient mechanism that linked "the nation" to "the land" was the Jewish religion. The place of the Jewish religion, the religious symbols, and the agreements that stemmed from the demands and the political strength of the religious sector in a basically modern and secular state can only be explained in terms of the contribution of the religious symbols to the feeling of "the right to the land." This is in accordance with a statement made by a minister of religions (Zerah Warhaftig) in the 1960s: "You [the secularists] will see to it that we live in this country according to our way, and we [the religious] will offer you the charter to the Land of Israel." It appears that the more severe the problem of legitimation has become (primarily since the 1967 war, where Israel assumed the control of the Arabs of the West Bank of Jordan), both as an external-political problem (where some of the countries refuse to recognize Israel and some have broken off diplomatic relations with it)[18] and as an existential-internal problem, the more the entire system has tended to gather about and fall back on religious symbols. As a result, there is an ever greater tendency to solve the tension between Israel's universalistic values and its particularistic ones by falling back on the latter.

It is already worth noting here that in regard to the problem of the internal legitimation, one should differentiate between the immediate effects of the wars and the effects of the Israeli-Arab conflict in its broad context (moral, political, and psychological). Conditions of actual warfare do not arouse doubts as to the right of the collectivity to exist. On the contrary, when one's physical existence is seen as being threatened immediately, the existential problems also enjoy a moratorium and the cohesion of the system increases. However, when the salience of the conflict in its broad context is great, the question of legitimation becomes all the greater. This is the explanation we gave when we found a significant and large positive link between the salience of the conflict over the years and the number of suicides in Israel (see Table 5.4).

The problem of legitimation is to a large extent similar to anomie, or may even be classed as a type of anomie, and therefore it is not at all surprising that the classic indicator of anomie[19] is linked to it. We also found a correlation between the number of suicides and various indicators of variations in the number of cases of mental illness discovered in Israel.[20] However, when one only takes the component of the use of force in the conflict, the link evaporates. It is most interesting to note that when the initiators of the use of force are Arabs, there is no significant

TABLE 5.4

Correlation Coefficients between the General Salience Index of the Jewish-
Arab Conflict and the Salience of Use of Forces, by Identity of the Initiator
and Suicide Rates in Israel, 1949-1966

	General Salience Index	Use of Force Initiated by	
		Arabs	Israelis
Total Suicides	.558*	.049	.372
Suicides -- male	.448*	.136	.250
Suicides -- female	.406*	.306	.400

*Level of Significance p < .05.

Source: Baruch Kimmerling, "Anomie and Integration in Israeli Society and the Salience
of the Arab-Israeli Conflict," *Studies in Comparative International Development* 9
(1974): pp. 75, 76.

correlation between the conflict and the number of suicides. On the other
hand, when the initiators are primarily Israelis, there is a tendency for
a drastic increase in the correlation (even if there are no significant links;
see Table 5.4). A certain type of anomie, a lack of physical security, and
uncertainty as to the continued existence of the collectivity and, as a
result, the "social and cosmic order," are some of the salient prices that
individuals pay for belonging to the Israeli society—a society involved
in an extended conflict. But exposure to all these subjective costs is
differential, and we suppose that the more the individual is located in
a central position, the more exposed he is to these "prices." On the
other hand, the patterns of reaction also change in accordance with one's
location. For example, at the end of July 1981, Palestinian forces shelled
areas in northern Israel and the civilian population was exposed to
artillery shelling and missiles (the Katyushas) for a number of days.

The differences in behavior among various segments of the population
was extremely salient. While the established population (of the northern
settlements), primarily those living in urban areas and who stemmed
from Europe, as well as the members of the kibbutzim (primarily born
in Israel, but descended from European parents) remained in their own
places and attempted to continue with their regular patterns of work to
the best of their abilities, a sizable proportion of the population of the
development towns (which are composed primarily of people from Asia
and Africa or their descendants) abandoned the area. The local leadership

collapsed and the local services were almost totally paralyzed. The army was forced to intervene and to supply those who remained behind with essential services, and even to try to sustain the morale of those remaining. A team of psychologists, brought in from outside the region, dealt with the population even after the shelling had stopped and after most of the population had returned.[21] This was a new phenomenon for the Israeli society, and the team that submitted a report to the local authorities attributed the collapse of the civilian system primarily to the absence of shelters and of security awareness, or, in other words, that the people were not aware of, and were not prepared for, what must be done in such circumstances.[22] In June, 1982, when the area was again exposed to Palestinian artillery (in the first stage of the 1982 war), the phenomenon of leaving the area was not observed. But this time the physical (shelters) and moral preparedness were better. This case study possibly indicates that the reaction of the population at large to a situation of direct impact is a combination of its location in the system and its physical and moral preparedness.

Another price that the individual (and the entire collectivity as well) must pay as a result of the conflict is the total amount of time that the individual must "waste" in military service. In Israel there is compulsory military service for all those young men who are capable of it (physically, mentally, and socially) and for most young women (even though women may be exempted for religious reasons).[23] The males must serve for three years, and thereafter they must serve in the reserves until the age of 39, for up to 40 days yearly. Thereafter, until the age of 55 they must serve for shorter periods of time. In the event of war the minister of defense can extend the service to whatever extent is deemed necessary. In any event, the length of the service and, to a large extent, the difficulty and the dangers involved in it depend on the rank of the individual and on his functional importance in the armed forces. Since both of these are normally in direct correlation with the location of the individual in the system (i.e., the more central he is, the higher his rank and the more essential the roles he fills), the social equation is that, in general, the more centrally located an individual is, the higher the price he pays as a result of the conflict. Young women only serve two years, and they are called up for reserve duty only on a selective basis and less frequently (again in accordance with the functionality of their skills) until they have their first child.

The cost invested is not only measured by the amount of time spent in military service, but also by its quality—the young Israeli is normally forced to serve between the ages of 18 and 21, which is a vital time in the formulation of his personality and career. Whereas most young men of the Western world complete their undergraduate work during this time, the Israeli is only released from the army by that time. But for many young men, as for the entire collectivity, there are also gains from this military service. Thus, those of the underprivileged strata can acquire an education and some of them will acquire a technical skill that will help them later in their civilian life. At one time the army was regarded as the tool for integrating the immigrants from different countries,[24] but data that were recently obtained by us deny this to a certain extent, even though the army still does serve as a *rite de passage* for acceptance into the Israeli society.[25]

And if service in the military forces is a type of endorsement of their acceptance in the Israeli society, and if in this immigrant society the symbolic differentiation between the "old timer" and the "immigrant" is not the number of years that the person has been living in the country, but whether he has lived in the country during a war or not, then for all the other members of the population, participation in the armed forces (a task that was already defined in the first chapter as a central goal in this society) grants a feeling of intense participation in the society. The participation is not only at the level of the individual but also at the level of the family, when the entire family, whose representatives serve in the armed forces, feels itself as contributing to and participating in the central goal; a feeling that no doubt offers a certain amount of compensation for the risks and inconveniences involved in the duty to serve. In this case, the link between the external conflict and social phenomena is made by the mediation of the military.

In general, Israeli society is defined and regarded as a "highly involved community."[26] The intensive involvement of different strata is not only a result of the external conflict, but also of the fact that it is a product of the Zionist movement, which is almost like a permanent revolution,[27] meaning that at least in part this is an immigrant society. In other words, immigrants not only came to solve their own individual problems but also wished to solve the collectivity's problems. Another factor that influenced the great involvement of many strata in the political processes was the trauma of the Holocaust of the Jewish people, and the feeling that such a Holocaust might happen in Israel as well (see Table 5.3). The small population of the collectivity also has a great deal of influence both upon the feeling of participation and upon the intensity of this participation. However, this participation is not only "functional." Political arguments and debates sometimes assume proportions above and beyond their real importance, and various old debates and causes célèbres are stirred up from time to time, with great vigor.[28]

The Conflict and Social Integration

This also explains the intensity with which internal social struggles can occur in Israel: between those of Asian-African descent and the establishment, which is regarded as being dominated by those of European and American descent; between the religious and the secular elements; between those with a moderate view and those with a radical view on the Jewish-Arab conflict; between Israeli-Arabs and Jews; and so on. We have already hinted above that there are certain indicators that show that the external pressure unifies and moderates the internal social conflicts in Israeli society.[29] Others have found that the intercommunity tensions and conflicts between the religious and nonreligious decrease as the external conflict becomes more intensive.[30] Frequently, but not always when the salience of the external conflict is high, in terms of the military dimension the internal dissension regarding the policies on the territories occupied by Israel in 1967 decreases.[31]

Yohanan Peres claims that the unifying effects of Israeli-Arab conflict upon the internal groups in Israel are composed of three components: (1) interdependence of fate, as a national loss is perceived as a loss to all (Jewish) Israeli ethnic groups (Peres dealt only with ethnic groups, but seemingly the same generalization is applicable to other groups in this society); (2) a common goal, since cooperation is perceived as necessary for survival; and (3) an outlet for aggression, as antagonistic impulses have a legitimate target.[32]

There are those who, as a result of this correlation between the external pressure and the degree to which internal conflicts erupt, whether explicitly or implicitly, wish to claim that Israel's foreign and military policy (which is regarded as sometimes being aggressive and uncompromising) manipulates the external conflict for its internal needs.[33] But here one should differentiate between two areas: (1) the internal problems that stem directly from the Israeli-Arab conflict, and (2) those whose focus is not the conflict (e.g., intercommunity tension, tensions between the religious and non-religious, labor disputes, etc.). We have no evidence of any single concrete example of the latter that can be shown unequivocally to corroborate this hypothesis.[34] However, there is no doubt that in regard to those internal problems that stem from the conflict and the way it is handled (where this is a cause of disagreement in Israeli society), there have been sizable parts of the Israeli government that have been influenced by public opinion, or by what was seen as "functional" under the conditions of the conflict. Thus, for example, Aharonson and Horowitz investigated the retaliation policy of Israel between 1951 to 1969, by analyzing the retaliatory actions taken by Israel during that period.[35]

These actions came about because of the minor skirmishes in which irregular forces of the Arab states and the Palestinians engaged in against Israel, and for both sides these were substitutes for all-out war. The authors arrived at a number of conclusions, four of which affect our discussion: (1) retaliatory actions were taken to answer the internal needs of the civilian and military morale, because it could not be imagined that Israel would allow attacks on its civilian population to take place with impunity; (2) these actions supplied the needs of a social consensus, without having to embark on a full-scale war (thus here the retaliation served the needs of the moderates); (3) these actions served to protect the political elite from public criticism for being ineffective and weak; and (4) provided a tool in the internal struggles for political positions (primarily between the Ministry for Foreign Affairs and the Ministry of Defense in the 1950s). The authors claimed that these were "latent functions" (based on Merton's definition),[36] as opposed to conscious, systematic, and cynical use of the conflict for internal political use. However this matter has remained a source of disagreement, and, as mentioned (see note 34), the term "securitism" (i.e., the abuse of the symbol of national security) became common among the public. However, since the governments knew they were accused of "securitism," we have the impression that in most cases they refrained from the direct use of the conflict for internal manipulistic needs. (But from time to time the suspicion of the public arose. In June-July 1982, Defense Minister Ariel Sharon was suspected of attempting to make political capital—for the future struggle over the prime minister's position—as one of the reasons for the outbreak of the 1982 war. As a result of the 1982 war and the partially interrupted social system, additional distinction appeared in the public opinion, between wars engaged in for immediate defense and for the ensurance of the survival of the collectivity, and wars for the improvement of the political and military position of Israel. An intense controversy arose in the system around two questions: [1] Was the 1982 war strictly necessary to the very existence of the collectivity, and even if not [2] may a polity based on a "nation-in-arms" military system, composed mainly of reserve forces, manage a war for considerable political benefits, but which is not strictly necessary for the collectivity's survival?)

Both perceptually and substantively, there is a direct link here to our basic contention as to the interrupted system: the common assumption is that, in general, in order to recruit the entire public for dealing with problems that arise as a result of the external conflict, there is need to recruit them solely in terms of this aim, and not for any other political or social aim, whether this other aim is desirable or not among different elements of the public. The borders between what is "security" and what is "not security," or between military and civilian, are very clear in many areas, but they are very poorly defined in a number of other areas (and we will discuss this below). And, finally, a few words on the reasons why the conflict should be an agent for social integration. Sociological theory does not offer an unequivocal answer as to whether an external conflict decreases or increases internal solidarity. But Coser and Simmel[37] recognize that a conflict with some external group can make a system disintegrate, and not necessarily unify it. What then is the best predictor? The answer, as usual, is "it depends."

The question whether the external conflict will harm the social system, will disintegrate it, or, on the contrary, will solidify it and increase its efficiency and creativity in different areas, depends on a number of factors or preconditions. Sorokin[38] was already aware of this when he attempted to ascertain the internal results of wars between nations. Kriesberg[39] surveys these reasons, and we are of the opinion that the most important factors for our study, as factors that determine the way the conflict will affect the society in question, are (1) The degree of prior or basic cohesion in the system. Or, in any event, if the system is one with a low degree of solidarity and is split by fierce internal conflicts, then external pressure (all other factors being equal) will act toward fostering disintegration. (2) The degree to which the management of the conflict or war is seen by the majority of the members of the collective as being "just." One of the differences that Coser lists between the reactions of the American public to the Second World War, as opposed to the Vietnam War, is the degree of difference in the feelings of "the justice of the cause." (3) The degree to which the conflict is managed in a "successful" or efficient manner. A system that is able to act efficiently (or "to win") or is perceived as being efficient by its members in dealing with an external conflict, will find that the conflict will be a unifying factor rather than one leading to disintegration. (4) The balance of the cost-benefit equation as a result of the conflict cannot tip too much in the direction of loss. If the price that the system has to pay is perceived (subjectively) as being much greater than the "profits" that the system is gaining from the conflict, then the conflict will be more likely to bring about disintegration. This last point is somewhat problematic, since, at least in our case, it contains a partial tautology—for integration itself is seen as a profit and disintegration as a loss. But these are definitely not the profits and losses that we are dealing with here.

As to the basic cohesion, or that which preceded the conflict, in our case it is very difficult to determine these matters unequivocally. On the one hand, the conflict with the Arab environment has accompanied the Jewish system at differential levels almost from the outset, so that the conflict has become a part of world order or of "nature." On the other hand, the Israeli society has no shortage of internal conflicts and tensions, as pointed out above. "The justice of the cause" is also a very complicated question. We have already pointed out here briefly, and elsewhere at length,[40] that the very conflict and its form have resulted in a permanent problem of doubts as to the "right" of the Jews to the land, as opposed to the "right" of the Arabs. However, these problems of legitimation have been dealt with and have been answered both on the moral and philosophical level and on the institutional level, even though they were never eliminated. Together with the problem of legitimation, the conflict and the Zionist enterprise have been accompanied throughout with a feeling of "there's no alternative" (both in terms of the fate of the Jews in the Diaspora throughout 2,000 years of persecution and in terms of the Arab opposition—two factors that have often been linked together). It appears that the problem of legitimation and the feeling that "there is no alternative" cancel one another out. This whole question was weakened after 1967, from which time Israel began regarding itself as a "military power," at least on the regional level, and, at the same time, assumed control of a substantial Arab population. The questions of the conflict had already been a source of contention previously, between the "hardliners," who even sometimes advocated territorial expansion, and the "softliners" and liberals,[41] with this argument intensifying greatly after the 1967 war. In addition, as we have already shown above, the other major foci of the central conflicts were also aroused that this time, just as they were also intensified somewhat after the peace treaty with Egypt.

Almost without a doubt, the Jewish-Arab conflict was conducted, in Israeli eyes, generally in a most successful military (not political) manner. The opening stages of the 1973 war did indeed cause a certain trauma, but it is difficult to judge the degree to which it was influential, because the war ended in victory for Israel. From this point of view, it appears that the influence of conflict upon the country's cohesion was a direct one, except for the 1982 war, which raised questions about its "justness" and deeply divided the country. The fourth point, which deals with the cost-benefit balance of the conflict, is in fact the central motif of this chapter, so it will be better for us to leave discussion about this until the end of the chapter.

The Financial Burden

In 1948 the British Mandatory regime was transferred to the Provisional Council of the sovereign State of Israel. One of the first pieces of legislation adopted was increasing the tax rate by 100 percent for those of the middle and lower income groups. This increase was explained as stemming from the needs of pursuing the war and furthering the general social aims that the new state set for itself. While the Mandatory regime had had only minimal ambitions as to supplying services to its citizens, the new state saw itself as marching toward the construction of a welfare state, which would at the same time have to absorb new immigrants. At the same time, it was promised that once the emergency situation would pass, there would be a revision, and that taxes would be decreased.[42] Since then, the emergency has not been terminated, and thus Harold Wilkenfeld could claim that "for years the average Israeli taxpayer has been among the most heavily taxed in the world, and since 1970, he may have achieved the dubious distinction of being the most heavily taxed."[43]

And, indeed, when Israel is compared to other developed countries and when one calculates the direct and indirect taxes as a percentage of the gross domestic product, one finds that Israel is in the highest group in the collection of those indirect taxes (see Table 5.5).[44] However, even when the major component of direct taxation—income tax—is taken into consideration, one finds that the tax rate for even those with a middle income is extremely high, and amounts to 35-50 percent. Where the Israeli paid a marginal income tax rate of 45 percent, the Briton paid 33 percent; the West German, 22 percent; and the American, 18 percent. Similarly, where the Israeli paid a marginal rate of 50 percent, the British rate was 33 percent; the West German, 25 percent; and the United States, 20 percent. Finally, where the Israeli paid at a 60 percent rate, the figures for Great Britain, West Germany, and the United States were, respectively, 60 percent, 37 percent, and 24 percent.[45] All of these calculations refer to the gross taxation calculations;[46] it is very difficult to determine the net taxes. While Israel is a relatively moderate welfare state (compared, for example, to Great Britain or the Scandinavian countries), it is basically a "giving" country, with all types of benefits whose real values are very difficult to assess (e.g., heavily subsidized basic foodstuffs, transportation, and fuel; and parcelled out state lands and properties—for long periods of time extending over decades).[47] The Israeli economic system is characterized by the fact that throughout it has had an infusion of capital into the system, with this capital passing

TABLE 5.5
International Comparison of the Tax Burden as a Percentage of the Gross Domestic Product, 1972[a]

		Product	Taxes as Percentage of GDP		
		per capita	Total	Direct[c]	Indirect[d]
No.	State	in dollars[b]			
1	Norway	3,889	46.5	27.8	18.7
2	Denmark	4,170	43.9	26.2	10.7
3	Sweden	5,157	43.7	29.2	14.5
4	Holland	3,437	43.1	30.8	12.3
5	Germany	4,218	37.2	23.2	14.0
6	Austria	2,747	37.0	20.8	16.2
7	Israel	2,279	36.3	16.1	20.2
8	Belgium	3,664	35.5	23.4	12.1
9	France	3,823	34.4	19.3	15.1
10	Gt. Britain	2,742	34.4	19.6	14.8
11	Canada	4,805	32.7	17.9	14.8
12	Italy	2,164	31.6	19.3	12.3
13	Ireland	1,834	31.1	11.7	19.5
14	USA	5,551	29.4	19.7	9.7
15	Chile	649	27.5	14.8	12.7
16	Australia	3,769	25.1	13.9	11.2
17	Greece	1,374	24.4	10.2	14.2
18	Spain	1,340	22.0	12.8	9.2
19	Portugal	989	21.7	10.7	11.0
20	Japan	2,797	20.5	13.2	7.3
21	S. Africa	843	19.4	11.0	8.4
22	Rhodesia	311	16.2	8.1	8.0

a. Arranged in descending order by taxes as a percentage of GDP
b. At the official exchange rate
c. Direct taxes include: taxes on corporate profits, income taxes, taxes on non-profit organizations including payments for social security, taxes on accumulated worth, inheritance tax
d. Indirect taxes include: purchase tax, inventory tax, value-added tax, customs duties, stamp tax, fees, property tax, local authority taxes

Source: State of Israel, *Report for Fiscal Years 1971–1974* (Jerusalem, Ministry of Finance, 1976), p. 6.

through many institutional filters to various individuals and groups, even though this was done in a differential manner.[48] One should not, therefore, be overimpressed with the gross taxes paid by Israelis, and should remember that the taxpayer receives very many goods and services in return, even though these do not appear as official receipts of funds. Some of these distributions, as we will prove below, are related either directly or indirectly to the Israeli-Arab conflict.

At the same time—because of the high direct taxes, because of a lack of awareness of the differentiation between net and gross taxes, and above all because of the open statements of the political center—the tax

TABLE 5.6

Military Expenditures of Selected Countries, by Manpower and Financial
Resources, 1976–77*

Country	Manpower in the Military (for each 1,000 inhabitants)	Military Expenditure per capita (in 1976 $)	Military Expenditure as percent of the GNP
England	5.91	195	4.9
USA	9.49	432	5.4
West Germany	8.00	251	3.5
Netherlands	8.00	224	3.5
Norway	9.7	230.50	3.2
France	10.3	258	3.9
Sweden	8.2	289	3.3
Israel	49.8	831	30.7

*Annual average.

Source: United States Arms Control and Disarmament Agency, *World Military Expenditure
and Arms Transfers, 1968–1977* (Washington, D.C., 1979).

burden in Israel is perceived as being very high, and this high level of
taxation is justified at least partially in terms of the needs engendered
by the Israeli-Arab conflict. This is the cost for the individual.

What is the cost for the entire system? This too is a complicated
question, one that is very difficult to answer unequivocally. By taking a
glance at Table 5.6, one can see that Israel stands at the top of the list
of developed countries on three scales of expenses for national security:
defense expenditures as a percentage of the gross national product (Israel
with 31 percent compared to the United States in second place with 5.4
percent), defense expenditures per capita (Israel $831 and the United
States slightly more than half this figure), and the number of individuals
employed by the armed forces and in national defense jobs (almost 50
persons per 1,000 inhabitants in Israel, compared to about 10 in the
United States and slightly more than 10 in France).

The burden that is seen here from the table is dramatic, and the
immediate question aroused is how any system can sustain such a burden,
and yet allocate funds for other social needs without collapsing upon
itself. The answer is found in Tables 5.7 and 5.8, which dissect the

TABLE 5.7
Allocation of Economic Resources

Percent of GNP (annual average)	1954-55	1957-61	1963-64*	1968-72	1971-72	1974-48	Change in percentage points 1954-55 to 1957-61	1963-64 to 1968-72	1971-71 to 1974-78
Private consumption	74.6	71.1	69.9	61.6	57.6	63.0	-3.5	-8.0	5.4
Civilian public consumption	11.8	10.9	10.4	10.8	10.5	11.6	-0.9	0.4	1.1
Defense expenditure	7.0	8.5	10.0	21.6	22.0	29.7	1.5	11.6	7.5
Investment	31.2	29.0	32.0	28.9	32.5	29.0	-2.2	-3.1	-3.5
Import surplus	24.6	19.5	22.0	22.9	22.8	33.0	-5.7	0.9	10.5

*1963–1964 is used for prewar to postwar comparison, because 1965 and 1966 were years of recession.

Source: Eitan Berglas, "The Indirect Costs of Defense Spending: The Israeli Experience." Conference paper on Defense and National Economy in the 1980s (Tel-Aviv University, Center for Strategic Studies, 14–17 December 1981). Reprinted with permission of the author.

TABLE 5.8
The Composition of Foreign Aid

	1964-66	1967	1968-72	1973	1974-80
	($ million, annual averages)				
Defense Expenditure					
Direct	108.1	285.5	436.6	1180.0	1419.0
Indirect	37.7	71.0	151.4	277.0	481.1
Foreign grants					
U.S. government grants					
Defense	-	-	-	820.0	616.4
Defense, including grant component of loans*	-	9.8	66.0	898.2	774.8
Civilian	28.8	13.8	10.0	50.4	417.6
Civilian, including grant component of loans*	28.8	23.6	76.0	327.4	1257.7
Institutional transfers including grant component**	114.3	357.0	273.8	817.0	477.4

*The grant component is an estimate of the implicit current value of the subsidy in subsidized loans.

**The grant component implied by the low interest rate on Israeli Bonds.

Source: Bank of Israel, *Annual Report 1979*, pp. 186-87 (Hebrew).

defense expenditures into the sources that finance them and the length of time over which these are to be paid. Table 5.7 shows that until 1964 the defense expenditures varied between 7 to 10 percent of the GNP, and never exceeded the total other public expenditures. Between 1968 and 1978 (1973?)—in other words, as a result of the 1967 war—there was a doubling of the national defense expenditure in terms of the percentage of the GNP (as the GNP also grew during this time, the absolute defense expenditures grew by even more). Table 5.8 shows that these expenses were still paid for by internal sources.[49] The next great leap took place as a result of the 1973 war, with defense expenditures reaching an average of 29 percent of the GNP for the years 1974-48 (30.7 of the GNP of 1976-77). However, already in 1973, 61.6 percent of these costs were financed by American grants and loans, while between

1974 and 1980 close to 41 percent was financed by American foreign aid. This aid represents a sizable portion of the growth, but does not represent any added financial burden for Israel.

Table 5.7 should convey a macro-economic idea of what internal goals suffered as a result of the burden of the defense costs. First, while it is true that Israel's foreign debt grew, this was due primarily to the growth in defense expenditures (had it not been for these import expenses, the debt in the second and third periods would evidently have been small). The civilian public expenditures (and we will still discuss these later) were not harmed in the last two periods (even though they did not grow a great deal in comparison with the GNP). Individual expenditures were curtailed greatly (when compared to the GNP—even though, in absolute terms, they generally did grow) in the first two periods, and the growth in the GNP was not enough to fuel a raise in the standard of living. However, what declined consistently over all three periods were investments in the economy. One may thus state that there were two central internal factors that bore the burden of the defense expenditures: the standard of living and the future growth of the economy.

However, the domestic defense needs were much greater than those envisioned in the national budget, for many of those costs that were the result of the conflict were included in other budget sections, and there are a number of very important economic factors that cannot be calculated and that one may not even be able to estimate. In addition to the three years of military service for all adults, which include about 7 percent of all one's productive time (which is generally 40-45 years), and which can be estimated as equivalent to about 5 percent from the GNP,[50] it is very difficult to estimate the cost of reserve army duty, and it is even harder to estimate the damage caused to the different manufacturing or service units as a result of people's absence at frequent intervals, and thus the neglect of routine functions.

In chapter 2 we described the emergency warehouses of the emergency economy, but we did not mention in that context that there are heavy prices to be paid in maintaining supplies and storing them for a lengthy period of time. There is an economic cost resulting from all those who are killed and who are no longer in the production cycle, and this is all the more true with the wounded: while it is true that some of the medical and rehabilitation costs (as well as the pensions of those injured in hostile acts) are listed in the budget of the Ministry of Defense, the cost of losing these people from the production cycle (either temporarily or permanently, in one measure or other of severity) cannot be calculated or quantified. Another example of a major expenditure that does not appear in the defense budget, and is paid in one fashion or other by the individual citizen, is the cost of building bomb shelters, which are required in Israel. One can estimate that this expenditure alone amounts to about 0.5 percent of the GNP.[51] Another example of a major expenditure that does not appear as a defense cost but which is nevertheless an expenditure stemming directly from the Israeli-Arab conflict, is the money expended on internal security, most of which is carried out by the police force (here we refer to dealing with what is called the Palestinian terror).

Berglas summarizes the value of the items related to national defense, even though they are classified for budgetary purposes under other rubrics or cannot be calculated at all, as follows: "Although it has not been possible to assign even rough orders of magnitude to most of these items, it emerges from such figures as I have been able to suggest that the missing amounts (unreported or not ascribed to defense) come to more than half of the reported expenditures in local currency."[52]

But the picture will not be complete if we fail to note that a number of components of the budget that do appear under the heading of "national security" are in fact civilian expenditures, and that some defense expenditures do indeed have a "positive" impact, in economic terms, upon the Israeli system. Thus, for example, the army is involved in both formal and nonformal educational programs.[53] To the credit of the military, thousands of soldiers who hail from the weaker strata, and whom the educational system has had difficulty reaching, receive basic educational skills (reading and writing, improving and enriching one's vocabulary, etc.). Similarly, and in addition, the army supplies a number of teachers, primarily in the development towns and in places where there is a shortage of teachers. However, more important than this, in terms of the army as an educational agent, is the thousands of soldiers who receive technical and administrative skills each year, beginning with the lowest ranks and extending to administrative experience at the highest levels. The fact that the borderline between what are listed as defense expenditures and what are not, and what actually is spent on defense and what on other areas, is so unclear, has wide-ranging political and social effects, which will be discussed below—but here we are only analyzing the economic influences.

However one of the economic influences for the long range of the wars and conflicts upon the Israeli system is the growth of a large and complex military industry, whose sophistication is constantly increasing. Based soley on official publications, Israel produces almost all types of weapons and ammunition (and might even have been able to produce more, had not a part of the U.S. aid been conditional on acquiring weapons from the American arms industry). At present, Israel produces items ranging from submachine guns and automatic rifles, which are known throughout the world (the Uzzi and the Galil), to tanks, various types of missiles, missile boats, and sophisticated fighter planes and bombers that can compete favorably with those produced by the super-powers. Much of this equipment is produced for the Israeli military, while some is exported. (Israel has two serious problems in exporting military equipment: [1] various components, such as certain aircraft engines, are imported from the United States, and their transfer to a third party is conditional upon American approval, which is not always forthcoming when an order might compete for a market with the American arms industry; and [2] because of Israel's foreign relations problems, there are many nations that might have been potential buyers but refrain from entering into any contracts due to fears of the Arab boycott and Arab political reactions. Some of these nations do purchase arms from Israel—but secretly.)

There are no exact figures regarding the extent of Israel's arms exports (because it is evidently impossible for Israel politically to publicize some of these contracts), but, for example, the *New York Times* (24 August 1981) estimates the extent of Israel's arms exports for the year 1980 as high as $1.3 billion, or about 0.5 percent of all arms transactions in the world. The major selling point of these arms—and this is the point emphasized in marketing them—is that they have been tested in battle. The speedy expansion of the military industry has had a number of far-reaching effects: the modernization and the introduction of new tech-nologies into Israeli industry, primarily in the field of electronics;[54] the allocation of funds for research and development; the establishment of a human infrastructure with a high degree of skills; and the introduction of the highest standards of quality in at least one segment of industrial production. In a very similar vein to the findings of Baran and Sweezy, who claimed that as expenditures on national defense rise in a capitalistic society the scope of the economy grows,[55] one can hypothesize that in Israel too there was such a link between these variables (while at the same time with the reservation which we already noted above that some of the increased expenditure on defense needs was not financed by local sources). Beginning with the year 1972, the Ministry of Defense began decreasing its orders from the local market—a fact that hurt those enterprises that did not find any alternate markets for their products, or which were not able to convert to the production of civilian products, both for local consumption and for export.[56]

The societal results of the growth of a large military industry were even more far-reaching than appears at first. This growth brought about the creation of a military-industrial complex,[57] which expressed itself primarily in a constantly increasing influence upon determining national priorities and upon the societal decision-making process.[58] One example, which caused a public debate in Israel, was the decision by Israel Aircraft Industries to invest a huge amount of money on an advanced fighter plane for the 1990s, without waiting for the go-ahead from the government. In his 1981 report, the state ombudsman criticized the very fact that money was invested without any authorization, with the government being presented with a fait accompli. The state ombudsman also asked the following questions that Aircraft Industries (which is a government enterprise) should have answered before investing in the project:

> Will the IAI [Israeli Aircraft Industries] be able to supply the Air Force with an airplane which will meet its future needs, when the economic and political alternatives in the world market have not been investigated? Does the state have the resources to finance a project of these dimensions? Does the investment financially and in terms of manpower [using some of the most skilled workers in the system] coincide with the economic, social, and political priorities of Israel? Will the orders of the Air Force and of the foreign customers be large enough to justify the costs of the investment in development?[59]

Similar or identical questions can be asked about most of the weapons systems developed in Israel, and the answers given will almost certainly be the ones given here; in other words, the development of weapons is not simply an economic question. In order for Israel to decrease its political dependence upon other countries (i.e., the United States), primarily in managing its own foreign and defense policy, there is a need to maximize Israel's ability to produce weapons systems. This consideration is one of those to be examined together with other economic and social considerations.[60] When the system operated under basic principles that give primacy to political considerations over economic ones, the concept of the economic "burden" upon the system (as opposed to the burden upon groups or individuals within it) lost its importance to a large extent.

In such conditions, with the combination of a system that is absorbing immigrants while at the same time carrying the burden of an external conflict, where this is partially financed by a continuous infusion of money from the outside, the economic considerations of whether any action is financially worthwhile or relevant lose their importance when weighed against comprehensive (internal and external) political considerations. The economic system loses its autonomy and is to a large extent controlled by extra-economic considerations. One cannot state that this is purely the influence of the conflict, but the conflict does have a marked influence upon it, both as a catalyst and as a direct factor.[61] The degree of autonomy of the economic sector has not been uniform and has increased and decreased at different times, but in general one can say that the rule that political considerations have primacy is correct.[62]

A Militaristic Society?

The fact that the political sphere predominates over the economic sphere brings us to a more comprehensive question: Has the extended conflict resulted in having the other social activities and processes also subservient to the political sphere, or, even more radically, has it become subservient to that group in the political system that manages the external conflict (those who are known as "managers of violence")—i.e., the armed forces, or the civilian and military elite whose main role is to manage the conflict? In a less sophisticated fashion, one can ask the question as to what extent Israel has developed as a totalitarian society, where militarism is classically characterized, in the definition of Vagts,[63] as a domination of the military man over the civilian, an undue preponderance of military demands, and an emphasis on military considerations, spirit, ideals, and scale of value, in the life of states. It has meant also the imposition of heavy burdens on a people for military purposes, to the neglect of welfare and culture, and waste of the nation's best manpower in unproductive army service.

A number of scholars have tried to deal with this problem, or with similar questions, where they have assumed a priori that there is such a problem in Israeli society, and then the question becomes whether Israeli society is a "garrison state"[64] or a "nation-in-arms."[65] Others have used the terminology of Luckham,[66] who investigated the degree of permeability of the boundaries between the military establishment and the political institutions. The permeability of the boundaries runs along a continuum on one pole of which the boundaries are "integral"; i.e., "the extent to which the interchange between persons holding roles at various levels of the military hierarchy and the environment are under the control of those with responsibility for setting the operational goals of the armed forces . . . boundaries are permeated to the extent to which there is a complete fusion both in respect of goals and of organization between the possessors of the means of violence and other social groups."[67]

The "fragmented" boundaries are an intermediate category between the integral and permeable poles. Luckham, following Ben Halpern,[68] locates the Israeli case on the integral pole. But recently, Lissak, after examining the whole spectrum of institutional linkages, concluded that "with the exception of a few cases . . . there are really no integral boundaries between the defense and the civilian sectors in Israel."[69]

Lissak came to this conclusion after he examined the unbelievably numerous functions of the institutionalized and the noninstitutionalized, the formal and the nonformal, between the military and defense establishment, and the other strata of the elite in Israel. These junctions occur mainly in the realms of politics, economics, education, culture, and mass communications; between professionals (economists, doctors, lawyers, psychologists, sociologists, etc., whose reserve duty includes work in their own field), as well as in the area of nonformal social relationships. These relationships stem primarily from the minuscule size of Israeli society, where "everyone knows everyone else," or where everyone studied with everyone else, and, of course, all serve together in the army, both in the regular army and in the reserves. However, at these junctions, which make the boundaries permeable, there is no unequivocally predominant force in determining the rules of the game, and there is definitely no clear-cut superiority of the defense sphere.

In any event, even in cases of cooperation, as in the case of competition and even in cases of conflict between the spheres, there is no guarantee whatsoever that the military and defense sphere will prevail, and, in many cases, it is the civilian norms that predominate over the defense and military spheres. Dan Horowitz, who primarily investigated and analyzed the political aspects, reached similar conclusions. In Israel there is a tendency "toward convergence of the military and civilian systems in terms of (a) organizational modes of operation (particularistic, non-authoritarian), (b) elite perception of international environment (*Realpolitik* and power-politics oriented), (c) dominant political culture (democratic-coalescent). Convergence . . . thus represented a limited and normatively restricted militarization of the civilian political institutions, and a partial civilization of the military institutions."[70]

The conditions that have resulted from the extended conflict in which Israeli society finds itself are much more complicated than those found in the classical definitions of militarism (e.g., Vagts' version), and, in reality, one must independently examine each area involved, as these too can change from one period to another—and the degree to which the civilian population is militarized or the military population is "civilized" can change from time to time. This can be deduced implicitly from the very concept of social interruption, as developed in this study. In reality, in spite of the claim that there is convergence between the military and the civilian values, Horowitz claims that there is an institutional compartmentalization between the two, or a lack of consistency in tendencies and processes, where the civic values continue to persist even under conditions of acute conflict. This is the way he sums up:

> The inconsistencies inherent in the Israeli response to this challenge [the preservation of the democratic system] led a former commander of the Israeli air force to label Israel as a "schizophrenic" society . . . [but] at least as far as civilian-military relations are concerned, this "schizophrenia" has been instrumental to the ordinary functioning of Israeli society as a stable multiparty democracy.[71]

Horowitz thus speaks of a differentiation in the institutional and mental spheres, which to a certain extent preserve the Israeli society from phenomena of militarism or of a garrison state, while the concept of the interrupted system, as presented in this volume, speaks of the ability of differentiation in the dimension of time—between the times of social interruption and routine times as a built-in mechanism that permits activity which is to a large degree freed of the symptoms of a society that is in acute conflict, even when this is the objective reality. These two views are not mutually exclusive but are to a certain extent complementary.

By most criteria and in spite of a protracted conflict and the absence of any democratic tradition of its founders, Israel is recognized as a democratic society. However, immediately after making this statement, two serious problems arise regarding the question of defining the limits of the system. Israel is a democratic country in terms of the Jewish majority within the country, but the degree to which it is open and flexible is different in regard to its Arab citizens,[72] and all the more so for those who live in territories occupied by Israel since 1967. Until 1965, Israel maintained a military government, which was in effect for almost all its Arab citizens. By means of this and by expropriation of lands and by formal and informal means barring Arab citizens from attaining certain positions within the society, (1) the state infringed upon the civil rights of its Arab citizens, and (2) discriminated between its Jewish and Arab citizens.[73] This discrimination was not only a product of the majority-minority relationship, which is common in many societies, but stemmed to a large extent from a certain conception of the Israeli-Arab conflict—the Israeli system was not able to free itself from a number of codes and rules of the game that had been formulated in the period of the confrontation between the two communities during the Mandatory period, and which continued to relate to its Arab citizens as a potential threat, primarily in terms of control of the land resources.[74]

The problem becomes more severe when we come to the population in the territories occupied in 1967, which were not annexed to Israel, although they were almost completely integrated into it economically.[75] In addition, these areas have been marked by a considerable degree of Jewish settlement.[76] Thus, a condition was created where more than a million people have been living for over 15 years under Israeli military occupation. It is the nature of things that this population is denied, at least partially, some of those rights that are accepted in Israel, and this is true even when one compares the rights granted this population to those granted to Israeli Arabs. One interesting fact mitigates this situation somewhat: the government of Israel decided to permit the inhabitants of these territories to have access to Israeli law courts, including the Supreme Court, and to receive the protection of the courts when faced with administrative arbitrariness. This is an unprecedented situation in terms of international practice, and the Supreme Court, sitting as the high court of justice, has struggled with the question of what degree of authority it has over these occupied territories. The Supreme Court finally decided that beyond the mere question of international law, one cannot in humanitarian terms simply abandon the population to the arbitrary whims of the military government, and the court assumed for itself the right to intervene.[77] But the presence of the Israeli courts has only somewhat alleviated the conditions prevailing in the military government—primarily at times of tension and a political struggle between the local population and Israel.[78] The sociological and political analyses in Israel (as opposed to a number of works published outside Israel)[79] have tended to exclude the inhabitants of these territories from any analyses of the Israeli system, because (1) they are not formally part of Israel, and (2) the latent assumption has been that the occupation and the retention of the vast majority of the territory and population is merely a temporary stage. The question, however, is whether, after holding onto the territories and their inhabitants for 15 years, one can still see in this a phenomenon that is "beyond the limits of the Israeli system." Answering this question either way is likely to change drastically the analysis of Israeli society as a single-nationality society, with all the consequences that follow. However, even if one relates to Israel and the territories as two separate units, there are still many questions as to how long Israel can maintain two separate sets of the rules of the game, one for the country and one for the territories, and to what extent those norms formulated in the occupied territories will spill over into Israel.[80] In addition, the economic integration of the territories—with unskilled laborers streaming into Israel and Israeli products and money streaming into the territories—has changed to a noticeable extent the Israeli occupational structure, and has created a limited congruence between national origin and occupation. Even where there is no national conflict (e.g., where foreign workers are employed in Western Europe), such conditions are liable to cause social tensions and the potential for the outbreak of conflict, and this is all the more true in the circumstances prevalent in the Middle East. On the other hand, until this time the absorption of these workers of the territories into the Israeli economy has created—at least in a partial manner—an interest in coexistence while refraining from escalating the national and political differences. The macro-social profits and losses from the retention of the territories depends to a large extent on the different aspects that constitute this reality, and also, possibly, upon the values of the person analyzing them.

Immigration and Emigration as a Reflection of Cost-Benefit Balance

As stressed previously at the beginning of this chapter, Israel is not only an active immigration country, but it was also built and readied to serve as the home of some, or the majority (this question is still being argued), of the world's Jews. In fact, in abridged form, the Zionist ideology is to gather the Jews once again in their old country and to achieve a sovereign nation for them, so that they can be like all the nations of the world. Immigration to Israel is not merely an aim, but is also perceived as an indicator of the degree of the "correctness" of the solution proposed to the Jews by the Zionist movement, as opposed to the other alternatives.[81] The opposite process—the Jews leaving the country—has the same significance, but, of course, in reverse. Leaving the country is seen as infringing upon the proper order of society. This is an act that is unacceptable in terms of Zionist ideology, similar in its portent to leaving many of the communist countries behind the Iron Curtain. Here, though, there is added significance to such an act, stemming directly from the Jewish-Arab conflict: The human resource is regarded as one of the most important resources in the balance of power between the Jews and the Arabs in general, and between the Israelis (the Jews) and the Palestinians in particular. Each person who leaves the collectivity is regarded as weakening Israel (and, on the other hand, each entry is seen as strengthening it) and as engaging in a treacherous act. Such an action is also often defined as the personal weakness of the individual who leaves.

And yet there is emigration from the country, just as there is emigration from every other active immigrant country. The extent of this emigration is a major source of disagreement, primarily due to the fact that there are no criteria and effective tools for measuring it. The estimates that exist of Israelis who left the country from 1948 to 1979 vary from 250,000 to 500,000.[82] The low estimates regarding emigration (about 270,000) amount to 16 percent of the immigration,[83] but even if we add the highest estimates Israel still will not one of the leaders, when compared with other countries during periods of mass immigration (Table 5.9). But one cannot compare these figures exactly. Most of those who im-

TABLE 5.9
Percentage of Emigrants of the Total Immigrants, Israel and Selected Countries

Country	Years	Percentage of Emigrants
Australia	1906-1924	70
Argentian	1857-1948	46
U.S.A.	1821-1924	34
Brazil	1872-1940	26
Israel	1948-1979	16-30

Sources: United Nations, *Demographic Yearbook 1977: International Migration Statistics* (New York, 1978); M.R. Davie, *World Migration: With Special Reference to the United States* (New York: Macmillan, 1946); G. Beijer, "Modern Patterns of International Migratory Movements," in J.E. Jackson (ed.), *Migration* (Cambridge: Cambridge University Press, 1969), pp. 11–59; B. Thomas, *Migration and Economic Growth* (Cambridge: Cambridge University Press, 1954); Etan Sabatello, "Emigration from the Country and Its Characteristics," *Bitfutzot Hagola* (Summer, 1978), pp. 63–76; *Ha'aretz,* 17 October 1975.

migrated to Israel came from countries where there was no possibility for Jews to "return to the homeland," or where return to the homeland would involve far greater difficulties than, for example, an Italian returning to Italy, a Pole to Poland, etc. The more likely opportunity available to these Jews was integration into a third country, primarily North or South America. Taking into account these facts and the fact that emigrants are castigated, in terms of Zionist ideology even an immigration rate of 16 percent, where only some of those leaving were new immigrants while others had been in the country for years or had even been born there, is a major problem. How much is the conflict and the burden that it has imposed upon the Israeli population responsible for emigration? In a survey conducted in 1974, 19 percent of the Jewish population of Israel claimed that they had either little or no desire to stay in Israel.[84] When asked why they wished to leave, they classified their reasons as follows: (1) the heavy taxation (31 percent); (2) the low standard of living (28 percent); (3) the bureaucratic problems involved in living in Israel (25 percent); (4) the political regime (22 percent); (5) the future of their children (21 percent); (6) the chances of better employment (20 percent); (7) military service (19 percent); (8) the social gap (18 percent); (9) working conditions (16 percent); and (10) physical security (12 percent).

TABLE 5.10
Israelis' Readiness to Leave the Country, 1973–1981 (in percent)[a]

Date of Survey	would very much like to	would like to	would somewhat like to	would not want to particularly	would not want to	would very much not want to	N
November 1973	1	2	2	4	29	61	668
March 1974	3	6	7	12	30	43	563
March 1975	4	4	6	6	32	47	543
July 1975	5	3	3	4	32	53	596
September 1976	2	4	4	5	31	54	1900
January 1977[b]	5	4	–	8	28	53	506
December 1977	5	3	2	5	39	46	573
March 1978	5	7	3	5	28	53	–
November 1978	5	5	3	4	28	55	–
December 1979	7	4	4	7	28	51	–
April 1980	7	3	4	8	18	59	–
November 1980	7	3	3	9	24	54	–
August 1981	5	5	4	7	21	58	592

a. Based on the question: "If you had the opportunity, would you prefer living [permanently] outside the State of Israel?"
b. The category "would like somewhat" was not included.

Source: Based on data supplied to the authors by the Israel Institute of Applied Social Research. Our sincere thanks are due to Louis Guttman and Shlomit Levi.

At first glance, the two factors that relate directly to the conflict (military service and physical security) are marginal in terms of the desire to leave. However, there are other factors (such as the tax burden, the standard of living, and certainly the future of one's children) that nevertheless have some connotation in terms of the conflict. When one examines the readiness to leave the country over a period of time (see Table 5.10), one sees a slight connection, even though it is still a weak one, between the existence of the conflict and the readiness to leave the country. During these years, when the Palestinians were involved in guerrilla tactics that caused civilian casualties in Israel (such as Beit Shean and Ma'alot in 1974, the Savoy Hotel in 1975, the bus on the coastal road in 1978, Kibbutz Misgav Am in 1980, etc.), it was found that the percentage of those willing to leave the country rose, but in a short time the levels fell to their normal ones, or about 12-14 percent. (Compared with other countries, Israelis demonstrate low motivation to emigrate. In February 1971 the Gallup Poll surveyed citizens of nine nations, asking: "If you were free to do so, would you like to go and settle in another country?" The distribution of positive answers was: Great Britain, 41 percent; Uruguay [Montevideo], 32 percent; West Germany, 27 percent; Greece, 22 percent; Finland, 19 percent; Sweden, 18 percent; Brazil [São Paulo, Rio de Janeiro], 17 percent; Netherlands, 16 percent; United States, 12 percent [Special Survey, #824-K, Question 6a, p. 2292].)

The complementary problem is that of immigration to Israel, which, as mentioned above, is one of the major components of Zionist ideology, which sees Israel, among others, as a "secure" refuge for the Jews of the world. It is not difficult to prove that at present Israel is unable to fulfill this function, and that the Jews of Israel as a community are perceived as being in the greatest (although not the only) danger of annihilation in the world. When the Jews of a large American suburb were asked whether they would feel "a personal sense of loss" if Israel were destroyed, only one percent of them saw Israel as a "personal haven" (but 28 percent did still regard it as a "haven for the Jews" in general).[85]

It is very difficult to determine to what extent the existence of the conflict prevents the Jews from coming to Israel to settle there, but one may assume that when three specific factors interact, they limit the attraction of Israel tremendously. These factors are (1) the delegitimation of Israel; (2) the physical threat to the existence of individuals and the existence of the entire collectivity (and one should again recall here the findings of Tables 5.2 and 5.3); and, added to this, (3) the inability of Israel to ensure that immigrants to the country will have a standard of living close to that in the Western world, which also to an extent seems a result of the conflict. But one should stress that throughout the Jewish setttlement in Palestine there was always a sizable number of Jews who immigrated to the country for religious reasons or because they had no alternative, who to a large extent neutralized the problem of legitimation.[86] The conflict is thus also to a certain extent a "selection tool" as to *who comes* and *who does not come* to Israel. It is thus not surprising that in such conditions the social system moves slowly from a more open and universalistic orientation to a population in which those with a particularistic orientation predominate.[87] When one investigates the self-identity of youth in Israel and compares them at two different points in time—1965 and 1974—one sees a much greater tendency to identify oneself as "Jewish" (which is more particularistic) than identifying oneself as "Israeli" (which is more pluralistic and universalistic).[88] This social change evidently mediates as a result of the internal and external problems that were thrust upon Israel as a result of the confrontation with the territory on the West Bank with its population of a million Arabs.[89]

Summary: Routinization of the Conflict Situation

There is no doubt that the existence of the Israeli-Arab conflict has had an accumulative effect upon the structure, the rules of the game, and the rules governing the allocation of resources in Israeli society, in the sense that these would certainly have been different had it not been for the fact that the conflict is not unidirectional, and that it involves both "profits" and "losses" to the society and to its individuals. We hope that we have been able to illustrate some of these profits and losses in this chapter.

At the same time, one should not exaggerate the influence of the conflict upon Israeli society. It would appear that it is just because of its "chronic" nature, that the Israeli society developed mechanisms for dealing with these problems, that the conflict has arisen. The very existence of these mechanisms is due to the influence of the conflict, but the result of their existence has evidently worked in a single direction—the routinization of the conflict situation. The Israelis have converted the conflict to a permanent phenomenon of Israeli society, just as every society has more or less permanent phenomena (for example, class conflicts, ethnic conflicts, religious conflicts, etc). The conflict is not perceived as dominant or radical, but as one of the normal political and social facts of life. While it is true that this conflict has sometimes shown differential salience, and has sometimes become a central topic or goal, it has eventually "died down" among the other societal problems.

Another important question in this context is how this routinization of the conflict has affected the motivations of the system to take steps in order to terminate the conflict, since this termination may involve costs to the collectivity (e.g., giving up occupied territories and evacuating settlements). But the desire for peace seems to be still a very strong symbol and social code in this society, and the price that Israel has paid for the peace treaty with Egypt could be an indicator that the "routinization" does not mean resignation to a state of conflict and periodical warfare.

In its radical form, it becomes salient and for a time changes the rules of the game during periods of "acute" outbreaks or when the society is uninterrupted or partially interrupted (as occurred at the time of the so-called Peace for Galilee Operation in June-July 1982). However, as we have stated throughout this work, the system learned how to return in a comparatively short time to the normal patterns of "no peace–no war."

Notes

1. In 1948 the Jewish community in Palestine numbered about 60,000, whereas by 1952 the number of Jewish residents of Israel was 1,450,000. No parallel is known in history, to a time when, within less than four years, an entire social system more than doubled.
2. The motives for immigration of the Jews to Israel were somewhat different from one group to the next. The motivation of those who came from the European countries was a mixture of national attraction and repulsion from their homelands (this having acquired much greater intensity after the Holocaust, which had primarily affected the Jews of Europe). On the other hand, modern nationalism was foreign to most of the immigrants from the Asian and North African countries, as was the additional intention of building a "model" society, in the terminology of utopian socialism or liberalism, held by some of the immigrants from Europe and North America. Thus, the common motivating factors around which both categories united were the various religious symbols. See Baruch Kimmerling, *Zionism and Economy* (Cambridge, Mass.: Schenkman, 1983).
3. The idea here is that when the first massive and unselective immigration of the 1950s took place, a partial congruence was created between one's location in the stratificational system and one's ethnic origin, whereby most of those who came from Asia or Africa were directed into agriculture or were absorbed in the periphery of employment in industry and the services. Symbolically, too, the Eastern culture these immigrants brought with them was perceived, even by the immigrants themselves, as "inferior" to the "Western" culture of those already living in the country and the new immigrants from Europe. This location in the lower end of the stratificational system and the cultural differentiation tended to pass in a partial form to the second and third generations as well. See Yochanan Peres, *Ethnic Relations in Israel* (Tel Aviv: Sifriyat Poalim and Tel Aviv University, 1977) (Hebrew); Sammy Smooha, *Israel: Pluralism and Conflict* (London: Routledge and Kegan Paul, 1978); or Shlomo Swirski, *Orientals and Ashkenazim in Israel: The Ethnic Division of Labor* (Haifa: Mahbarot L'mehkar Ul'bikoret, 1981) (Hebrew).
4. As a result of the 1967 war, Israel achieved control over 1,500,000 Arabs in the Gaza Strip and the West Bank of Jordan. In very short order an almost complete merger was accomplished between the labor markets in Israel and those in the West Bank and the Gaza Strip, with workers from the latter being absorbed in the lower strata of employment in Israel. From this point of view, the Jews from Oriental countries achieved collective mobility, moving from the lower to the middle strata, remaining between the Arabs of the occupied territories and the Jews with a Western background. This is a somewhat simplified presentation of this complicated matter (see Kimmerling, *Zionism and Economy*).
5. We use the concept of the "Jewish-Arab conflict" and not the "Israeli-Arab" one, not because we wish to stress the religious element in the conflict (even

though this too exists), but in order to indicate that the conflict began considerably before the State of Israel was established. See, for example, J. Khouri, *The Arab-Israeli Dilemma* (Syracuse: Syracuse University Press, 1968), and Baruch Kimmerling, *Zionism and Territory: The Socioterritorial Dimension of Zionist Politics* (Berkeley: Institute of International Studies, University of California, 1983).

6. Such an approach allows for a moratorium on the solving of social problems in Israel for some future utopian time.

7. One can find almost no reference in print to this approach. At the same time, all modern Israeli historiosophy is full of terms that express the dialectic of the Jewish-Arab conflict: The more the Arabs attempt to harm Israel, to limit its strength and even to wipe it out as a political entity (to commit politicide), the stronger it becomes. See, for example, Jehuda Slotzky, *History of the Hagana: From Defense to Struggle* (Tel Aviv: Am Oved, 1967) (Hebrew).

8. Beginning with the Zionist colonization of Palestine, Jews and Arabs were killed as a result of the confrontations between them. What is possibly surprising is the small number of those killed on both sides, especially when one summarizes this over a long period of time. Between 1882 and the beginning of the 1920s, no more than a few dozen were killed. In the riots of 1920-21 about 50 Jews were killed, and in what appeared to be a national Arab revolt in 1929, 135 Jews were killed—including most of the community of Jews in Hebron (which, incidentally did not belong to the "Zionist settlement"). In the general rebellion of 1936-39, 545 Jews were killed and about 700 were wounded.

9. Statistics of casualties attributable to wars will be found in Quincy Wright, *A Study of War* (Chicago: The University of Chicago Press, 1942); Pitirim Sorokin, *Social and Cultural Dynamics,* vol. 1 (New York: American Book Co., 1937), appendix 21; Raymond Aron, *The Century of Total War* (Boston: Beacon Press, 1954), pp. 75-77; Alan S. Milward, *War, Economy and Society 1939-1945* (Berkeley and Los Angeles: University of California Press, 1977), pp. 200-212. For the British casualties in World War II, see Richard M. Titmuss, *History of the Second World War: Problems of Social Policy* (London: HMSO and Longman, Green, 1950), appendix 8. As for Great Britain, it is very difficult to calculate the casualties in relationship to the population, because those listed as injured or killed in the armed forces included soldiers from throughout the British Empire.

10. The Israeli army does not publish statistics regarding casualties by rank, and even less so by socioeconomic status. But according to our computation, the relative distribution of the fatalities in the 1973 war was the following: Of a total of 2,358 surveyed fatalities, 23.8 percent were officers, or about 2.7 times their weight in the Israeli armed forces officer's population. The ethnic origins of those soldiers killed (based on their first and last names or their parents' names) were: occidentals, 61.94 percent (of the identifiable—because 10.5 percent of the total were unidentifiable), or 1.16 times their weight in the country's total population; and Orientals, 0.82 times their weight. The representation of the fatalities according to their place of residence was: cities and metropolitan areas, 0.98; small towns and development towns, 0.27; kibbutzim, 4.0; and other rural areas, 2.04 (data computed from Israel Defense Forces, *The Fatalities of the Yom Kippur War,* 1974).

11. *Ha'aretz Magazine,* 2 July 1979.

12. The phenomenon of the gap between subjective estimations of the probability of events occurring and their "true" probability is well known, but in general the tendency is to exaggerate upward with "good" events (winning the lottery or any other game of chance) and to do the opposite (i.e. exaggerate downward) with "bad" events. For a full discussion on this, see John Cohen, *Psychology of Probability* (London: George Allen and Unwin, 1972). In our case, the gap between the subjective and objective probability is even greater than usual.

13. Broadcast on Israel Radio, 26 April 1982.

14. See, for example, Yehoshafat Harkabi, *Arab Strategies and Israel's Response* (New York: Free Press, 1977).

15. One can find sharp expressions of this in some Israeli prose and poetry. Thus, for example, Hebrew historiosophy commonly draws a comparison between the Crusader Kingdom of Jerusalem and the State of Israel. In both instances—it is claimed—foreign invaders came to this territory, temporarily conquered the Muslims, and established kingdoms that were a "foreign element" in the region. However, these entities cannot maintain themselves for an extended period of time, since they are opposed to historical and sociopolitical logic. Just as Saladin defeated the Christians, so the Arabs will eventually defeat the Israelis. Whether consciously or not, whether explicitly or implicitly, the Israelis are attempting, both in their scientific research and in their literature, to contend with the "Crusader model"—to deny the analogy, or "to learn from the Crusader attempt," in order to prevent its repetition. On this, see Ehud Ben-Ezer, "War and Siege in Israeli Literature (1948-1967)," *Jerusalem Quarterly* (winter 1977):94-112.

16. See Kimmerling, *Zionism and Territory*.

17. See, for example, Charles Liebman, "Myth, Tradition and Values in Israeli Society," *Midstream* (January 1978).

18. Kimmerling, *Zionism and Territory*.

19. See Emile Durkheim, *Suicide* (Glencoe: Free Press, 1952), and Marshall B. Clinard, "The Theoretical Implications of Anomie and Deviant Behavior," in M.B. Clinard (ed.), *Anomie and Deviant Behavior* (Glencoe: Free Press, 1954).

20. Baruch Kimmerling, "Anomie and Integration in Israeli Society and the Salience of the Israeli-Arab Conflict," *Studies in Comparative International Development* 9, no. 3 (fall 1974):64-89.

21. A psychological team that investigated the topic, primarily from the point of view of the pressure imposed upon the children who had been shelled, concluded that some of the established population (of the town of Metulla) acted in the same way as the new population and that fleeing stemmed more from a feeling of inequity rather than from low morale, because all the other residents of the country were safe, and only in this relatively small area were the residents under fire. Thus, a trip of but a few kilometers put the person and his family in a "safe" area. See "Platform for Discussion," in "The Presidential Conference on Children," mimeographed (Jerusalem, 5 October 1981).

22. Remarkably similar findings are reported in other cases of casualties suffered in development towns. See Chaya Zukerman-Bareli, "Outmigration from a Development Town in Israel," *International Journal of Comparative Sociology* (September-December 1979):260-62.

23. See Dan Horowitz and Baruch Kimmerling, "Some Social Implications of the Military Service and Reserve System in Israel," *Archives Européennes de Sociologie* (1974):262-76; Baruch Kimmerling, "Determination of the Boundaries and Frameworks of Conscription: Two Dimensions of Civil-Military Relations in Israel," *Studies in Comparative International Development* 14, no. 1 (spring 1979):22-41.

24. See Moshe Lissak, "The IDF as an Agent of Socialization and Education: A Study of Role Expansion in a Democratic Society," in M.R. Gills (ed.), *The Perceived Role of the Military* (Rotterdam: Rotterdam University Press, 1971), pp. 325-40; Maurice M. Roumani, *From Immigrant to Citizen: The Contribution of Army to National Integration in Israel* (The Hague: Foundation for Study of Plural Societies, 1979); Samuel Rolbant, *The Israeli Soldier: Profile of an Army* (New York: Thomas Yoseloff, 1970); and Tom Bowden, *Army in the Service of the State* (Tel Aviv: University Publishing Projects, 1976).

25. Victor Azarya and Baruch Kimmerling, "New Immigrants in the Israeli Armed Forces," *Armed Forces and Society* (spring 1980):455-82.

26. Simon N. Herman, Yochanan Peres, and Ephraim Yaar (Yuchtman), "Reactions to the Eichmann Trial in Israel: A Study in High Involvement," *Scripta Heirosolymitana* 14 (1965):99.

27. See Shlomo Avineri, *The Making of Modern Zionism: The Intellectual Origins of the Jewish State* (London: Weidenfeld and Nicolson, 1981), pp. 217-27.

28. "Historical" events still arouse the state periodically, and these are constantly mentioned in actual political debates. Some examples of this are: periodical debates about the dismemberment of the particularistic armed forces that had existed before the state (included here is the sinking of the Etzel ship *Altalena* in 1948, which was perceived as an attempted rebellion); political murders that occurred in 1932 and 1957; or intelligence failures in Egypt in the 1950s, which brought about widespread repercussions in the political regime. And there are those who claim that these events brought about an undermining of the Labor party regime that reigned in the 1960s, eventually leading to its defeat in 1977.

29. See Kimmerling, "Anomie and Integration."

30. Ze'ev Ben-Sira, *The Present Situation in the Eyes of the Public* (Jerusalem: Institute for Applied Social Research, Communications Institute, Hebrew University, 1937), p. 68; Shlomit Levi and Louis Guttman, *Social Indicators in Israel* (Jerusalem: Institute for Applied Social Research, Communications Institute, Hebrew University, 1974), p. 15. See also Peres, *Ethnic Relations in Israel,* p. 97.

31. See Rael Jean Isaac, *Israel Divided: Ideological Politics in Israel* (Baltimore: Johns Hopkins University Press, 1976).

32. Yochanan Peres, "Ethnic Relations in Israel," *American Journal of Sociology* 76, no. 6 (1971):1027.

33. Sometimes the argument is extremely sophisticated. Thus, for example, three scholars who investigated the conflictual behavior of six Middle Eastern countries (Israel and its direct neighbors) found that there is no link between Israel's behavior in the conflicts with its neighbors and in internal conflicts and that 71 percent of the variance in Israeli behavior in the conflict is explained by the actions of its neighbors toward it. See Jonathan Wilkenfeld, Virginia Lee Lussier, and Dale Tahtinen, "Conflict Interaction in the Middle

East, 1949-1967," *Journal of Conflict Resolution* (June 1972):135-54. However, these findings prove not necessarily any unwillingness to use the external conflict for internal needs, but simply an inability to do so. But there is no doubt that the high degree of variation in the conflict, which is explained as stemming from the reactions of the other side, hints that the perception in Israel, at least between the years 1949 and 1967, was that Israel's behavior in the conflict with its neighbors is dictated primarily by the behavior of the opposing side.

34. But there were at least three salient events in which it was claimed that the ruling political elite had used defense symbols, or carried out actions in this sphere, in order to harvest internal political profits. In June 1961 Israel launched a rocket (named Shavit 2), which was hailed as a "rocket for investigating the atmosphere," while its military value was stressed by those involved in the launching, including members of the Ministry of Defense and the armed forces. Afterwards, it was claimed that the action was taken as a deterrent to Egypt, which was intent on producing rockets; however, segments of the Israeli press claimed that the launching and the publicity surrounding it were meant for internal consumption, given the imminent internal elections. As a result, a new word entered the Hebrew language: *bitchonism,* which can be translated into English as "securitism." The word connoted the abuse of the idea of national security for internal political needs. The second event, which was also a cause of debate, was the destruction of the Iraqi nuclear plant a short while before the elections in 1981. But the most salient event, which raised a violent public controversy, was with regard to the reasons and aims of the 1982 Lebanese war.

35. Shlomo Aronson and Dan Horowitz, "The Strategy of Controlled Retaliation—The Case of Israel," *State and Government* (summer 1971):77-99.

36. Robert K. Merton, *Social Theory and Social Structure* (Glencoe: Free Press, 1949), pp. 19-84.

37. Georg Simmel, *Conflict* (trans. Kurt H. Wolff) (Glencoe: Free Press, 1955); Lewis Coser, *The Functions of Social Conflict* (Glencoe: Free Press, 1956).

38. Pitirim Sorokin, "Sociological Interpretation of the 'Struggle for Existence' and the Sociology of War," in *Contemporary Sociological Theories* (New York: Harper, 1928). See also Robert E. Park, "The Social Function of War," *American Journal of Sociology* 46 (1941):551-70.

39. Louis Kriesberg, *The Sociology of Social Conflicts* (Englewood-Cliffs, N.J.: Prentice-Hall, 1973), pp. 247-57.

40. Kimmerling, *Zionism and Territory,* chap. 7.

41. See Harkabi, *Arab Strategies and Israel's Response.*

42. The struggle over the amount of the marginal tax continued into the 1970s. Those who advocated high taxation were divided into two camps: the pragmatists, who claimed that the circumstances demanded high taxation, and the ideologues, who wished to redistribute the national income. For this, see Alex Radian's article "Tax Rates as Goals, Tax Rates as Outcomes: Israel, 1948-1975" (forthcoming). In 1979, 38 percent of all employees in Israel paid taxes at the 25 percent rate (in 1972 this included 72 percent of all employees), 27 percent paid 35 percent, 12 percent paid 45 percent, 14.5 percent paid 50 percent rate, and 12.5 percent paid 60 percent. Joseph Baggay and Eytan Sheshinski, "The Influence of Taxation Transfer Payments and Subsidies on Inequality of Income Distribution" (unpublished paper).

43. Harold C. Wilkenfeld, *Taxes and People in Israel* (Cambridge: Harvard University Press, 1973), p. 3.

44. The recommendations of a committee appointed in 1974 to reform taxation in Israel stated among other things, that "the Committee on Taxation was established due to public demand for a significant reform in the taxation system which has an extremely high taxation rate, where the taxation rate is incredibly high even for those earning extremely low incomes. . . . In the circumstances, inequities developed, which took two major forms: The first was that those who were supposed to pay taxes evaded doing so. The second was 'institutionalized evasion' with full knowledge of the government and the tax authorities . . . the high tax rates on low incomes lead people not to exert any effort in work and productivity, and direct financial activity to those areas where it is easier to conceal income" (The Committee on the Reform of Taxation, *Recommendations for Changing the Direct Tax* [Jerusalem, The Government Printer, March 1975] [the "Ben-Shahar Report"], p. 3 [Hebrew]).

45. The Committee for Changes in Taxation (the Gross Committee), *The Committee Report* (April 1982), p. 3.

46. The gross taxation is the sum total of all the taxes the state collects from its citizens, either directly or indirectly. In order to arrive at the net taxation, one must calculate the payments the citizens receive in return from the government, such as national security, welfare support for the needy, government subsidies for health-care services, the subsidies on major foodstuffs, the subsidies on gasoline, etc. It is not customary to include as returns to the public any costs for internal and external defense.

47. See H. Rosenfeld and S. Carmi, "The Privatization of Public Means, The State-Made Middle Class and the Realization of Family Value in Israel," in Jean C. Peristiany (ed.), *Kinship and Modernization in Mediterranean Society* (Rome: The Center for Mediterranean Studies, American Universities Field Staff, 1976). But Rosenfeld and Carmi see the process of the transfer of the national property to individuals as a directed process, while if there was such a process it was but a by-product of a socioeconomic policy meant to gain political support for the center, and it was distributed throughout all the strata in a differential manner.

48. See Moshe Lissak and Dan Horowitz, *Origins of the Israeli Polity: Palestine under the Mandate* (Chicago: The University of Chicago Press, 1978), passim; and Kimmerling, *Zionism and Economy*, 1982.

49. Since its establishment, Israel has enjoyed substantial financial support from Jews throughout the world, and primarily from those in North America. In the 1950s and 1960s it received compensation payments from Germany. But from our point of view, all of these are included in the "internal sources," for Israel was able to determine for itself how to spend this money. The American support is in most instances meant to cover defense expenses; and this, to a large extent, is based on American choices concerning types of weaponry, quantity, price, etc.

50. Eitan Berglas, *The Indirect Costs of Defense Spending: The Israeli Experience.* Conference Paper on Defense and National Economy in the 1980s (Tel Aviv: Center for Strategic Studies, and Tel Aviv University, 1981).

51. Ibid.

52. Ibid., p. 28. See also Haim Barkai, *The Cost of Security: A Restrospective View* (Jerusalem: Falk Institute Research Paper no. 115, 1981) (Hebrew).
53. Victor Azarya, "The Israeli Armed Force," in Morris Janowitz and Stephen D. Westbrook (eds.), *The Political Education of Soldiers* (Beverly Hills: Sage, 1982).
54. Marshall Sarnat and Haim Levy, *The Impact of the Six Day War on the Metalurgic and Electronic Industry in Israel* (Jerusalem: Eshkol Institute, Hebrew University, 1973).
55. Paul Baran and Paul Sweezy, *Monopoly Capital* (New York: Monthly Review Press, 1966). For a criticism of this finding see Albert Szymanski, "Military Spending and Economic Stagnation," *American Journal of Sociology* 79 (July 1973):1-14.
56. Sarnat and Levy, *Impact of the Six Day War.*
57. E.g., Stanley Lieberson, "An Empirical Study of Military-Industrial Linkages," *American Journal of Sociology* (January 1971); or Sidney Lens, *The Military-Industrial Complex* (Philadelphia: Pilgrim, 1970).
58. See Kimmerling, *Zionism and Economy.* See also Alex Mintz, "The Military-Industrial Complex: The Israeli Case," in M. Lissak (ed.), *Israeli Society and Its Defense Establishment* (London: Frank Cass, 1984); Yoram Peri and Amnon Neuibach, *The Israeli Civil-Military Complex* (Tel Aviv: International Center for Peace in the Middle East, 1984).
59. State of Israel, *The State Comptroller's Report: 1981* (Jerusalem: The Government Printer, 1981).
60. The predominance of the political institution over the economic, in the context of the Jewish-Arab conflict, is already rooted in the rules of the game that developed during the Mandatory period, within each of the opposing forces and between them. See Baruch Kimmerling, *The Economic Interrelationship Between the Arab and Jewish Communities in Mandatory Palestine* (Cambridge: MIT Center for International Studies, 1979).
61. See Baruch Kimmerling, "A Model for Analysis of Reciprocal Relations between the Jewish and Arab Communities in Mandatory Palestine," *Plural Societies* 13, no. 1 (1982).
62. See Kimmerling, "Boundaries and Frameworks of Conscription," and idem, *Zionism and Economy.*
63. Alfred Vagts, *A History of Militarism: Romance and Realities of a Profession* (London: Allen and Unwin, 1938), p. 12.
64. See Amos Perlmutter, *Military and Politics in Israel: Nation Building and Role Expansion* (London: Frank Cass, 1969). Perlmutter emphasizes that Israel is *not* a "praetorian state, and gives the garrison state a positive meaning, in contrast to al-Qazzaz" ("Army and Society in Israel," *Pacific Sociological Review,* no. 16 [1973]:143-65).
65. A.R. Luckham, "A Comparative Typology of Civil-Military Relations," *Government and Opposition* 6, no. 1 (1971):24.
66. Ibid.
67. Ibid., p. 18
68. Ben Halpern, "The Role of the Military in Israel," in I.J. Johnson (ed.), *The Role of the Military in Underdeveloped Countries* (Princeton: Princeton University Press, 1962).
69. Moshe Lissak, "The Defense Establishment and Society in Israel: Boundaries and Institutional Linkages" (unpublished paper, April 1981).

70. Dan Horowitz, "The Israeli Defence Forces: A Civilized Military in a Partially Militarized Society," in Roman Kolkowicz and Andrzej Korbonski (eds.), *Soldiers, Peasants, and Bureaucrats: Civil-Military Relations in Communist and Modernizing Societies* (London: Allen & Unwin, 1982), p. 96.

71. Ibid., p. 97.

72. See Ian Lustick, *Arabs in the Jewish State: Israel's Control of a National Minority* (Austin: Texas University Press, 1981), and a more politically biased Elia T. Zureik, *The Palestinians in Israel: A Study in Internal Colonialism* (London: Routledge & Kegan Paul, 1979), passim.

73. In general, this discrimination has no basis either formally or legally, except for the existence of the famous Law of Return, which sees each Jew in the world as a potential citizen of the State of Israel (as opposed to non-Jews, whose entry into the country is limited and conditional). There are also certain benefits that Israeli law offers to those who have completed army service, whereas the Christian and Muslim Arab citizens do not have compulsory military service (unlike the Druze and Circassians). For other aspects of this discrimination, see the items listed in the previous footnote, as well as Jacob Landau, *The Arabs in Israel* (London: Oxford University Press, 1969).

74. See Baruch Kimmerling, "Sovereignty, Ownership and Presence in the Jewish-Arab Territorial Conflict: The Case of Bir'im and Ikrit," *Comparative Political Studies* (July 1977):155-76.

75. See Brian Van Arkadie, *Benefits and Burden: A Report on the West Bank and Gaza Strip Economies Since 1967* (New York and Washington: Carnegie Endowment for International Peace, 1977); Arie Bregman, *The Economy of Administered Areas, 1974-75* (Jerusalem: Bank of Israel, 1976); Kimmerling, *Zionism and Economy.*

76. See Kimmerling, *Zionism and Territory.*

77. See Israel National Section of the International Commission of Jurists, *The Rule of Laws in the Areas Administered by Israel* (Tel Aviv: TZATZ Print, 1981), p. 36.

78. The situation became especially severe, for different reasons, in two of the areas at the beginning of 1982: Israel annexed the Golan Heights, and the Druze inhabitants of that area showed violent opposition to this move, primarily because of their concern that they might be drafted into the army and that their lands might be expropriated to enable the government to set up further Jewish settlements. The opposition of the Druze focused on the refusal to accept Israeli identity cards. The authorities attempted to force the Druze to accept them by imposing a curfew on the area for a number of weeks, by preventing them from receiving certain services or from going to work, and by preventing their flocks from grazing, etc. These actions elicited strong opposition in Israel as well, and "The League for Citizens' Rights" (headed by retired Supreme Court Justice Haim Cohn) termed what was taking place in the Golan Heights a "barbaric law." At that time, approximately, in order to influence the autonomy talks with Egypt regarding the land occupied by Israel, the residents of these areas attempted to protest by means of violent demonstrations. These demonstrations were dispersed using violent means unparalleled in the area, and a few dozen demonstrators (mainly young people) were wounded or killed by the gunfire of the armed forces. Here too

the events brought about public protests in Israel, a fact that forced the government to moderate its actions.

79. E.g., Joel S. Migdal, *Palestinian Society and Politics* (Princeton: Princeton University Press, 1980), pp. 3-96.

80. The most prominent proponent of this argument is the philosopher Yeshayahu Leibowitz. See his *Judaism: The Jewish People and the State of Israel* (Jerusalem and Tel Aviv: Schocken, 1975), pp. 418-22 (Hebrew).

81. The other alternatives the Jews had open to them, at different times and in different places, were the following: (1) migration to other countries (primarily in North and South America, an the modern era), (2) religious or at least social assimilation, (3) integration into those movements that strove for far-reaching social changes, and (4) enclosing themselves within their own religious and traditional system and awaiting the Messiah. The Zionist alternative was one of the less common until the time of World War II.

82. See Etan Sabatello, "Emigration from the Country and Its Characteristics," *Bitfutzot Hagola* (summer 1978):63-76 (Hebrew); or Ezra Zohar, *In the Clutches of the Regime: Or, Why No One Has Stood Up* (Jerusalem: Shikmona, 1974), p. 146-47 (Hebrew). A study conducted in 1974 on Israeli emigration to the United States showed that most of the Israeli emigrants to the U.S. were between the ages of 25 and 40. It is assumed that they number about 250,000—about a third of all the Israelis in this age bracket. (*Ha'aretz,* 17 October 1975.) This finding is consistent with the trends observed by Sabatello.

83. Sabatello, "Emigration from the Country," p. 67.

84. The Israel Institute of Applied Social Research, "The Will to Remain in the Country," mimeographed (Jerusalem, 1974) (Hebrew).

85. Marshall Sklare and Joseph Greenblum, *Jewish Identity on the Suburban Frontier* (New York and London: Basic Books, 1967) p. 216.

86. The religious factor was strong especially among the immigrants from the Asian and African countries, beginning with the Jewish immigration from Yemen in 1881 until the waves of immigration from Asia and North Africa at the beginning of the 1950s and 1960s.

87. The small number of immigrants from the United States also based their immigration more and more on religious convictions. See Araon Antonovski and Abraham David Katz, *From the Golden to the Promised Land* (Darby, Pa., and Jerusalem: Norwood and Jerusalem Academic Press, 1979), chap. 4.

88. Uri Farago, "Stability and Change in the Jewish Identity of Learning Youth in Israel," mimeographed (Jerusalem: Levi Eshkol Institute for Research of the Economics, Society, and Policy in Israel, Hebrew University, 1977) (Hebrew).

89. See Kimmerling, "Zionism and Territory."

6

Limitations of This
Study and Other
Concluding Reflections

Chapter 5 attempted to consider the topic of Israeli society at war within a broader context. In this manner, we determined that the cumulative influence of the conflict situation resulted in oscillation between routine and social interruption. In the latter case, most social resources are recruited either for attaining the predominant objective—victory in active war—or for eliminating a threat to the system's survival. The 1973 war period was studied intensively, yet our findings also pertain to the brief interruption periods of 1956 and 1976. The 1982 war and the waiting period that preceded that of 1967 indicate that there need not be any overlap between the situation of war and social interruption. Furthermore, they underscored an interesting feature of the system's behavior, namely the mechanisms constructed to prevent "unnecessary" interruptions (i.e., those which are difficult to justify in terms of internal politics).

We claimed that Israeli society has largely succeeded in preserving its openness, flexibility, and democratic rules of the game (at least for Jewish residents). This success is due to Israel's ability to pass rapidly from one phase (that of routine activity) to the other (that of a recruited and interrupted society) and back again, absorbing the conflict within the system. It then becomes one of a number of phenomena that constrain the system itself. At this point, however, we encounter one of the primary difficulties and limitations of our conceptual and intellectual framework. This very interruptive capacity, which enables Israeli society to maintain its routine processes and preserve Western style political and social rules (with certain reservations—although no different from those that characterize virtually all Western societies), also constitutes a reason for the existence of this capacity itself. At first glance there appears to be a logical fallacy or tautology, yet we contend that the two are distinct, mutually reinforcing social phenomena.

This emphasis upon routinization of the conflict situation, on the one hand, and the claim that the ability to function during periods of social interruption differs among Israeli society's various segments and strata (along the center-periphery continuum, for example), on the other, lead us to one of the most prominent shortcomings of this study—and perhaps of the overall conceptual framework presented here. Ability to function is undoubtedly affected by the essential features and characteristics of Israeli society, which were not analyzed systematically in this work. We assumed that interruptive capacity is a component of a modern society's optimal adaptive ability (How shall we determine what is "optimal"? How do we measure it? Optimal for whom?). Further research must account for the influence of other key factors, such as religion, culture, ethnic features, economics, and employment, upon the interruptive capacity and conflict routinization. The relevant points to be found in this study still require systematic development and inclusion within a unified conceptual framework.

In this context, it is also interesting to determine the differential extent to which interruptive capacity is to be found in other societies and the reciprocal relations between such capacity and social change or disruption. We note that several case studies (primarily those of Britain and Germany at the first stages of World War II) have indeed attempted to develop the concepts of routinization of war and interruption on the home front. Chapter 1, which compared disaster studies with the study of interruption, pointed out several common characteristics and many differing ones. Several of the smaller and medium-sized states (such as Yugoslavia, Romania, and Sweden) institutionally plan for social interruption—or a parallel political/socioeconomic pattern—as an integral part of their doctrine of military deterrence. In the introduction we noted that totalitarian states attempt to mobilize the periphery for extended revolutionary activity, in order to attain collective (economic, social, political, military, and other) goals against a background highly reminiscent of the *structural* aspects of interruption. We claimed that one of the key distinctions between these patterns of mobilization and social interruption is the promise to return to the previous situation. In all other cases, the goal is to change rather than restoration of prior conditions. We contend that the difference is manifested not only in terms of mobilization slogans; rather, there is a substantial difference between the phenomena themselves. Even if this be the case, we may ask: Is it possible to impose a moratorium on most social processes in order to attain individual objectives— temporarily defined as top-priority goals and unrelated to the state of war or emergency? If so, have such phenomena been discerned in political cultures other than that of Israel? The present study offers no answers to these questions. These demand future comparative research, transcending the case studies on relatively small communities affected by natural disaster. However, only limited comparisons can be made with the Israeli case, as these studies deal with communities that can always rely upon the intervention and support of a broader system.

Another point of dissatisfaction with this work—but which also constitutes an advantage—concerns the delimitation of the collectivity under study. The book represents a study of the sociology and social psychology of war and is therefore highly fragmented. Notwithstanding the comprehensive survey included in the preceding chapter, it almost ignores several very important aspects of the Israeli-Arab conflict, such as: relations with Palestinians living under Israeli rule (especially their effect upon the economic and stratification system); the territorial characteristics of this conflict; the penetration and influence of cultural aspects upon the conflict; etc. We have also ignored the conflict's interesting effect upon the internal Israeli battle over the role of Jewish religion and culture; the conflict and its varying patterns have in fact served as a catalyst in the overt and covert *Kulturkampf* taking place within Israeli society and between this society and world Jewry.[1]

A further limitation is the deliberate and virtually total lack of attention to what sociologists call the "world system,"[2] namely the international division of labor and mutual dependence of great and small states upon each other, which also influences the internal structure of society, economy, stratification, and domestic politics. One need not be a "radical sociologist" to recognize its importance. The Israeli-Arab conflict plays a distinguished role in the development of these international systems. We may explain several aspects, patterns, and components of this conflict (which we currently believe to be marginal in Israel's social structure) within this intellectual framework. The preceding chapter recalled that Israel depends upon the import of capital from the West and from world Jewry. However, it is even more important to analyze the problems of Israel's integration within the world system, or at least her desire to occupy a place different from that which she has been "assigned" (as noted, although not analyzed, in chapter 5). Moreover, Israel's optimal position and influence within the world system are also subjects for internal debate.[3]

All in all, the most serious limitation inherent in this work is apparently characteristic of all monographs: concentration upon a single topic and the consequent impression of a deterministic thesis. The reader might feel that all phenomena that occur in Israeli society are the direct or indirect result of the Arab-Israeli conflict and that those that are not demand explanation. This is a necessary outcome of concentration upon analysis of a problem at middle-range theory level and the attempt to bridge the gap between empirical findings and the conceptual framework derived from macro-sociology, utilizing psycho-social variables. We do stress that numerous processes within Israeli society are not connected with the Israeli-Arab conflict. Routinization of this conflict, as indicated above, has also largely isolated its effects. The Israeli-Arab conflict is not as dominant a variable in the development of the Israeli society of immigrants as might have been expected—and as perhaps may be reflected in this work.

Interruption versus Disaster

Chapter 1 has already indicated that in Israel, war is regarded both normatively and psychologically as a disaster; hundreds of people are killed, while many others (individuals, families, and, in the Israeli context, the entire collectivity) find themselves in direct danger of annihilation. However, comparing the 'civilian system in Israel at a time of social interruption with the findings and paradigms developed in the framework of disaster studies, we find very little in common. It thus becomes apparent that this paradigm, at least in its present state, is not effective for understanding the Israeli case.

In order to examine the similarities and the differences between social interruption and a disaster, as defined succinctly in the professional literature, we will examine the different stages in the occurrence of disasters, as they appear in two well-known sources (see Table 6.1), comparing them with parallel stages of interruption.

The first stage, the predisaster period, which precedes both disaster and interruption, is not included in the model of Powell, Rayner, and Festinger, but is stressed by Barton. It constitutes an integral part of perception of the interrupted Israeli system. This difference is not purely coincidental. While certain disasters can be foreseen (although one cannot forecast their exact time or estimate the probability of their occurrence), most are not predictable at all. Furthermore no social system can be constructed based upon anticipation of such a disaster occurring—particularly not when it threatens the very existence of the entire social order; or all the more so, when the physical survival of the entire collectivity is in danger. If nevertheless there is awareness of such possibilities, they are perceived as so remote that preparation for dealing with them appears to be no more than ritual, remaining a question of political and/or psychological lip-service, rather than involving any serious measures. Similarly, routine political processes do not overly encourage

TABLE 6.1

The Fit of the Interrupted System to Characteristics of Stages in the Development of Disasters (According to Powell, Rayner & Festinger,* and Barton)**

Stage	Barton	Powell, Rayner & Festinger	The Interrupted System
i	a. pre-disaster period		pre-interruption period: accumulated learning of the system: preparedness against possible acute outbreak of the conflict
ii	b. The discovery and transmission of warnings of a specific threat (this stage may be very short or sometimes even non-existent)	warning: the arousing of awareness, justified or otherwise, to the creation of conditions which might bring about a disaster.	increase in security tension
iii		threat: the people are exposed to messages or to signs which indicate an immediate and specific danger	partial mobilization of the reserves (whose scope is not clear or whose extent cannot be foretold)
iv		impact: the actual disaster strikes	social interruption
v		inventory: those exposed to the disaster begin to form a first impression of the damages	
vi	c. immediate, relatively unorganized and non-structured response	rescue: spontaneous, local and unorganized actions assume the form of first aid to the injured wounded, etc.	spontaneous reaction at the individual level as a result of the emergency

TABLE 6.1 (continued)

vii	d. organized social response of rehabilitation	remedy: initiated aid and rescue activities; both professional and formal, by those who were spared and by external aid agents	organizational activites: utilizing the institutional framework to interrupt the system
viii	e. long term balance as a result of the disaster once the society has completed reconstruction and has absorbed the disaster's permanent influences. This balance may or may not be identical to that prevailing before the disaster	recovery: a long period of returning to local social stability or stable adjustment to the new conditions, as a result of the disaster	gradual return to the routine of the societal pr0cesses

*As adapted by A.F.C. Wallace, *Tornado in Worcester: An Exploratory Study of Individual and Community Behavior in an Extreme Situation* (Washington, D.C.: National Academy of Science, 1956).

**A.H. Barton, *Communities in Disaster: A Sociological Analysis of Collective Stress Situations* (New York: Anchor, 1969).

the allocation of funds for an event that has a low probability of occurrence, whose exact time cannot be forecast, and whose results are not pleasant. Institutional arrangements to prepare the population for a disaster are normally the result of extended social learning and historical experience. Alternatively, they constitute an integral part of a comprehensive project that includes risks in its calculations (such as building dams, nuclear reactors, etc.), even when there has been no experience with any disaster envisioned.

This is not so in the Israeli case. We have already noted that interruption is an integral part of the chronic conflict situation, whose acute eruptions cannot always be precisely foretold. Nevertheless, the probability of their occurrence is perceived as high, and sometimes even essential—or as part of the common "fate" of this immigrant society senenced to live upon this arid land. In May 1956, Moshe Dayan, then chief of staff of the Israeli Defense Forces, eulogized a soldier named Ro'i Rottenberg as follows:

> Yesterday morning Ro'i was killed. The quiet of the morning blinded him and he did not see the murderers lying in wait for him along the furrow. Today, let us not condemn the murderers. What do we know of their fierce hatred for us? For eight years they have been living in refugee camps in Gaza, while before their eyes we were cultivating the lands and villages they and their ancestors lived upon. We should demand blood not of the Arabs of Gaza, but of ourselves. . . . Let us take a reckoning today. We are a generation of settlers, yet without a helmet or a gun barrel we will be unable to plant a tree or build a house. Let us not be afraid to perceive the enmity that consumes the lives of hundreds of thousands of Arabs around us. Let us not avert our gaze, for it will weaken our hand. This is the fate of our generation. The only choice we have is to be armed, strong and resolute or else our sword will fall from our hands and the thread of our lives will be severed. The light in [Ro'i's] heart blinded him, and he did not see the slaughterer's knife.[4]

Dayan's message was short and unequivocal, apparently requiring no further interpretation or analysis.[5]

Returning to a comparison of different kinds of disasters we noted that, at least in certain cases, it was Israel that initiated war (in 1956, 1967, and 1982); hence the collectivity had a certain degree of control over events within the interrupted or partially interrupted system. Preparedness, in this case, is an integral part of interruption. This is not true in the event of a disaster.

Just prior to the 1947-48 war, the preliminary signs of preparedness stemmed primarily from two earlier events: the Arab revolt of 1936-39 and the British experience of World War II.[6] In the second case, part of the Jewish collectivity was involved at the front, but the majority were only marginally involved in the war. In 1947 the Jews had neither the resources nor the time to prepare themselves (although they did possess a limited amount of information as to their opponents' plans). Nevertheless various types of preparations commenced at the periphery, primarily as a result of local initiatives by individuals, families, or various organizations. Yet there is no doubt that the perception of interruption was only formulated subsequently, evidently as a result of the social learning that followed the 1948 and 1956 wars. From this point of view, Israel is always in a state of preinterruption.[7]

The first stage, according to Powell, Rayner, and Festinger, and the second according to Barton, is that of warning. At this stage, questions are asked regarding the degree to which the warning is clear, specific, and unequivocal, and the amount of time the community has left before the disaster. The warning may be true or false; the degree to which it is perceived as being truthful is certainly a significant factor. Sometimes the mere warring itself (even if false) suffices to bring on part of the disaster, or a different type of disaster (as in *The War of the Worlds* broadcast); it may even become a self-fulfilling prophecy. Powell, Rayner, and Festinger introduce an intermediate stage, wherein the first sign of the actual disaster appears, thus making it clear that the message was genuine. In the Israeli case, an increase in security tensions may serve as a warning, but this is not a decisive indicator. From this point of view, the 1973 war broke out without any prior warning, while one may—possibly only post facto—perceive the increase in security tension before the 1956 and 1967 wars as warnings. However, the very conception of social interruption imparts litle significance to the warning stage, because the system is always ready for interruption (for the military, of course, there is far greater value in prior warning based on intelligence sources, as was shown in the 1973 war). Security tension accompanied by partial reserve mobilization may be analogous to the threat stage of Powell et al. (even though it is normally undertaken to avert war and warn the enemy, or to indicate that the country is engaging in only a limited war, as was the case in 1982-83).

The fourth stage, that of the disaster itself, is not identified by Barton, yet there is no doubt that this stage is essential for the following ones. In our case, there was no disaster, but rather an optimal mobilization of resources to implement the predominant goal, brought about by interruption of a majority of overall social processes. As indicated earlier, this stage is not identical to war. Theoretically and practically, such an interruption is possible without the outbreak of war. The waiting period in May 1967, during which Israel was mobilized but did not go to war, is the clearest example of social interruption. It is precisely this stage that illustrates the great difference between the perceptions prevailing in disaster studies and the concept of social interruption.[8]

At the fifth stage of Powell et al., which likewise does not appear in Barton's division, those who are exposed to possible injury begin to gain their first impressions of the situation, the extent of the damages, and the degree to which their world order has been destroyed. As disaster and interruption are not wholly analogous, it appears that this stage does not exist in the Israeli case, unless one considers it to be the point at which initial information is received regarding the scope of interruption and the functioning or nonfunctioning of various systems.

The sixth stage in both models of reactions to disaster is the one at which people are involved in spontaneous and unorganized rescue and aid activities among the injured. In general, this refers to individuals who react immediately to the disaster situation. In our case, it is characterized by spontaneous reactions at the individual level, as a result of the interrupted situation and the potential threat. However, this parallel between stages is purely technical, as our own case does not deal with a disaster, but rather with social interruption, which is substantively different.

The seventh stage in both models is that of organized and professional aid activities by other organizations charged with these duties (the police, Red Cross, national guard) or by those that have accepted such responsibility (the army). In this case, the parallel is very clear, referring to the entire Israeli emergency system (which was considered in detail in chapter 2), and other organizations outside this institutional structure, which have attempted to deal with problems and conditions created by personnel shortages occurring during the interrupted period (e.g., in the educational system). Emphasis is placed upon maintaining activities considered to be routine under abnormal conditions and using unusual means to ensure their maintenance. Insofar as the disaster paradigm is concerned, one cannot speak of efforts aimed at "routinization of routine," and nor may any activities be considered routine at this stage. Note that in the interrupted system, stages six and seven do not occur consecutively, but rather simultaneously.

The eighth stage in Barton's and Powell's model concerns long-term rehabilitation of the system. In many cases, this stage is utilized not only to reconstruct the "old world" and its order, but also to build a "new world" that promises to be better; in some instances, there is an undertaking by external agents (the government, etc.) to that effect. As stressed above (primarily in the first chapter), in the event of social interruption the message and promise are diametrically opposed to one another. In this case, an attempt is made to return to the previous social situation as rapidly as possible. This is a stage in which the predominant goal is perceived as attainable and absolute; the system needs to return to its routine situation, primarily by releasing the manpower resources from the military and restoring them to the civilian sphere. In the long run, as we have already claimed, this need not be the case, and the system that had prevailed prior to the interruption need not be identical to the one thereafter.

Refraining from Continuous Mobilization

One of the effects of extended external conflict with the Arab states upon Israeli society is undoubtedly the achievement of interruptive capacity and the construction of its attendant institutional arrangements. This ability enables Israeli society to engage in extended conflict without being mobilized on a permanent basis, minimizing the economic, psychological, and societal costs. This type of social flexibility (which generally characterizes modern societies) has contradictory social results. In an early version of this study, the senior author considered the concept of the interrupted society,[9] "going out on a limb" to claim that this has prevented Israel from adopting the characteristics of a "besieged society." This idea has not been totally disproved, as one of the essential conditions of a society under siege is that it is at least partially mobilized on a permanent basis.[10]

This ability to effect a speedy transition (at minimal cost) from a routine situation to a mobilized one, coupled with the return to the routine situation (without any major dislocation), enables the society to maintain a routine lifestyle during periods of "no war," or of a limited war (primarily against the Palestinians). The ability to interrupt the routine and return to it anew allows for institutional and psychological compartmentalization—in terms of time and the social rules of the game—between war and no war, despite the ongoing situation. Here, one may differentiate between external conflict and war. One of the major reasons that the 1982 war aroused fierce controversy within the system, as well as vocal and active opposition to it (for the first time in the nation's history), was that the boundaries between active warfare and routine conflict were blurred.

One may thus ask two questions, which differ from one another substantively, yet which may both be stated analytically and empirically: How do these *wars* influence Israeli society, and how does the *continuing conflict* affect it?

The ability to interrupt society is a necessary condition for the existence of a society that is not permanently mobilized, and is thus both open and free. It is not a sufficient condition, however. As mentioned above, the content of Israeli society is detemined to a certain extent by the other elements of the Israeli-Arab conflict, together with additional factors that are not necessarily related to the conflict; for example, Israeli society's ethnic make-up, relations between religious and nonreligious Jews, Diaspora-Israel relations, the ethical and practical aspects of economic processes, etc.[11]

The Influence of the Continuing Conflict

To a great extent this issue constitutes a problem distinct from that of the influence of war. In this case, we found influences in different areas and directions that at times contradicted one another. The conclusions noted in chapter 5 were only tentative, as no comprehensive study of the topic has been undertaken, although a number of relevant issues have been considered in detail.

Conflict with the external environment, which takes place simultaneously on different levels—political, economic, and military, for example—is, at least at first glance, a heavy social burden upon both the individual and the community as a whole in Israel. A very large percentage of the gross national product is earmarked for national defense, precluding its use for other purposes, such as welfare, education, and improving social integration. A sizable proportion of local manpower resources is involved directly (military service, reserve duty) and indirectly (military industry) in the "security field," rather than in producing consumer items and civilian services. Housing and population dispersal policies are influenced by ideologies and perceptions that follow directly from the conflict and its consequences. National priorities are apparently determined by the conflict, even when society is not in a state of interruption. Even if this is the case, this aim is not seen as predominant in routine situations, and allocation of resources involves a constant struggle between civilian needs and those of the conflict management—a phenomenon that virtually disappears during times of interruption.

At the individual level, every member of the Israeli "club" pays very high membership dues, in comparison to those of other "clubs" resembling it politically and socially (i.e., Western democratic states): (1) compulsory military service (primarily in the case of males) at a crucial time in building one's personal career; (2) high taxes—especially in light of welfare services provided; and (3) the individual psychological burden felt by most members of the collectivity and the danger to the entire collectivity.

Israel is an immigrant society, with poor natural resources (including land, water and primary sources of energy). These features, when combined with permanent external pressure, should, ostensibly, have been devastating to Israeli society. However, considering the historical and ideological background of the state's creation, this very combination of external pressures and internal conflicts—together with Israel's social structure and appropriate social arrangements—strike a balance that enable this society to exist. These arrangements accord a feeling of intensive participation to relatively large segments of society (when compared with other societies). Thus, they constitute a mechanism that balances the costs demanded for such participation with a large measure of social compensation. However, there is no doubt that this balance—between external and internal pressures, between the "price" of participating in the collectivity and the compensation for doing so—is extremely fragile and any disturbances may place it in danger. It is almost impossible to predict what will happen if this balance is indeed disrupted.

There were three such disturbances in the past; two occurred a number of years ago, while the third happened recently. The first two events (which were not necessarily independent of one another) were the occupation of the West Bank (of Jordan), Sinai, and Gaza following the 1967 war and the change in the ruling party following the 1977 elections. The system has still not returned to its former state since these changes. The occupation of the territories, especially Judea and Samaria, has utterly shattered the national consensus, rendering the political system more right wing and power oriented. These processes too, are not unequivocal, and are still taking place at present.

The third disruption occurred in the midst of the 1982 war, when the national consensus that had been cracking in any event, ultimately broke apart completely.[12] Although the majority supported the war, this was the first time that a sizable population stratum, with access to the mass media, objected to the aims of the war at the time it was being conducted. The political leadership reacted with visible anxiety, accusing the war's opponents of "stabbing our soldiers [who were also divided on the issue: one colonel was discharged from service when he refused to participate in an attack on Beirut] in the back."

The seeds of a centralistic and paternalistic social and political regime were actually already present in the system. These stemmed from another historical characteristic of the Israeli-Arab conflict—namely, the question of territory. The conflict's primary concentration on land was largely responsible for two distinct consequences: an increased challenge to the system's legitimacy and the conversion of the political leadership into a nearly monopolistic landowner, rendering it stronger than any other political, economic, or social body. The first problem, legitimation of the existence of the system—or "its right to exist"—in light of Arab moral quasi-legal claims to that same territory, strengthened the religious elements (among others) in both the symbolic and the political power spheres, within a society that was basically secular. It was only the adoption of religious symbols that enabled the society to provide a link between the Jewish "nation" and "the land," and to claim, both internally and externally, that it had a "right" to the territory; it thereby legitimitized the Zionist settlement movement, which primarily consisted of emigration from the European countries to the Middle East, and the creation of a social and political entity that differed culturally and primordially from the "Levintine" surroundings.

The completion of this book was arbitrary in nature. Most of the processes indicated (especially in chapter 5) are still developing at this time, as are the internal struggles regarding Israel's character and her relationship with both the Jewish world and her Arab neighbors. Israel signed a peace treaty with Egypt and withdrew from the territories it had captured from her (excluding the Gaza Strip). Nevertheless, Israel's relationship with Egypt, not to mention the rest of the Arab world, is fluid and has certainly not been determined in any decisive way. There will be no great risk in predicting that the next stage of the Israeli-Arab conflict will be nuclearization. This process will surely alter the patterns of the conflict, although it is difficult to determine in which direction. There is no reason to assume that the "balance of nuclear terror" that functions among the superpowers will necessarily be followed by small states that are divided by far greater cultural differences than the superpowers, especially since ideological and religious motives are far more important in this region than are rational considerations. On the other hand, the introduction of nuclear weapons may force the political systems on all sides to adopt more rational behavior in their relationships and in their social and political processes. Hence, we perceive the situation as moot, rather than an apocalyptic vision. The concept of social interruption is also likely to undergo a change in a nuclear-armed world.

Notes

1. Baruch Kimmerling, "Between Primordial and Civil Definition of the Collective Identity: The State of Israel or *Eretz Israel?*" in Moshe Lissak, Erik Cohen, and Uri Almagor (eds.), *Modernity and Tradition: Essays in Honor of Shmuel N. Eisenstadt* (Boulder, Colo.: Westview, 1985).
2. See, for example, the most eminent representative of this approach, Immanuel Wallerstein, *The Modern World System* (New York: Academic Press, 1974 and 1980), vols. 1 and 2.

3. The moral and material basis of relations with the United States has often been subject to debate in Israel. Certain sectors of Israel's political leadership tend to present their country—both towards the United States and towards herself—as a (military and political) strategic asset for the United States in the Middle East. This stance justifies Israel's demand for increased American military and economic aid, adding a "commercial" dimension to the U.S. "moral obligations" towards a democratic state with a "similar way of life," whose people have faced severe persecution throughout history and are subject to the danger of extinction even at present. Those who objected to defining Israel as a strategic asset—and hence also to "strategic coordination" with the United States—claimed that this situation would increase Israel's dependency upon the Americans, suspecting that the Israeli political leadership was ready to fight wars other than those of Israel herself (against the Syrians, for example, to ensure the departure of the U.S. Marines from Lebanon in 1984).

4. Quoted in Shabtai Teveth, *Moshe Dayan* (London: Steimatzky, Weidenfeld & Nicolson, 1972), p. 240.

5. Dayan later changed his approach to the topic; his last book, which sums up his efforts to bring about an agreement between Begin and Sadat at Camp David, is entitled *Shall the Sword Devour Forever?* (Jerusalem: Edanim, 1981) (Hebrew).

6. See, for example, Tom Bowden, "The Politics of the Arab Rebellion in Palestine: 1936-1939," *Middle Eastern Studies* 11, no. 2 (1975):147–74.

7. Many small states, such as Switzerland, Sweden, Yugoslavia, and Rumania, which, for various reasons, desire to maintain sizable armies, employ the citizen army model. All, except for the Swiss model, from which Israel learned a great deal, differentiate between the regular and auxiliary soldiers; the latter, despite their training, are not considered an integral part of the armed forces. These conceptions are normally based on what is called "territorial defense" (i.e., military activity—occasionally attempting to mobilize the entire country, as in Rumania) against an invading army. It constitutes a literal interpretation of the phrase "nation-in-arms." The Israeli conception is different, not only because it does not consider the possibility of partial or full invasion of Israel and the attrition of the conquering force (as conquest implies the dismemberment of the entire system), but also because Israel maintains a sharp division between the battle and the home fronts, which operate according to entirely different rules. Only military mobilization will be optimal. In Israel, the reserves are indeed highly professional and skilled—qualities that are not normally expected when dealing with mass mobilization. For further information on citizen armies, see Adam Roberts, *Nations in Arms: The Theory and Practice of Territorial Defense* (New York: Praeger, 1976); David P. Burke, "Defense and Mass Mobilization in Romania," *Armed Forces and Society* (fall 1980):31–49; Robert C. Hasenbohler, "The Swiss Militia Army," in Louis A. Zurcher and Gwyn Harries-Jenkins (eds.), *Supplementary Military Forces: Reserves, Militias, Auxiliaries* (Beverly Hills: Sage, 1978), pp. 239–58; and Theodore F. Cook, Jr., "The Japanese Reserve Experience: From Nation-in-Arms to Baseline Defence," in *Supplementary Military Forces*, pp. 259–74.

8. Even severe disruptions on the home front, such as bombings (which result in death, injury, and widespread destruction of property), probably do not lead to any essential change in the social interruption situation: the system

is built to adjust to such circumstances. For example, during the first period (including the German blitzkrieg that swept through Central Europe and Poland), the German social perception of life on the home front relatively untouched by war was based upon similar (but *not* identical) perceptions to those of Israeli's regarding social interruption (there is, of course, a vast difference between a totalitarian and a democratic, free regime). In addition, even at the height of the Battle of Britain, in which most of the British institutional system was gravely affected, life continued routinely, in a fashion similar to that of the Israeli social interruption. In Britain, too, there was an accumulation of social learning (both from the previous war and the immediate experience). There were also major debates concerning British social perceptions and basic assumptions, related to the form of British society after the war and the role of the war in social changes—either desirable or undesirable—that would occur as a result thereof. On Germany, see the United States Strategic Bombing Units, *The Effects of Strategic Bombings on German Morale,* vols. 1 and 2 (New York and London: Garland, 1976); Allan S. Milward, *War, Economy, and Society: 1939–1945* (Berkeley and Los Angeles: University of California Press, 1977), pp. 23–31 and passim; Albert Speer, *Erinnerungen* (Berlin: Ullstein, 1969); and William L. Shirer, *The Rise and Fall of the Third Reich* (New York: Simon & Schuster, 1960), chapter 8. On Britain, see Angus Calder, *The People's War: Britain 1939* (London: Jonathan Cape, 1969); Tom Harrison, *Living Through the Blitz* (London: Collins, 1976); and Richard M. Titmuss, *History of the Second World War: Problems of Social Policy* (London: HMSO and Longmans, Green 1950).

9. Baruch Kimmerling, *Social Interruption and Besieged Societies: The Case of Israel* (Amherst: Council on International Studies, State University of New York at Buffalo, 1979).

10. We may see an antithesis to the concept of "social interruption": the cases of attempts at permanent mobilization of considerable parts of one collectivity. The most striking example may be Chinese society during Mao Tse-tung's "Great Leap Forward" and later his "Cultural Revolution." For these mobilizations the "military" was used as a symbol, and thus "220 million men and women of a predominantly agricultural population were to be transformed into an 'ocean of soldiers.' " John Gittings, *The Role of the Chinese Army* (London: Oxford University Press, 1967), p. 202.

11. Shmuel N. Eisenstadt, Israeli Society (New York: Basic Books, 1967), and Baruch Kimmerling, *Zionism and Economy* (Cambridge, Mass.: Schenkman, 1983). Dan V. Segre, *A Crisis of Identity: Israel and Zionism* (Oxford: Oxford University Press, 1980).

12. See D. Horowitz, "Israel's War in Lebanon: New Patterns of Strategic Thinking and Civil-Military Relations," in M. Lissak (ed.), *Israeli Society and Its Defense Establishment* (London: Frank Cass, 1984); Yael Yishai, "Dissent in Israel: Opinions on the Lebanon War," *Middle East Review* (winter 1983-84).

Methodological Appendix

The data on which this study is based were gathered from several sources, in order to cover as many aspects as possible of the functioning of the civilian system and the individuals within it during the 1973 war and the period of emergency following it.

The 1973 War Questionnaire

In this study a sample of Jerusalem's population was administered a questionnaire.

The Questionnaire

The questionnaire was composed of two parts. The first included about 180 items covering SES background variables of the respondent as well as items relating to his or her attitudes, opinions, and activities. All respondents were asked to respond to this section.

The second part was a questionnaire for volunteers, with 32 items referring to various aspects of volunteer activity. Those respondents who had volunteered during the war were asked to respond to this section.

Most of the items were closed-ended questions. Some of them included an open category of "other," in which the respondent could indicate a response different from those listed in the questionnaire. A few items were left open after we found in a pilot study that we could not determine the entire spectrum of responses in advance.

In each case the interviewer read the question to the respondent but did not read the response categories, and noted the appropriate category according to the response given. In the attitudinal items, in which the respondent was asked to indicate his attitude on a given scale, the interviewer read the scale's categories to the respondent.

The respondents were told that the questionnaire was anonymous and that its findings would be used for research purposes only. Each interview lasted between 45 and 60 minutes. (Note: The complete questionnaire in Hebrew may be obtained from the Department of Sociology, Hebrew University, Jerusalem 91905, Israel.)

Sampling Method

All of Jerusalem's neighborhoods were included in the study, except for the very religious neighborhoods in which cooperation could not be obtained and several new neighborhoods that were not yet fully populated during the war (Neve Yaakov, Gilo, Ramot, Armon Hanatiziv).

In each neighborhood two streets were sampled randomly. We interviewed the person who was the head of the household during the war in the first house on the first street, on the first floor, in the apartment on the right. Subsequently, the interviewer went to house number 2, to the apartment on the left-hand side of the second floor, from there to house number 3, to the apartment on the right-hand side of the third floor, until he had completed 20 questionnaires on those streets. The interviewer was asked to return to the same address several times at different hours of the day in the event that the respondent was not to be found at home.

This sampling method was preferred to random sampling for two reasons: First, at least some of Jerusalem's neighborhoods are characterized by concentration of specific populations clearly differentiated from one another demographically and in terms of socioeconomic characteristics. Neighborhood-based sampling enabled us to include a broad spectrum of population groups in the sample. Second, our method was economical in terms of the interviewer's time, since all the addresses he had to reach were located in the same area.

Such a method of sampling does not ensure proportional representation of Jerusalem's population, but it seems that our sample deviates only slightly from the general population in terms of socioeconomic characteristics (see the Other Sources section).

It is also worthwhile emphasizing that compatibility between the sample and the population was not of decisive importance for the purposes of our study, because we were dealing with the connection between certain characteristics of groups of the population and the behaviors and activities of those groups, as well as with comparisons among the groups. Thus, the primary consideration taken into account in choosing the sampling method was the inclusion of subsamples of varied groups of the population that would be large enough to be dealt with statistically, and not necessarily that the sample be a representative sample of the population of Jerusalem.

Interviewers

The interviewers were about 30 undergraduate students in sociology who participated in a research seminar on the subject. Each student

TABLE A.1
Sex Distribution of Samples as Compared with Sex Distribution of the
Jerusalem Population

	Sample	Population
Males	32.1	50.0
Females	67.9	50.0
Total	100.0	100.0

Source: Central Bureau of Statistics, *Census and Housing Survey, 1972: Demographic Characteristics of the Population,* pt. 2—Country of Birth, Period of Immigration, and Religion (Jerusalem: Publications of the Census and Housing Survey, 1972, no. 10, Table 3, 1976), data from Stage A.

TABLE A.2
Distribution by Father's Continent of Birth in the Sample and in the
Jerusalem Population, Age 29 and Over

Father's Continent of birth	Population n = 97,763	Sample n = 548
Israel	7.9	10.6
Asia-Africa	46.6	35.6
Europe-America	45.5	53.8
TOTAL	100.0	100.0

Source: Central Bureau of Statistics, *Census and Housing Survey, 1972: Demographic Characteristics of the Population,* pt. 2—Country of Birth, Period of Immigration, and Religion (Jerusalem: Publications of the Census and Housing Survey, 1972, no. 10, Table 3, 1976), data from Stage A.

conducted 20 interviews within a given neighborhood. The interviewers indicated the names and addresses of the respondents to enable supervision of their work.

The Sample

The questionnaires were transmitted in May-June 1975 to a sample of 575 persons in Jerusalem. In each case the person interviewed was the one who was the head of the household during the war; that is, the head of the family or the main breadwinner if he was not mobilized, or the person who was responsible for most of the household obligations while the head of the family was mobilized.

This definition of the population necessarily led to a situation whereby the proportion of women in our sample was much higher than their proportion in the population (see Table A.1).

As noted (see the Sampling Method section), we could not expect total compatibility between the characteristics of our sample and those of the population, but it can be assumed that our sample was representative of Jerusalem's population as it existed in the 1973-74 period of interruption.

A comparison of the sample to the population in terms of father's continent of origin and the respondent's continent of birth will be found in Table A.2.

It is clear that the high concentration of those having 0-8 years of schooling in the Central Bureau of Statistics (CBS) data as compared with our data stems, at least partially, from the fact that the CBS data include young respondents, most of whom are still studying. A similar situation also exists in the comparison of data on participation in the labor force. According to the census data, 48.2 percent of Jerusalem's residents (age 14 and over)[1] participate in the regular labor force, as compared with 59.9 percent of our respondents reporting employment. Here it should be noted that a certain gap may exist as a result of differences in the definition of a worker between the present study and the census. There is a possibility of bias in our sample because of the overrepresentation of women, while according to the census data their percentage in the labor force is low (32.7)[2] when compared to that of men (64.4).[3] It should be noted that there is no conspicuous difference in the data analysis for other variables and our data resembled that of the census, for example 23.9 percent in the sample owned cars, as compared with 21.2 percent in the census data.[4]

Qualitative Content Analysis of Newspapers

Information as to the nature and level of functioning of the system in times of emergency was obtained from the daily newspapers. For this

TABLE A.3
Distribution by Continent of Birth in the Sample and in the Jerusalem
Population, Age 29 and Over

Respondent's Continent of birth	Population n = 90,711*	Sample n = 514
Israel	27.5	38.7
Asia-Africa	35.0	23.9
Europe-America	37.5	37.4
TOTAL	100.0	100.0

*The differences in the size of the population in Tables A.2 and A.3 stem from the fact that in the CBS publications there are data on the father's origin only with reference to the entire Jerusalem district ($n = 261,103$), whereas on the respondent's continent of birth we could find data more appropriate for the purpose of comparison, which related only to the city of Jerusalem ($n = 230,315$).

Source: Central Bureau of Statistics, *Census and Housing Survey, 1972: Demographic Characteristics of the Population,* pt. 2—Country of Birth, Period of Immigration, and Religion. (Jerusalem: Publications of the Census and Housing Survey, 1972, no. 10, Table 11 1976), data from Stage A.

TABLE A.4
Distribution of Sample by Age

Age	n	Percent
0-25	66	13.3
26-35	126	25.5
36-45	130	26.3
46 plus	173	34.9
TOTAL	495	100.0

Source: The sample.

TABLE A.5
Distribution by Years of Schooling in the Sample and in the Jerusalem
Population, Age 14 and Over

Years of Schooling	Sample n = 479	Population n = 158,843
0–8	23.0	45.2
9–12	44.1	34.5
13+	32.9	20.3
TOTAL	100.0	100.0

Source: Central Bureau of Statistics, *Census and Housing Survey 1972: Housing, Labor Force, and Education* (Jerusalem: Publications of the Census and Housing Survey, 1972, no. 7, Table 46, 1976), temporary data from Stage 2.

purpose the three large daily newspapers (*Ha'aretz, Ma'ariv,* and *Yediot Achronot*) were surveyed from 31 December 1972 to 10 July 1973. We gathered all the information relevant to the functioning of the institutional system in Israel during that period.

Other Sources

To complete the picture we used three additional sources:

1. Reports of the Labor and Welfare Research Institute of the Hebrew University of Jerusalem. This institute conducted studies on labor and welfare in routine times. The war's outbreak almost completely paralyzed its routine activity. The researchers who were not recruited were divided into small teams, and on their own initiative conducted surveys of the situation prevailing in various parts of the city and in various spheres of functioning (and in certain cases organized several services). The reports that the researchers submitted in the wake of their surveys and general summaries of the institute's activities were printed for internal use and the material was placed at our disposal.

2. Interviews with people who held key positions in the system during the war. The interviews were conducted between April and June 1975 by students of a research seminar and by research assistants. In this framework, we interviewed the spokesman of the Employment Bureau in the Ministry of Labor, representatives of various groups that organized volunteer activities, the spokesman of the Jerusalem bus company, the manager of a bakery, broadcasting authority personnel, representatives

of groups that gave psychological counseling, the head of the municipality's education department, the person in charge of volunteers at Hadassah, etc.

3. A series of surveys conducted during the war and the period of emergency by the Bureau of Applied Social Research and the Communications Institute at the Hebrew University. These reports, which were submitted to the Supreme Committee of the Emergency Economy, dealt with various aspects of disturbances in the regular civilian services and in shortages of products and services. The reports included findings of a national survey.

Notes

1. Central Bureau of Statistics, *Census and Housing Survey 1972: Housing, Labor Force, and Education* (Jerusalem: Publications of the Census and Housing Survey, 1972, no. 7, Table 17, 1976), temporary data from Stage 2.
2. Ibid., Table 19.
3. Ibid., Table 18.
4. Ibid., Table 2.

Index

Academic Women's Organization, 58
Activities: institutional arrangements and, 36–38; interrupted system and, 20, 28, 32, 36–38, 83–117; situationally dependent, 89–101; women and routine, 99, 102. *See also* Individual behavior; Volunteering
Age, volunteering by, 122–23, 128
Agriculture, 72–73, 123
Aharonson, Shlomo, 159–60
Alcoholism, 117n27
Asian-African born Israelis. *See* Ethnic origin

Banking services, 54–55, 79n16, 124
Bankruptcies, 47, 72
Bar-Lev, Haim, 71, 73
Bar-Yosef, R., 14, 16, 21–22, 25
Barton, A.H., 7–8, 9–10, 11, 13–14, 17–18, 19, 31, 194, 198–200
Berglas, Eitan, 169
Books, reading of, 95–97

Cantril, H., 10
Caplan, G., 58
Car ownership, 29, 59, 76, 98, 99, 115n6, 136–37, 138. *See also* Transportation
Carmi, S., 186n47
Casualties, 4, 50–51, 149–53, 168, 182n8, 182n9, 182n10. *See also* Cost-benefit analysis
Catering halls, 75
Change, social, 22, 25–29, 58, 192
Child care, 132–33. *See also* Educational system
Civil Defense, 50–51
Collectivity: disasters and the, 12, 13, 14, 38n8; individuals and the, 149–58, 184n28; influence of conflict on the,

193, 202; role fulfillment and the, 32–33, 42n73; social contacts and the, 97–98; stratification and, 15–16, 22; temporariness and the, 22–23; threats to, 5–6, 153–56, 179. *See also* Social integration; Social system
Commerce, 75–76
Communications system, 25, 58–59, 80n38, 115n7, 115n8, 116n9, 116n10
Communications, Ministry of. *See* Communications system
Community. *See* Collectivity
Conflict: financing of, 47–48, 79n17, 163–72, 186n47; influences of continuing, 147–89, 201–3; management, 20–21, 161, 201; mobilization for, 3–4, 5, 20, 22–24, 78n2; social integration and, 159–62, 184n33, 184n34; stratification and, 21–22, 23, 25, 30; studies about, 7–19, 78n2, 191–200, 201n8. *See also* Disasters; Interrupted system
Construction industry, 73–74
Coser, L., 22, 97–98, 161
Cost-benefit analysis, 148–80, 202; financing the conflict, 163–72, 186n47; immigration/emigration and, 176–80; militarism and, 172–76, 188n73, 188n78. *See also* Casualties
Cost of conflict. *See* Casualties; Conflict, financing of; Cost-benefit analysis
Costs, volunteering, 129–32
Craftsmen's Union, 72
Crime rate, 47
Crusader model, 183n15

Dayan, Moshe, 149, 197, 204n5
Democracy, Israel as a, 172–76
Deutsch, Karl, 108